THE WORLD
OF IMAGERY

THE

WORLD OF IMAGERY

*

METAPHOR AND KINDRED IMAGERY

BY

STEPHEN J. BROWN, S.J.

Author of *The Realm of Poetry*

HASKELL HOUSE

Publishers of Scholarly Books

NEW YORK

1965

published by

HASKELL HOUSE
Publishers of Scholarly Books
30 East 10th Street • New York, N. Y. 10003

Library of Congress Catalog Card Number: 65-26462

CONTENTS

v

CONTENTS

THE WORLD OF IMAGERY

INTRODUCTORY

METAPHOR, simile, synecdoche, metonymy, personification, allegory, parable, fable, symbolism, emblems—can these things have any but an academic interest, remote from life ?   Can they be of importance to any but the grammarian, the rhetorician, the philologist, in short the scientist or the professor ? I would ask the general reader not to answer straightway with a hurried negative and turn the page.   For the writer believes—whether rightly or wrongly the reader must be judge—that he can make out a case for the study of the things represented by this string of Greek words, things which he has ventured to range under the general term " Imagery ".   And if he does not convince his readers that the subject is full of interest and significance for them personally, he may at least hope to show how full of interest and significance it is or ought to be for a great many people.   And that will be something gained.

I

Imagery in the sense in which it is taken for the purposes of the present work may be defined as " words or phrases denoting a sense-perceptible object, used to designate not that object[1] but some other object of thought belonging to a different order

[1] Or at all events not that object for its own sake.

or category of being ". The sense-perceptible object or image in question becomes a medium for conveying to the mind some notion regarding that other object of thought. The image is momentarily substituted for that object. This substitution may involve a comparison or it may not. The relations between the different ways of speech that fall within this definition may be roughly indicated by means of the following table :—

	Literal Comparison		
	Explicit Figurative	In Narrative	Parable
	Comparison, i.e. *Simile*	Form	Fable
Substitution with Comparison	Implicit Figurative Comparison, i.e. *Metaphor*	In Narrative Form	*Allegory*
	Minor forms of imagery—*Personification*		
		Metonymy	
		Synecdoche	
Conventional Substitution without Comparison.	*Symbolism*—literary, artistic, religious, etc.		
	Emblems and Emblem Literature		

Strictly speaking, symbolism is in the sphere of things what metaphor is in the sphere of speech. " Both these terms," says Professor König, " stand for something which is not used in its bare literal sense or for its proper purpose. Both describe methods which are employed to give concrete expression to ideas belonging to the realm of spirit. But whereas ' metaphorical ' applies to expressions, ' symbolical ' is an attribute of objects and actions. How closely allied the two conceptions are is shown by the fact that in familiar speech the terms are occasionally interchanged ".[1] Indeed, it may fairly be said not only that the terms " symbolism ", " symbolical " are now commonly used to describe forms of literature, but that all symbolism whether

[1] Hastings's *Dictionary of the Bible*, Extra Vol., p. 169.

INTRODUCTORY

literary, artistic, or religious, is expressible in speech and may be dealt with as a form of imagery in speech.

In the present volume I deal with metaphor and its kindred imagery alone, reserving for future treatment, God willing, the imagery derived from metaphor and simile, viz., parable and allegory, and the whole subject of symbolism.

The figurative element in language and literature has been studied many times and from many different points of view. There exists, in fact, a very considerable body of literature dealing with the subject. Some writers have dealt with figurative language of every kind, others have confined themselves to such figures as may properly be described as imagery. Some, again, have taken literature at large as the field of their survey, others a certain province of literature—a literary period or a literary group. Others, finally, have studied from this point of view the works of particular authors.

We shall more than once have occasion to mention a curious work, *The Might and Mirth of Literature*, by John Walker Vilant Macbeth.[1] The scope of this work is literature in general and every form of figurative language. It is a vast miscellany of some five hundred and fifty pages dealing *seriatim* with two hundred and twenty different figures of speech.[2] Though discursive and somewhat tiresomely effusive in style, the work is of no small value. It is also interesting and at times amusing, were it only for its profuse quotations from a great variety of sources. It records and distinguishes with considerable accuracy almost every conceivable departure from the original and simplest form, construction, or application of words and phrases. Out of the two hundred and twenty

[1] London, 1876.
[2] Holmes, in his *Rhetoric Made Easy*, 1755, enumerates and expounds no less than 250.

figures dealt with by Mr. Macbeth seven only fall within the scope of the present work—Metaphor, Simile, Metonymy, Synecdoche, Personification, Allegory, Parable ; and these are not much more fully treated by him than the rest. Indeed, his discussion of metaphor, the most important figure of all, is quite inadequate.

The author is, no doubt, justified in his claim to be the first to take figurative language as a point from which to survey a whole literature. And, not-withstanding such a work as Lord Kames's *First Principles of Criticism* wherein figures are dealt with at considerable length, we may allow his contention that there existed, when his book appeared, no thoroughly satisfactory treatise on figures.[1] He observes that, even among the best writers on the subject, great confusion of thought and much inaccuracy prevailed. We would venture to add that though, among writers on rhetoric subsequent to that time, there are some who have treated the subject of figurative language with accuracy and sometimes with fullness, it is still true to say that in the majority of such works that department receives scanty and perfunctory treatment. Whole groups of figures are entirely neglected ; the different types are carelessly and inaccurately defined and still more inaccurately distinguished from one another [2]; the same stock samples are repeated by one writer after another ; and little or no attempt is made to explain the *raison d'être*, nature, and functions of the principal figures. Finally, the very false impression is created that figures are mere excrescences and irregularities of speech, at best extrinsic ornaments.

[1] Mr. Macbeth says, indeed, "no even tolerably good treatise," but I do not think this can be maintained in view of the existence of Lord Kames's excellent work, which appeared as far back as 1779.

[2] We must venture to quarrel, in this connexion, even with Mr. H. W. Fowler and his *Dictionary of Modern English Usage*, Oxford, 1926.

INTRODUCTORY

Very shortly after the appearance of Mr. Macbeth's work another fairly comprehensive work was published, viz. *Figurative Language: Its Origin and Constitution*, by Leo H. Grindon.[1] This author is equally at home in literature, classical and modern, and in philology, and writes with enthusiasm and charm. It is a delightful as well as a valuable book and fully accomplishes the author's design " to show that the study of Figurative Language introduces us by new avenues to the noblest themes on which the mind can employ itself ". It confines itself, however, almost exclusively to the part played by metaphor in the making of language. Only in Chapter XVI does the author step aside from his main theme to dwell on the underlying basis of metaphor. Two pages are devoted to simile and a brief chapter to personification.

These would seem to be the only books in English that have attempted a comprehensive treatment of the subject. The Germans, on the other hand, have, as we might expect, worked out the theory and explored its bearings with considerable thoroughness. There is, for instance, Friedrich Brinkman's unfinished treatise, *Die Metaphern, Studien ueber den Geist der modernen Sprachen*.[2] This is an extended statement of the theory of metaphor, with suggestions and illustrations of various points of view in the study of metaphor : it is by no means a full treatment of the subject of imagery. There is the ponderous and learned work of Gustav Gerber, *Die Sprache als Kunst* [3] (Speech considered as Art), and there are the writings of A. Biese, *Das Metaphorische in der dicterischen Phantasie* and *Die Philosophie des Metaphorischen*.[4]

A French work which dealt with the subject on such broad lines and in so ample a fashion as, in spite of its date, to be still of value is the *Traité des Tropes*

---

[1] London, 1879.
[2] Bonn, 1878.
[3] Bromberg, 1871–3 ; Berlin, 1885.
[4] Hamburg, 1893.

5

of César Chesneau du Marsais.[1] Together with various works by the same author on rhetoric, logic, and other subjects, it enjoyed considerable vogue in its day and passed through several editions : but it is now very difficult to obtain.

Besides these and other such attempts to deal with the general principles of the subject as a whole, there have been published a very large number of books dealing with particular aspects of it. These shall be indicated as occasion arises in the course of this work.

II

Numerous as these books are, however, they are very far from exhausting the subject. Much, as I hope to show, remains to be done, much that is worth doing. The study has, from more points of view than one, an interest and significance which, to the writer's mind,[2] justify such pains as he, at all events, has bestowed upon it.

It may in the first place be claimed for the study of imagery that from it much light may be derived for the study of *language*. In fact, the branch of the science of language known as Semantics[3] is mainly concerned with imagery. Our everyday speech, as a very little study may show us, is largely made up of metaphor and simile [4] (some of it in the fossil stage, some of it still living), of synecdoche and metonymy,

[1] New edition published at Leipzig, 1757 ; 3rd ed., Paris, 1775. Included in collected edition of *Oeuvres*, 7 vols., Paris, 1797.

[2] That this significance is pretty widely acknowledged witness the booklet *Metaphor*, issued (1922) by the Society for Pure English ; *Poetic Imagery*, by Henry W. Wells, Columbia Press, New York, 1924 ; *Similes and their Use*, by Grenville Kleiser, Funk & Wagnells, New York, 1925. And an able and suggestive leading article, "Metaphors," in the Literary Supplement of *The Times* for 14th Oct., 1926.

[3] The standard work on this subject is still Michel Bréal's *Essai de Sémantique*, 1896, 5th ed., 1914 ; English translation by J. P. Postgate, under the title *Semantics*.

[4] Three-fourths of our language may be said to consist of worn-out metaphors," A. H. Sayce, *Introduction to the Science of Language*, 3rd ed., 1890, vol. i, p. 181. "Language is a dictionary of faded metaphors," Jean Paul Richter.

personification, and even symbolic expression. Metaphor, in one form or another, is of the very warp
and woof of speech. *Tout mot est un résidu de métaphore.* This being so, it is clear that a close study of
the nature and functions of metaphor ought, speaking
generally, to result in a better grasp of language,
it ought to contribute to our power of wielding language
at once more accurately and more effectively. For
ability to distinguish between figurative modes of
speech and plain literalness ought to conduce to accuracy
in the expression of ideas, while a thorough grasp of the
figurative element in common speech, with its appeal
to the imagination and the emotions, gives a certain
power to use language with impressiveness and force.
Then, again, it is scarcely possible, without some study
of this subject, to realize the vast resources which
language has at its disposal for the freshening and
heightening of literary style and for the expression
of the finer shades and *nuances* of thought.

Thus leading, as it well may, to greater power in
the handling of speech and to closer discrimination
of its capabilities, it would seem clear that the study
of imagery may lead also to a fuller appreciation of
literature. This must surely be obvious as regards
poetry : imagery is its very life. It is clear also as
regards the more imaginative and impassioned forms
of prose, such as oratory. But even in a form which
belongs so essentially to prose (though I am not
forgetting Pope's famous Essay) as does literary
criticism, the function of imagery is of much importance.
Witness the writings of Coleridge or James Russell
Lowell or Matthew Arnold. From another point
of view there are few things that throw such light on
the antecedents, the habits, and the temperament of a
writer as a study of his imagery.[1] It is not too much

[1] This has been well shown by Professor Minto in his *Manual of
English Prose Literature,* and more recently by J. Middleton Murry
in *The Problem of Style,* London, 1925.

INTRODUCTORY

to say that this study is essential to training in rhetoric and style and to the education of literary taste.[1]

Certain forms of imagery have no small importance for literary history. Literary *genres* that have prevailed at certain periods are distinguishable mainly by their use of imagery or their relation to it. To take examples almost at random, there was the curious emblem literature which began in the fifteenth and lasted on into the seventeenth century.[2] It would seem to have considerably influenced Shakespeare.[3] In our own days we have seen the Symbolist movement in poetry.[4] While another type of imagery, allegory as a literary form, runs right through literature. We owe to it such strangely different masterpieces as Dante's *Divina Commedia*, Bunyan's *Pilgrim's Progress*, Spenser's *Faerie Queene*, and Goethe's *Faust*, to say nothing of the mediaeval " mysteries " and " moralities ".[5]

But if imagery be significant for literature in general, it is doubly significant for the sacred literature of the Bible. Imagery, as we shall see, is indispensable for the expression of religious ideas ; it is the natural language of religion. For religion must convey in human speech to human understandings its message from the unseen and supernatural world. It is, then,

[1] " Some understanding of them (figures) is fundamental to any intelligent study of literature, and nothing in language teaching is more important than helping children to an appreciation of their value." E. Greening Lamborn, *The Rudiments of Criticism*.

[2] The greater part of this is now quite forgotten. Best remembered, perhaps, is the work of Francis Quarles, *Emblems Divine and Moral*.

[3] This influence has been studied in a very interesting book by Henry Green, *Shakespeare and the Emblem Writers*, London, 1870.

[4] See Kahn, *Symbolistes et Décadents* ; Lentillon, *A propos de Symbolisme* ; A. Symons, *The Symbolist Movement in Literature*, etc. Among contemporary symbolist poets may be mentioned Rabindranath Tagore.

[5] Mr. Chesterton's *The Ball and the Cross* is practically an allegory in the guise of an extravaganza. The allegorical movement in literature is studied in Professor Saintsbury's volume, *The Flourishing of Romance and the Rise of Allegory*, 1897.

to be expected that the literature of revelation should abound in imagery—allegory, parable, metaphor, symbolism. Moreover, revelation, as contained in both Testaments, was primarily addressed to a primitive and to an Oriental people, and it is natural to a primitive, and still more to an Oriental people, to think in images, to understand through images.[1] In point of fact, sacred literature throughout is full of figurative language and of symbolism. One of the causes of the obscurity that prevails in certain portions of the sacred writings is the fact that its imagery is the reflection of a world that has long passed away. It is true that the peoples of the East have changed far less than have any peoples of the West, and that a careful study of their present habits and customs throws much light on the text even of books as old as the Pentateuch ; still, much remains obscure even to an Oriental, still more remains difficult of understanding to the Western mind.

But this is by no means the whole of the matter. The Old Testament is not merely a collection of the literature of an ancient people of the East, it is a collection of *sacred* literature which, from the point of view that concerns us at present, presents peculiar features of its own. The literature of prophecy, for instance, constitutes a large portion of its contents.[2] One of the main characteristics of prophetical literature is the fact that it conveys its message in the form of symbols and in language charged with metaphor. The same is true of apocalyptic literature. For the past three years a series of illuminating studies on the symbolism of the Prophet Ezechiel have been

---

[1] It has been well said that, whereas the Western mind reasons by syllogism and induction, the Eastern thinks in parable and aphorisms.

[2] It is not confined to the writings of the prophets, but includes passages in the historical books, the Apocalypse of St. John, and even certain passages in the Gospels.

appearing in the *Revue Biblique* [1] : it is plain that the subject is far from exhausted. The late Dr. Sanday has enumerated [2] six different forms of symbolism that are found in the Bible, and he has omitted at least one other, the symbolism of numbers. Though not belonging to prophetic literature, the great dramatic poem known as the Book of Job is full of wonderful imagery. And there is the elaborate personification and allegorism of the later Wisdom literature.

In the New Testament, the rôle of imagery is not less significant, while, because of the more vital import of the issues involved, the task of the critic is here still more delicate. In the reply of our Lord to Nicodemus (John iii, 5) : " Unless a man be born again of water and the Holy Ghost he cannot enter into the kingdom of God," the word water must be understood in its literal proper sense, as the Council of Trent has defined, and not " twisted to some metaphorical sense ". That a great proportion of Christ's teaching was conveyed through various forms of imagery is a fact too well recognized to call for insistence. But it is not enough to say that here and there metaphor, simile, and parable are used to illustrate or adorn that teaching ; imagery is interwoven with the very texture of the thought itself. It is for exegesis to determine where the literal ends and the figurative begins. He who said " I am the true vine ", " I am the door ", said likewise, " This is My Body ".[3]

[1] By Denis Buzy, S.C.J. Since published in book form under title *Les Symboles de l'Ancien Testament.*

[2] *Life of Christ in Recent Research,* 1907. It is customary among certain writers to speak of St. John's Gospel as " saturated with symbolism ". E. F. Scott, *The Fourth Gospel,* p. 20.

[3] The following quotation from Dr. Hastings's *Dictionary of Christ and the Gospels,* 1913, vol. ii, p. 179, is evidence, we think, of the importance of the subject in this connexion : " A simple metaphor expresses the resemblance (or identity) between two dissimilar objects or ideas by applying to one a term which can literally designate only the other, as ' This is my Body ' (Matt. xxvi, 26)."

Again, it is a remarkable fact, that whereas in the Synoptic Gospels (Matthew, Mark, Luke) parables form one of the main features of Our Lord's teaching, in St. John there are allegories but no parables. The recognition of this fact has led to closer investigation of the nature of parable and allegory. From the materials supplied by these researches M. Loisy and his school have endeavoured to forge a new weapon for the disintegration of the Gospels. And, as the discussion involves the whole philosophy of imagery, on these grounds also a study of the subject would seem to impose itself on serious students of Scripture.[1]

From Literature we pass to *Art*. From the earliest times of which record remains we find, mingled with ordinary figures of men and beasts and representations of real or imaginary events, other drawings, paintings, and carvings that are symbolic ; they stand for something other than themselves, an abstract idea, a concept of the mind : they belong to the world of imagery. Ancient Egypt and Chaldaea had their symbols of eternity, of divinity. Religious art, like religious literature, is necessarily figurative, symbolic. Christian art was symbolic from the outset, first and principally because it sought to bring home sublimest truths to the minds of the lowest orders of the ancient world, the dregs of Roman society, and then for the practical reason that it needed to hide its mysteries under enigmatic appearances. "Depuis les catacombes," says Emile Mâle, "l'art religieux parle par figures. Il nous montre une chose et il nous invite à en voir une autre."[2] But the Middle Ages, and especially the thirteenth century, were the great ages of religious symbolism in art. Without a close study

[1] Treatises on Biblical Introduction and on Hermeneutics often fail to deal adequately with this subject.
[2] *L'Art religieux du XIIIe siècle en France*, 1902. There is, for instance, the fish that represents Christ and the crude pictures of Jonah and the Whale which represent the Resurrection.

of its symbolism the religious art of that period is entirely unintelligible. By the middle of the sixteenth century the religious art of the Middle Ages had become an enigma ; its symbolism was no longer understood. Our own age is rediscovering it, but not without fresh research into the whole subject of symbolism. The problem of the relation of symbolism to art is still a matter of controversy among art critics. Ruskin in his *Modern Painters*[1] gave his opinion emphatically : " The simple fact is that allegorical (and symbolical) painting has been the delight of the greatest men and of the wisest multitudes from the beginning of art, and will be till art expires . . . the greater and more thoughtful the artists, the more they delight in symbolism and the more fearlessly they employ it." But the debate is not yet closed.

If imagery has such significance for Language, Literature, and Art we might well expect to find that it has certain bearings on the domain of *thought*. " To attempt a fundamental examination of metaphor would be nothing less than an investigation of the genesis of thought itself."—*Times Literary Supplement*, 14th Oct., 1926. And such bearings it has, in more ways than we can at present pause to enumerate. We may mention, as an instance, its significance for philosophy, in particular for logic and for psychology. Even in this realm of abstract ideas the imagination plays an important rôle, bringing imagery into thought and statement, Such imagery may be a danger to clear thinking ; it certainly is a favourite resource of confused and feeble thinking. It is the business of logic to analyse statements ruthlessly with a view to distinguishing what is the clear enunciation of an intellectual idea from what is imagery used in the attempt to make an idea vivid for the imagination. Mere metaphors and symbols masquerading as literal statements of

---

[1] Part IV, Chap. VIII, § 86.

truth are responsible for many a false notion that is widely accepted. But though fraught with danger, images are not without their use in the development of thought. " Rien," says A. Sabatier, " n'est plus propre que l'allegorie à porter une idée à son complet épanouissement. Il faudrait étudier, à ce point de vue, la fameuse allégorie d'Agar et de Sarah.[1] On verrait que si l'idée a créé l'image, l'image à son tour a singulièrement aidé l'idée a se préciser et à développer toute sa richesse." [2]

If the misuse of imagery has led to philosophical error, it is to be expected that a similar misuse should lead to aberrations in *theology*. Indeed, in theological thought the possibility of error from this source is considerably greater just because the truths with which theology deals are more lofty, more remote from human experience, farther beyond the ken of sense and imagination. It has been pointed out that some of the early heresies originated with the uncompromising and indiscriminate following up of some metaphor that either was in current use or had been taken over from some philosophy. The metaphor of the " Word ", of Alexandrine origin, had been used in the Gospel of St. John as a designation of the Second Person of the Trinity. This metaphor was worked out according to the philosophy of human speech and was used as an analogy to describe the nature and generation of the eternal Son. Heresy pushed the comparison to extremes. The Sabellians seized upon one aspect of it to confound the two Persons, Arianism on another to belittle the Second Person. Yet, whatever be the dangers involved, imagery of some sort must be used. Its necessity arises out of the fact that there are no words which

---

[1] The passage in question occurs in St. Paul's Epistle to the Galatians iv, 21.
[2] *L'Apôtre Paul*, p. 74.

directly describe heavenly realities. The Master Himself taught His sublimest truths through metaphor and parable ; John the Disciple taught through allegory in his Gospel and his Apocalypse, and conveyed the deepest and best of his message in the metaphors of " light " and " life ".

It is not surprising, therefore, that the writings of the Christian Fathers should abound with imagery. It was part of their mighty task to present the truths of the new revelation in intellectual forms that could be grasped by the mind of their age. In carrying it out they seized upon the materials that lay to hand, not only the abstract concepts of some widespread philosophy but its accompanying imagery. One of the habitual methods of attack adopted by adversaries of religion is to seek to confound together the imagery and symbolism in which a religious truth is enwrapped —perhaps but temporarily—and that truth itself. " Misrepresentation of religion," says a recent writer,[1] " may be accounted for, to a certain extent, by insufficient attention to the subject of the metaphorical and symbolic nature of theological language."

On the other hand, if used with due measure and caution, analogy and metaphor furnish a method of investigation, and a help to progress of thought, which is useful in theology as it is in other sciences.[2] To give a single instance, the analogy of light has been used to illustrate and to elucidate, if I may say so, the theology of faith.[3] In much the same manner the analogy of water has been of service to the science of electricity. " The *Summa* of St. Thomas," says a writer in the *American Ecclesiastical Review*,[4] " is all

---

[1] Gilbert Clive Binyon in the *Pilgrim*, July, 1922.
[2] The theological bearings of these forms of imagery have been studied in a recent work, *Analogie et Symbolisme*, by Maurice Debaisieux, Professor of Philosophy at the Ecole Jeanne d'Arc at Lille, Paris, 1921.
[3] This analogy is developed throughout the entire work, *La Lumière et la Foi*, par le R. P. Hugon, O.P.
[4] December, 1920.

abloom with these flowers of the imagination, these natural emblems and symbols of the supernatural."

When we descend from the region of religious thought into that of the external manifestations of religion, we find imagery in the form of symbolism entering into every phase of religious *worship*. All the Sacraments involve symbolic actions signifying something other and higher than themselves. External worship is entirely symbolical and a considerable literature exists dealing with the symbolism of liturgy.[1] To one entirely ignorant of that symbolism, ritual or ceremonial is at best a series of graceful evolutions, at worst mere unintelligible formalism. Religious iconography and religious architecture are both full of symbolism,[2] the significance of which can, in our days at least, be grasped only at the price of study. The most sacred things of our religion, from the Cross to the Sacred Heart, are symbols or emblems. This entire aspect of imagery has been studied in the Abbé Auber's important work on the history of religious symbolism.[3]

Nor is imagery without its bearings on the common life of every day. The difficulties it creates in the domain of abstract thought have their echo in that of daily intercourse. For common speech is rich in figures, richer in proportion as one descends the social scale, until in the course of an altercation in the marketplace one might, within a very few minutes, hear every figure that, with much pomp of Greek nomenclature, the rhetoricians have recorded in their manuals. As Chesterton has it, " Keats never put into a sonnet so many remote metaphors as a coster puts into a curse." Du Marsais, two and a half centuries ago,

---

[1] A good introduction to the subject is *Histoire et Symbolisme de la Liturgie*, A. Lerosey, Paris, 1912.

[2] Cf. Sidney Heath, *The Romance of Symbolism and its Relation to Church Ornament and Architecture*, London, 1909.

[3] *Histoire et Théorie du Symbolisme religieux*, 4 vols., Paris, 1884.

had said the same : " En effet je suis persuadé qu'il se fait plus de figures un jour de marché à la halle, qu'il ne s'en fait en plusieurs jours d'assemblées académiques." All this profusion of imagery, the product of imagination and of passion, is a foe to clearness of thought. It may produce an atmosphere in which thinking of any kind is scarcely possible. It is fertile in misunderstanding. Its greatest danger is its liability to be taken literally by unimaginative persons. Now, as a steadying influence amid the whirl of images, the knowledge (a department of rhetoric or of logic according to the point of view) of the many ways in which speech can, legitimately or otherwise, be turned aside from its literal sense, would be of no small value to the plain man. And we can see no adequate reason why the plain man should not receive definite instruction in the elementary rules of clear thinking and plain statement. He might thus be less at the mercy of the journalist or of the mob orator, less prone also to fall foul of his exuberant friends.

Of the bearings of the science of imagery upon certain special branches of study a word may be said next. It is clearly indispensable for archæology, a science which is itself of prime importance to history, both civil and ecclesiastical. Then there is the science of heraldry, once in high honour,[1] now little better than a minor department of archæology. Mr. G. K. Chesterton says of it,[2] " Heraldry involves two things of enormous importance to normal humanity ; the combination of the two making that noble thing called co-operation ; on which rest all peasantries and people that are free. The art of heraldry means independence ; an image

---

[1] The seventeenth-century Jesuit Francois Menestrier devoted the greater part of his life to its study. Among the 164 items of his bibliography are such titles as *L'Art des Emblemes, La Science et l'Art des Devises,* etc.
[2] *The Everlasting Man,* 1925.

chosen by the imagination to express the individuality. The science of heraldry means interdependence ; an agreement between different bodies to recognize different images ; a science of imagery." Heraldry, it is hardly necessary to recall, employs throughout the language of emblems and symbols. The study of imagery likewise furnishes many a clue in that byway of history which deals with the secret societies. There is again the science of comparative religion and the closely allied science of ethnology,[1] both of which have in recent years given rise to an abundant literature. Lastly, the light thrown by the study of the metaphorical element in language on certain aspects of comparative philology can be judged from the single example of the series of articles by Père Dhorme, O.P., in the *Revue Biblique*, 1920–1,[2] on the metaphorical use of names of parts of the body in Hebrew and in Accadian, an ancient pre-Semitic tongue of Mesopotamia which, seven centuries before Christ, was already a dead language.

III

The study of imagery seems to the writer to have a yet deeper significance and a more fundamental. For imagery is, as we have seen, a using of objects belonging to one order of being to explain, represent, picture forth objects belonging to another order. In its most characteristic and distinctive form it is a using of material objects as images of immaterial,

[1] One may mention the rare work of Nicholas Caussin, S.J., *De Symbolica Aegyptiorum Sapientia*, published at Cologne in 1623, and Creuzer's *Symbolik und Mythologie der alten Völker*, 4 vols., Leipzig, 1836–43. This has been translated into French, with additions, by M. Guigniant under the title *Les Religions de l'Antiquité*. More recent German works are those of Grohmann, Prinz, and Gressmann. A very important problem is that of the extent to which the ancient myths were allegorical.

[2] Since published in book form.

spiritual things. It is founded on the existence of analogies and correspondences between the various objects or phenomena of nature, and between these again and human life—man's emotional, moral, and intellectual nature, between matter and mind. Imagery is a witness to the harmony between mind and matter, to the unity of all creation, and thus to the oneness of its Author.

That the visible world and the mind of man both bear upon them the stamp of Him who made them and in so far reveal forth His nature and attributes must have been felt, however dimly, from the beginning. On the one hand, man believes himself made in the image and likeness of his Maker, on the other that the world around him is the handiwork of the same Mighty Artist and bears His imprint and sign manual. The Book of Psalms in the Old Testament Scriptures is filled with the grandest expressions of this belief. In the thirteenth chapter of the Book of Wisdom the idea is set forth in express terms :—" For by the greatness and beauty of the creature the Creator may be perceived so as to be known thereby." St. Paul restated for Christianity the same thought—" Since the creation of the world God's invisible attributes—His everlasting power and divinity are to be discerned and contemplated in his works." [1] And if creation bears witness to its Author's power, wisdom, and beauty, must it not bear witness to His oneness ? May it not throughout its realms be recognized for what it is— the product of a single Mind ?

Great thinkers of all times have seen in various aspects the existence of this unity. Plato believed in a world of subsistent ideas, the counterpart of the world of palpable things. Plotinus saw the world as an imaged image : Tertullian taught that all

[1] Epistle to the Romans i, 20, Westminster version.

18

things in nature are prophetic outlines of divine
operations, God not merely speaking parables but
doing them : Bacon realized the multitudinous
" respondences " between the worlds of matter and
mind. Pascal saw in nature an image of the realm
of grace. " Les choses corporelles," he writes,[1]
" ne sont qu'une image des spirituelles, et Dieu a
représenté les choses invisibles dans les visibles."
" Analogies," writes Archbishop Trench, " may be
called as witnesses, the world of Nature being throughout a witness to the world of Spirit, proceeding from
the same hand, growing from the same root, and
being constituted for that very end. . . . The things
on earth are copies of the things in heaven." In the
same strain write thinkers so different as Emerson
and Carlyle. " All visible things," writes the latter,
" are emblems. What thou seest is not there on its
own account. Matter only exists to represent some
idea and body it forth." For matter after all is, no
less than spirit, the embodiment of some divine idea.
" Have mountains and waves and skies," writes
Emerson, " no significance but what we consciously
give them, when we employ them as emblems of our
thoughts ? The world is emblematic. Parts of
speech are metaphors, because the whole of nature
is a metaphor, of the human mind. The laws of
moral nature answer to those of matter as face to face
in a glass. The visible world and the relation of
its parts is the dial plate of the invisible. . . . This
relation between the mind and matter is not fancied
by some poet, but stands in the will of God."[2]

In a writer still closer to our days[3] we find, in
a different form, the same thought. " As always,"
he writes, " the seen is to Christ the emblem of the

[1] *Pensées*, ii, 249, 88.
[2] *Nature*, ch. iv, Language.
[3] Alfred Edersheim, *The Life of Jesus the Messiah*, i, p. 411.

unseen and spiritual ; Nature, that in and through which, in manifold and divers colouring, He ever sees the supernatural, even as the light lies in varying hues on the mountain, or glows in changeful colouring on the edge of the horizon. . . . To Jesus all things pointed upwards, because the God of Nature was the God of Grace, the one living and true God in whom all matter and spirit lives, whose world is one in design, workmanship, and purpose."

This ultimate unity of the spiritual and material worlds as expressions of the one divine intellect has been from the beginning seen or guessed at by the poets, from the nameless poet who sang :

> The heavens show forth the glory of God
> And the firmament declareth the work of His hands

to the very modern poet who wrote :

> Earth's crammed with Heaven
> And every common bush afire with God.

It is the poet's very nature to feel—

> The spiritual significance burn through
> The hieroglyphic of material shows,

And to wonder with Milton

> . . . if earth
> Be but the shadow of heaven, and things therein
> Each to other like more than on earth is thought.

In Christian writers of the Catholic tradition the thought of Nature uttering God, mirroring the eternal Mind is all but a commonplace. We meet with it again and again in the Christian Fathers, above all St. Augustine. We find it, ages after, set forth in the poetry—that wonderful Hymn of the Sun, and in the life, of St. Francis of Assisi. Cardinal Bellarmine's little treatise *De Ascensione Mentis in*

Deum [1] is but the working out of the idea. And in our own days it has been even more fully developed in such beautiful but, I fear, little known, books as Mgr de la Bouillerie's *Le Symbolisme de la Nature*, *The Voice of Creation* by Canon Oakeley, an Oxford Convert, and *Nature as a Book of Symbols*.[2] The writer of a work that has enjoyed an extraordinary popularity [3] has endeavoured to carry the thought still further and trace in the supernatural world the working of the same laws that rule the visible universe.

Such thinkers and a host of others have but followed where the great Thinker had led the way. He came, speaking of shepherds and merchants, fishes and pearls, bread and vines, harvest and sowing, and all these were images and symbols of diviner things. He has made the simple things of nature utter for all time to man eternal verities.

Indeed, one cannot long explore the world of imagery without coming to realize that it is a sort of intermediate region wherein the world of visible things seems to blend with the world of thought. And it would be strange if out of this realization did not spring that of the ultimate harmony and unity of these two worlds as common expressions of the Mind of God. The two writers whom I have singled out as noteworthy explorers of the world of imagery both reached this thought. " If one writer," says Mr. Macbeth, " pen *Paradise Lost* and *Paradise Regained*, many resemblances will it be possible to detect between the two. But outward nature and mental nature are from the same Author—the one great Thinker and Poet, who has developed His divine ideas on sea and sky ; on conscience, heart,

---

[1] Recently translated into English and published under the title, *The Mind's Ascent to God*, Mowbray, London, 1925.

[2] By W. Marshall, London, 1893.

[3] *Natural Law in the Spiritual World*, by Henry Drummond. The book has passed through some fifty editions.

and intellect : a basis God-given on which to rest all similitudes. . . . Our subject reaches up even to God." And Mr. Grindon, " The Divine Ruler of the realm of spirit is the sustainer also of the material world in which we dwell. The maintenance of each is governed . . . by the same laws. Therefore they harmonize at all points and nature is a representative and counterpart of the invisible."

If there be any substance in the foregoing considerations we may hope from an exploration of the world of imagery no slight repayment for such labour and pains as the exploring may cost. It is as yet imperfectly explored, and the present explorer cannot hope in a single expedition to discover all its secrets and throw light into all its dark places. But he will endeavour roughly to map it out, to trace its main features, and to place on record for future explorers such discoveries as have hitherto been made.

PART I

THEORY

CHAPTER I

Genesis and Raison D'Être of Metaphor

Every object in the universe may be said to have a twofold significance, a significance in itself as a fragment of reality—that is, necessarily, a fragment of goodness, truth, and beauty, and a significance as symbol, emblem, or image of something other than itself. A star, regarded solely in its own concrete nature, interests the astronomer, the physicist, the navigator. For one it is a mass of chemical substances in an igneous state ; for another it is a member of the hierarchy of the heavens ; for a third it is a guide point in the chart of the night skies. To the poet, to the poetic mind of the common man, it is first a thing of beauty in itself, an element in nature's loveliness, and then a symbol that calls up a world of association and of imagery. To a Shelley or a Milton (though in very different fashion) it is the symbol of abiding hope and of peace everlasting.

> The soul of Adonais like a star
> Beckons from the abodes where the eternal are.

So the former. And Milton :—

> So sinks the Day-Star in the ocean bed,
> And yet anon repairs his drooping head,
> And tricks his beams and with new-spangled ore
> Flames in the forehead of the morning sky
> So Lycidas sunk low but mounted high. . . .

23

For a Wordsworth, thinking of Milton, it is an image of aloofness :—

> His soul was like a star and dwelt apart.

While still another writer can speak of "a poem round and perfect as a star ".

Many an ancient race fancied its gods among the constellations, and the Hebrew people, yearning for a mighty Redeemer and Restorer, pictured him under the same glorious image : " A star shall come forth out of Jacob " [1]—doubtless the same *stella splendida et matutina* which John saw in vision on Patmos.[2]

And as with lofty things so with things most lowly. A field-mouse, to the peasant a thing of naught, to the naturalist a subject of curious observation, becomes for the poet Burns a homely symbol of one of the familiar aspects of our daily lives. Carlyle, in *Sartor Resartus*, drew a philosophy of life from the symbolism of clothes. And so common things may be ennobled, caught up into the region of poetry, of art, of religion itself. The mind may see in things that pass symbols of the everlasting and in things material images of the spiritual world. " Nature," says Emerson, " offers all her creatures to a man as a picture-language. Being used as a type a second wonderful value appears in the object, far better than the old value." The deeper meaning of this we shall presently see. Enough to remind ourselves for the moment that the things about us, however common and familiar, are replete for the soul with a significance beyond themselves. The dove, the lamb, the shepherd, the daylight, and the darkness are images of the highest things. A nation's enthusiasm is symbolized in a piece of coloured cloth, which we call a flag, and a world's adoration is summed up in two pieces of wood which we call a cross.

[1] Num. xxiv, 17. Cf. Isa. xiv, 12 ; Deut. viii, 10.
[2] Apocalypse xxii, 16.

24

So, as it were behind this visible, tangible world there is another attainable only to man's intellectual insight, a world of deeper meaning and of spiritual significance, which I have ventured to call the " world of imagery ". This " world " is not, as we shall see, a pure creation of man's imagination. Between it and the world of concrete sense-perceptible reality there is a mysterious harmony, which is not the less real because we may often fail to account for it. But whatever its foundation in reality, this world is of wonderful variety, richness, significance. We may feel confident on setting out to explore it that our toil will have its recompense.

Now, lest our exploration be a mere aimless wandering, it is well that we should possess at least an outline chart of the land. In the sphere of reality there are three regions—call them worlds within worlds, if we will, *the world of things, the world of thoughts, and the world of words*.[1] Each of these has its counterpart in the world of imagery. To the world of things answers the realm of symbols ; to that of words, the realm of metaphor. The world of thought is itself a world of images, yet even to thought corresponds a distinct realm of the world of imagery, that of symbolical and analogical ideas—a mysterious land, this, which must be entered with cautiousness, for it is fraught with perils.

Our first task shall be to explore as best we may that region of the world of imagery which lies behind *language*. I have given to it the name of metaphor, but it is in reality more diversified than the simplicity of the name would lead us to expect. We might have called it " figurative language ", were it not for the fact that there are many " figures of speech " which

---

[1] This is not, of course, a strictly philosophical " division ". These three worlds overlap, or rather interpenetrate, one another. But they are for our present purposes sufficiently distinct.

are in no sense imagery. These, as we are not concerned with them, we need not at present name. But the name metaphor is meant to cover the figures known to grammarians and rhetoricians as metaphor proper, simile, metonymy, synecdoche, personification. These will form the object of the first stage of our explorations.

There is a tendency, natural enough it must be confessed, to look on the figures of speech as a somewhat meaningless invention of the grammarians, or as at best flowers of language, literary graces, ornaments of style, scarcely worthy of serious attention. A recent writer has well said that " the popular estimate of their significance has suffered from early association with rhetoric, not, as one might wish, with religion, philosophy, idealism and humour ".[1] That the Greek *names* are an invention of the grammarians is indeed most true. And the figures of which they are the labels *may* serve merely as the trimmings of literature. But their significance lies deeper, and in the first place the study of them leads us to the very roots of language.

All language is a device, a more or less imperfect and clumsy device,—

> For words, like Nature, half reveal
> And half conceal the soul within—

whereby we seek to convey to other minds the ideas that have had their origin in our own. There exists no means of laying our thoughts open to the immediate intuition of others, though they may, indeed, at times be guessed from the expression of the features. Accordingly, a man must have recourse to sense-perceptible tokens, signs, symbols, into which he may translate his thought with a view to transmitting it to some other mind. A little vibrating breath

[1] *Poetic Imagery*, by H. W. Wells, New York, 1924.

or a few scrawled characters must represent ideas from the lowest to the loftiest. How these four black marks which I now write, *t r e e*, can convey to your mind any notion of the wonderful living thing which, as I look out of the window on this spring day, is putting forth its myriad leaves, each a marvel of delicate texture and design, each an elaborate breathing apparatus for the creature's sustenance as well as a delight to the beholder—how, I say, these black marks can call up all that before your mind, how a combination of three sounds made with teeth and tongue and throat, can do the same, must always be something of a mystery. How the like clumsy devices can transfer from mind to mind all lofty and spiritual thoughts—the soul, love, beauty, God, is a mystery greater yet. But so it is. First these thoughts must stand for things, truth as it is in the mind being the correspondence of thought to thing, as of images in a mirror to the objects that are reflected therein.[1] Next, as we have seen, signs and tokens which shall stand for thoughts must be sought and chosen. But here there presents itself a difficulty which at first sight might well seem insurmountable. The brain— the unified sense-perception, if you will,—is a truthful recorder, a faithful mirror of reality. But there is within us a faculty of wholly different nature to which the brain serves as an instrument[2]—the intellect. The images of things around us pass through the open casements of our senses and impress themselves upon the brain within, but once " in the quick forge and working-house of thought " they are wrought upon with mysterious alchemy by processes which philosophy has labelled " abstraction ", " generalization ", and

---

[1] *How* thought is representative of reality is one of the great problem of philosophy which it would be beside my purpose to consider here. The analogy of the mirror is, of course, very imperfect.
[2] Though not in the strict sense of that word.

the like, scarce knowing what it means. By these processes, however, be they what they may, we are conscious of possessing ideas purged to all appearance of every trace of materiality, ideas " of spirit all compact ", yet with a reality of their own—such ideas as goodness, virtue, personality, relation, being. Here, as I have said, there arises in the genesis of language a difficulty which, had it not long since been actually met, might well seem a problem beyond the wit of man to solve—what audible or visible signs to choose in order to embody such ideas and transmit them from mind to mind.

In what manner precisely the problem was solved at the birth of language we can but guess. We need not enter upon the old quarrel, in which Plato [1] (followed by St. Augustine in his *De Re Dialectica*) and Aristotle took opposite sides, as to whether the signs chosen had or had not some natural kinship with the things which they were chosen to designate. It is generally held, with Aristotle, that, except for some onomatopoeic words for sounds and the like, they had no such kinship. There is nothing to show that the root-words chosen to name quite simple and concrete objects and actions were in every case pictures or natural representations of such objects and actions, unless, as we have said, they could in some way be associated with sounds.[2] A sheep might be called a " ba-ba ", as babies call it,[3] a tree, even, might conceivably be given a name that would recall the wind whistling or sighing through it. But what natural name could be given to bread or a stone ? By whatever process men

---

[1] The subject is debated in his dialogue *Cratylus*. But the debate is older still. We find it in the literature of the Brahmans.

[2] See Max Müller, *Lectures on the Science of Language*, 2nd Ser., Lecture VI.

[3] Just as they may call a cow a " moo " and a dog a " bow-wow ". For the latter, French babies say " tou-tou ", which scarcely recalls the sound of barking.

may have arrived at what seemed proper designations of the things around them,[1] it would seem clear that they first gave names to simple concrete objects—domestic utensils, necessaries of life, animals, and to the simplest actions. These things first named were, there is every reason for believing, such only as man's senses could directly attain, what he could taste or see or smell or hear or feel in some way.[2] But almost from the first moment when the human soul came to the use of its powers and faculties the need for the expression of more or less abstract ideas and for the naming of things unseen must have made itself felt. How were words found for such notions and concepts?

Broadly speaking, we may answer : instead of inventing new and arbitrary signs or words, man used those he possessed already, but he used them in a new sense. Words so *transferred* ($\mu\epsilon\tau\alpha$ $\phi\acute{\epsilon}\rho\omega$) from their original and proper sense to a new sense are used metaphorically, they constitute metaphors.

> The fact [says Max Müller] that all words expressive of immaterial conceptions are derived by metaphor from words expressive of sensible ideas was, for the first time, clearly and definitely put forward by Locke, and is now fully confirmed by the researches of comparative philologists. All roots, i.e., all the material elements of language, are expressive of sensuous impressions, and of sensuous impressions only ; and as all words, even the most abstract and sublime, are derived from roots, comparative philology fully endorses the conclusions arrived at by Locke.

[1] It is unnecessary to adopt here any particular theory as to the primary origin of language.

[2] " The more advanced a language is the more developed is its power of expressing abstract or general ideas. Everywhere language has first attained to expressions for the concrete and special " (O. Jespersen, *Language, its Nature and Development*, London, 1922, p. 429). And Frederico Garlanda points out in his *Philosophy of Words* that language is in continual evolution from a meaning more or less material to meanings more and more ideal, more and more spiritual. " The process of language is a great metaphor " ; " The evolution of the meanings of words, nay, the very life of language is a continual metaphor " (pp. 36–7).

And again : " Let us consider that there was necessarily and really a period in the history of our race when all the thoughts that went beyond the narrow horizon of our everyday life had to be expressed by means of metaphors." Hudson Maxim, in his interesting and original, if somewhat erratic book, *The Science of Poetry and the Philosophy of Language*, attempts to carry the thought still further back : " Man parted company with the brute when he began to have ideas which could not be expressed by the qualitative and quantitative properties of sound or by the imitative use of sounds as arbitrary symbols of concrete ideas. It was when man entered the abstract that he parted company intellectually with the lower animals. This was when man first used metaphor, when he first employed the expedient of expressing insensuous thought by sensuous terms." [1]

In that fascinating little work *La Vie des Mots*, M. Arsène Darmesteter, co-author with M. Adolphe Hatzfeld of the great *Dictionaire général de la langue française*, says (p. 85) : " In none of the languages whose history it is possible for us to study is there an abstract word which, if its etymology is known, is not resolvable into a concrete word."

This is even more amply expressed by an English writer on figurative language [2] :—

" Every abstract term, so called, was primarily constructed, in obedience to the fundamental laws of the intellect, as the appellation of something physical, and this primary sense, in the very nature of things, it never really loses. . . . Emotions, sentiments, qualities apprehensible by the mind alone, cannot be described and spoken of except by a reference, more or less direct, to something in the

---

[1] Op. cit., p. 24. We do not endorse the writer's Darwinian implications.
[2] L. H. Grindon, *Figurative Language : its Origin and Constitution.*

material world. Neither is it possible to denominate or refer to any mental process or operation except by citing something objective, something which belongs to the outer world, and the contemplation of which assists materially, when we come to reflect upon it, in the comprehension of the spiritual co-ordinate. . . . No word is metaphysical without having first been physical."

This conclusion of the philologists is quite in harmony with the findings of philosophy. Two principles in particular may be recalled. The first is this : the mind does not and cannot do its thinking without images, *phantasmata* according to the School-men. This Aristotle had already remarked.[1] A certain school of philosophers would identify the image with the idea itself, in which we need not follow them. But all, even the Schoolmen so jealous of safeguarding the soul's spirituality, admit that all the mind's ideas are at least accompanied by images which are not purely intellectual but are organic, that is, a product of man's organism, a compound of matter and spirit. Even in its loftiest soarings into the immaterial the mind needs the wings of imagery, wings that may be gossamer as the wings of Ariel, yet are in some sort material. Without their aid thought cannot soar. In this there is no cause for surprise, seeing that in man spirit and matter, though distinct and separate, are fused into such perfect oneness that nothing can take place in either element of our being without at least an echo in the other. So, with every thought that forms itself, there hovers somewhere in the grey matter of the brain at least the wraith of an image. All this, theoretical though

---

[1] Διο οὐδέποτε νοεῖ ἄνευ φαντάσματος ἡ ψυχή (*De Anima*, iii, 7). R. P. Lahr, S.J., in his *Cours de Philosophie*, 23ᵉ ed., Paris, 1920, tom. i, p. 380, says : " No thought is wholly independent of the images of all kinds that accompany it. The course of our thoughts can develop only by relying constantly on a parallel development of images."

it seem, has a very practical bearing on literature
and on life.

The second principle is closely akin to the first.
It is at least as old as Aristotle and was a practically
undisputed axiom of the Schools. Certain modern
philosophers have rediscovered it, formulated it in
new terms, and put it forth as destructive of traditional
and spiritual psychology.[1] *Nihil in intellectu quod non
prius fuerit in sensu* ; all knowledge originates in
experience, which is to say that out of the perceptions
that pour through the portals of the senses all our ideas
must be wrought : out of no other material *can* they
be wrought. Imagination may seize upon them,
combine them afresh, and weave them into many an
airy fabric of fancy. The intellect may thrice refine
them from all taint of matter till they are etherealized
into concepts the most abstract. Yet the impressions
of outward palpable objects upon our senses constitute
the crude original stuff on which alone imagination
and intellect can work.[2] And now mark the interest
of this for our present subject. It would seem but
fitting that the idea should go forth on its errand
to other minds robed in the same raiment of matter
and sense—though perhaps with freshened colours
and richer embroidery—as that wherewith it once
had entered ours. This, as we have seen, is a practical
necessity for the makers of primitive speech. It
continues, however, and must ever continue, to be
altogether in harmony with the nature of the mind.

---

[1] In the second volume (p. 7) of his work on Psychology (Louvain,
9th ed., 1912), Cardinal Mercier demonstrates this truth in the following
form : " The human intellect borrows its proper object from sense-
perceptible things."

[2] " Sensations once experienced modify the nervous organism so
that copies of them arise again in the mind after the original outward
stimulus is gone. No mental copy, however, can arise in the mind of
any kind of sensation which has never been directly incited from
without. . . . The man *born* blind can never have a mental vision "
(William James, *Psychology*, vol. ii, chap. 18).

RAISON D'ÊTRE OF METAPHOR

We continue to need images and pictures in order to think and in order to express our thoughts. To describe, for instance, their mental states or processes men were and are fain to borrow words which first they had invented to describe states or processes of their bodily organism, such as fell under the observation of some bodily sense.[1] Their feelings were " warm " or " cold ", their pain was " sharp ", their mind " grasped " its ideas, these ideas are " broad " or " narrow ", " high " or " low ", their sympathies were " touched ". And all this with a view to rendering such soul states or mental concepts intelligible, or at all events more readily intelligible, to other minds. Nothing, then, in the mind that entered not first through the senses and nothing in language that does not smack of the origin of those ideas to which it gives a name.[2]

Metaphor, then, is in its origin an attempt to express in terms of experience thoughts lying beyond experience, to express the abstract in terms of the concrete, to picture forth the unfamiliar by means of the familiar, to express insensuous thought by sensuous terms.

Of course it is clear that language in its present stage of development, so distant from its far-off beginnings, with all its elements so rubbed and ground in their passage down the stream of time, fully reveals its origin in the sense-perception of material things only to the trained student.[1] Yet we have many

---

[1] " The material world has lent its entire vocabulary to the spiritual world : a breath, a wind gave its name to the soul. . . . The soul has been endowed with all the epithets and all the verbs which designate the qualities and the actions of sense-perceptible beings." Lanson, *Principes de Composition et de Style.*

[2] " Omnia," says St. Thomas Aquinas, " quae in praesenti statu cognoscimus, cognoscuntur per comparationem ad res sensibiles naturales " (*Summa*, Ia. pars. q. 84, a. 8). All things that in our present state we know are known through comparison with the sense-perceptible things of nature.

abstract words in daily use whose quite material origin is still easily traceable. "Spirit" has, among its many meanings, come to stand for immaterial substance itself, yet its origin is humble. The Latin word from which we have borrowed it, *spiritus*, like the Greek word *pneuma* that corresponds to it, meant a breeze. Then it came to mean the breath of life,[1] and then the immaterial principle that quickens us. Rising still higher, it was used to name a wholly disembodied being, and finally the Third Person of the Blessed Trinity.[2]

There is a passage in the Gospel of St. John which in the Douay Version is translated "the Spirit breatheth where He wills", and it may be so translated. But in many modern versions,[3] including some by Catholic translators,[4] it simply runs : "the wind bloweth where it listeth," and this is at least an equally possible translation. Let us set down the original and its Latin equivalent. They run :—

$$\tau\grave{o} \ \pi\nu\epsilon\hat{u}\mu\alpha \ \ddot{o}\pi o\upsilon \ \theta\acute{\epsilon}\lambda\epsilon\iota \ \underline{\pi\nu\epsilon\hat{\iota}}$$

*Spirit*us ubi vult *spir*at.

It will be at once seen that in both original and translation verb corresponds to noun as it cannot be made to do in English. This is a curious example of a word, in which the metaphorical sense had all but supplanted the original, suddenly reverting to the latter. From the same quite concrete and material

---

[1] Thus in Gen. ii, 7 : "And God breathed on his face the breath of life, and man became a living soul."

[2] It is a curious reversal of etymological history that this same word should come to be put to such uses as it is put to in the modern automobile industry with its *pneumatic* tyres and its motor *spirit*.

[3] Authorized Version, Revised Version (with the alternative in the margin), *The New Testament in Modern Speech*, *Twentieth Century New Testament*, etc.

[4] Crampon, "Le vent souffle où il veut" ; Father Spencer, O.P., *A New Translation of the Gospels*, and others.

root *spir*, " to blow," have grown various highly abstract and general notions [1] :—

in-spir-ation—originally " a blowing in " ;
a-spir-ation—" a drawing in of the breath " ;
con-spir-acy—" a breathing together " ;
ex-spir-ation—" a breathing forth " ; as well as
re-spir-ation—which retains the original sense ; and
per-spir-ation—in which the original sense is but little altered.

Professor Max Müller has pointed out the multitude of abstract terms in every Aryan tongue of which the primitive root, *mar*, " to grind," is the ancestor.[2] Elsewhere he has shown that from the simple notion " to be bright " came words for sun, moon, stars, the eyes of man, gold, silver, play, joy, happiness, love.

It will be instructive to go back to the roots of other familiar abstract terms, and to see their origin in sense-perception and therefore their originally metaphorical nature. Thus, the primary intellectual act " apprehend " was " to grasp at ", " comprehend ", " to grasp together ". " Explanation " is a " laying out flat ". To feel meant originally " to handle with the palm of the hand "—which it may still mean. " Instigation " came from the use of the *goad*, " tribulation " from that of the *flail*, and " conjecture " from the throwing of *dice*. " Independence " is the state of something that does not *hang* from another, " incentive " is that which sets the tune. " Define " is to put bounds to, and " refute " to " knock out " an argument, in the manner of a boxer. " Instinct," " distinguish," " stimulate," " stigmatize " come from a root which simply means to " prick " (English, " stick " and " sting "). " Attention " meant a " stretching to " and " reflection " a

[1] The Latin words for " mind ", " soul ", *animus, anima*, have a similar origin, the same as that of the Greek word ἄνεμος, " the wind."
[2] *Lectures on the Science of Language*, vol. ii, in the chapter " On the Power of Roots ".

"bending back"; to "perplex" was to "braid together", and to "develop" was to "unwrap". Again, "affliction" is derived from the figure of dashing against a rock; "anxiety" is based on the figure of choking or strangling; "grief" is from the figure of a burden heavy to bear; "trouble" from the disorderly pressure of a crowd. So of our vocabulary of psychical terms. Intellect is from *inter legere*, to choose between. Cogitate is from a Latin verb *coagitare*, to mix together, investigate from *vestigium*, the foot-print, examine from a word meaning the tongue of a balance.

Men at all times have seized upon aspects of nature, visible sights and sounds, to describe the invisible workings of the immaterial principle within them. How else, indeed, could they have put those workings into words? "No advance," says Max Müller again, "was possible in the intellectual life of man without metaphor." "Every expression that we employ," writes Professor Weekley, "apart from those that are connected with the most rudimentary objects and actions, is a metaphor, though the original meaning be dulled by constant use." And to illustrate the statement, he goes on : "In the above sentence *expression* meant "what is squeezed out"; to *employ* is to "twine in", like a basket maker; to *connect* is to "weave together"; *rudimentary* means "in the rough state", and an *object* is something "thrown in our way".[1] What more abstract than the word "idea", as we use it now? Yet it originally meant the visible organic form or outline of a thing. We find in Pindar[2] the expression ἰδέα το καλον, beautiful in shape, and

[1] *The Romance of Words*, by Ernest Weekley, London, 1913. See further George McKnight, *English Words and their Background*, Appleton, New York, 1923, p. 202.
[2] *Olympian Odes*, x, 22.

in Aristophanes[1] ἀθάνατοις ἰδέαις, immortal forms. So St. Matthew, describing in his Gospel[2] the angel of the resurrection, says, ἦν δὲ ἡ ἰδέα αὐτοῦ ὡς ἀστραπή, his countenance was as lightning. In the Platonic philosophy ideas were self-subsisting celestial representations of terrestrial things—a stage nearer the meaning we give to the word in modern speech.

It is only another aspect of this process that is envisaged in the law formulated by the Danish philologist, Professor Otto Jespersen, in his *Language, its Nature, Development, and Origin* (London, 1922) : " The more advanced a language is the more developed is its power of expressing abstract or general ideas. Everywhere language has first attained to expressions for the concrete and special " (p. 429). And Cardinal Mercier has pointed out that the findings of philology on this point agree with the well-known principle of Scholastic Psychology referred to above (p. 32). He proceeds to show the material origin of such terms as être, connaître, intelligence, sagesse, vertu, relation, justice, âme, Dieu.[3]

For our present purpose, however, it is not necessary to hold that all names for immaterial ideas, without exception, came originally from material sources.[4] We merely wish to make it clear how common and even universal a process in the making of language is this transference of words from material to immaterial objects. The *raison d'être* of such processes lies, as we have seen, in the very nature of our minds, and therefore we might expect the process to continue

---

[1] Clouds, 289.
[2] xxviii, 3.
[3] *Psychologie*, ii, p. 17. See Bréal, *La Sémantique*, p. 132, on the material origin of σοφος.
[4] " Every word without a single exception which has an immaterial meaning had originally a material meaning." Max Müller, *The Science of Thought*, p. 506.

long after language had passed beyond its tentative beginnings. That it is so in fact, a moment's reflection may convince us. The process of language-making is ever going on. Which of us cannot recall a dozen words now in use that were unknown when we were children, and a still greater number of old words that have acquired new meanings. Many of these new words are metaphors and many of these new meanings metaphorical, though we may be unaware of the fact. Therefore in the metaphorical use of words it is important to distinguish two stages— metaphor that is still *living* and metaphor in the *fossil* state. A metaphor has reached the fossil stage when the users of it are no longer conscious that it is not literal. From being a mere label or token standing for a given object of sense-perception it has come to be a mere label or token standing for some other object of quite a different nature.

This term " fossil " metaphor seems to me more expressive than Dr. Brinkmann's term " incarnate " metaphor. But however that may be, the two terms would seem to cover the same phenomena. The examples given by Dr. Brinkmann are such as one might give as samples of " fossil " metaphor. The central spot of the eye is called the *pupil,* in Spanish *la niña* (little girl) *de los ojos.* Again, the Greek ὄνος (donkey) used for windlass, the upper millstone, and a distaff : the same name given in Sanskrit to the plough as to the swine's snout, for reasons obvious enough : the familiar battering *ram* (in French *bélier*), and *crane* (in French *grue*). The " incarnate " metaphor is one that has been " completely absorbed into the blood of the language so as no longer to be felt as metaphor ".

Professor Max Müller prefers to classify metaphors as " radical " and " poetical ". By radical metaphor he understands the transference of one and the same root to different objects as when in Sanskrit both the sun and a hymn of praise are called *arká* from a root *ærk*, to shine, the one in the sense of what shines, the other in the sense of what makes shine or blazes forth the glory of a God—the blazer and the blazoner, we might say. The application of this root to various objects was the very process by which these objects were first given a name. But in poetical metaphor, metaphor as we commonly use the term, the process is different. Here you have two objects or concepts each with a name of its own, but, because of some analogy he perceives between the two, the speaker borrows the name of one of the concepts or objects and gives it to the other. The difference between these two processes may be illustrated by a diagram.

Radical

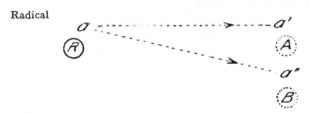

R is a definite object or concept with a name (generally a root-word) a. A and B are objects or concepts vaguely but not yet definitely realized and without names. The name a is given to them because of some real or fancied resemblance to R. The line is dotted to show that our awareness of the connexion ends by ceasing altogether.

Poetical

A is a well-known concept or object with a name a. B is another concept or object with a name b. Because of some perceived analogy between A and B, the name of A is transferred to B but does not displace its proper name, unless for the moment. But a has a new meaning.

In his later, and I think less known, work *The Science of Thought*, Max Müller revised some of the views set forth in his earlier work. He inclined to the opinion that in the process of metaphor there is not necessarily any transference of name, conscious or unconscious. Freqently all that happened was that the *differentia* of the term a making it peculiarly applicable to A gradually faded out of the mind. Thus *gubernator*, the steersman of a ship, gradually came to mean " the guider of a ship—or of anything else ", and therefore, naturally enough, the guider of the state, its governor.

The normal process of " radical " metaphor, which is also, practically speaking, the process by which a living metaphor gradually becomes fossilized, may be set forth somewhat as follows :—

A.—The word is a mere token for a particular idea.

AB.—It is metaphorically applied to a second idea carrying with it the first as an associated image which is not entirely absent from the consciousness either of the user or of the hearer of the expression.

B.—By the frequent and indiscriminate use of the word in this second meaning the associated image becomes dimmer and more blurred, till in the end it disappears, and now the word is a mere token for the second idea.

Of the process as it is still going on very simple examples readily occur. We speak of a " sheet " of paper without thinking of bedclothes, as the French speak of a *feuille de papier* without thinking of a tree. A more interesting example is the evolution of the word " vast ". Originally meaning a waste place, desert (cf. Latin *vastare*, " to lay waste "), it has come to mean simply large. Thus :—

A.—In the dark *vast* and middle of the night.

A + B.—As *long* as a journey across a vast.

BA.—A *vast* journey ; or Milton's *vast* vacuity and *vast* infinity when speaking of Chaos.

Ba.—*Vast* sea, *vast* regions.

B.—*Vast* strides, *vastly* pleased, a *vast* deal of pains.[1]

While words are passing through the transitional stage they are living, full of vitality, full also of poetry because of the suggestive, imaginative element they contain. When consciousness of the metaphor in them has quite faded away they are metaphors indeed still, but fossil metaphors, their poetical vitality is gone. Every language, says Michel Bréal, might constitute for itself its metaphor museum and in the specimens stored therein would be embedded a thousand relics of the history of the people that speaks that language. Nay, the study of fossil metaphor would throw many an interesting and curious side-light on the general history of civilization. To sum up with Carlyle : " Examine language ; what, if you except some few primitive elements (of natural sound), what is it all but metaphors, recognized as such or no longer recognized ; still fluid and florid, or now solid-grown and colourless ? If these same primitive elements are the osseous fixtures in the Flesh-Garment, Language—then are metaphors its muscle and tissues and living integuments."

[1] Here I am much indebted to Moulton, *Introduction to the Study of Literature*, and to Darmesteter, *La Vie des Mots*.

CHAPTER II

The Nature of Metaphor

We have studied the spontaneous need which, historically speaking, has given rise to the use of metaphor and kindred imagery. We have now to examine more closely the nature of metaphor. Such definitions or descriptions of it as are commonly to be met with give, correctly enough, no doubt, the meaning of the word, but they fail, as a rule, to afford us any very deep insight into the real nature of the thing defined. "Though the world's literature," says a recent writer,[1] " is full of the most consummate beauty introduced by the agency of metaphors, theory and analysis here seem to have lagged behind practice and construction, and the nature and function of metaphor retain much of their mystery still."

I

Let us, to begin with, glean what help we may from some of the current definitions.[2] According to the Standard Dictionary[3] metaphor is " the form of trope which is founded on a resemblance of relations ", or " a figure of speech in which one object is likened to another by asserting it to be that other or speaking of it as if it were that other ". The latter of these

[1] J. G. Jennings, *Metaphor in Poetry*, 1915.
[2] Mr. H. W. Wells in *Poetic Imagery*, Columbia University Press, 1924, considers that no strict definition of metaphor is possible, but suggests, as a " working test " that metaphor is " the recognition of a suggestion of one concept by another dissimilar in kind but alike in some strong ungeneric characteristic " (p. 21). One is not sure that this throws very much light upon the matter.
[3] Funk and Wagnall, 1903.

42

definitions gives us little help, the former contains in germ the theory which we hope to develop later. The Oxford English Dictionary defines metaphor as " the figure of speech in which a name or descriptive term is transferred to some object different from, but analogous to, that to which it is properly applicable ". Here is a metaphor from Thackeray : " He (Addison) was six and thirty. . . . He had not worked crop after crop from his brain, manuring hastily, subsoiling indifferently, cutting and sowing and cutting again, like other luckless cultivators of letters." " Work crop after crop from ", " manure ", " subsoil ", etc.—these are terms " properly applicable " only to the cultivation of fields. They are " transferred " [1] to an object, viz. the pursuits of literature, which is so " different " from agriculture as to belong to quite another order of things. Yet, in a flash, the writer has perceived that the two objects are " analogous ". Instead, however, of saying as much, he tacitly identifies them for the moment and uses of one the terms that belong to the other. It is an accurate and serviceable definition, but it leaves us wondering wherein this analogy lies, and by what mental process the identification of these merely analogous objects is effected. How is literature like a field, and how can the practice of literature be spoken of in terms of agriculture, not merely pleasingly and picturesquely, but also *truly* ?

Next to a dictionary definition it will be well to record definitions or descriptions given us by philosophers, writers on rhetoric and literary theory, exegetes, philologists, each from his particular point of view. The definitions I shall choose can be but average samples of countless similar definitions that might be given.

[1] The Greek verb μεταφέρω, to which we owe the word metaphor, means simply to transfer.

43

THEORY

Aristotle, in his *Poetic*,[1] defined metaphor as " the transference of a word to a sense different from its proper signification ". But, as is plain from a fuller treatment of the subject in another part of his works,[2] this definition covered what we now call synecdoche, the substitution of a whole for the part or of a part for the whole. Of the four kinds of metaphor that he enumerates, the first two really belong to the figure just mentioned, the third and the fourth, viz. transference from species to species and transference by analogy, are distinguished merely by a circumstance of minor importance. The one class of metaphors is direct, being founded on a perceived resemblance between two objects ; the other is indirect, being founded on the fact that the two objects in question bear similar *relations* to other objects. We may express the difference thus :—

(1) a (regarded in a particular aspect) $= x$.
   e.g. He (a) is a rock (x) of good sense. Behold the Lamb of God.
(2) $a : b$ (the mental world) $= x : y$ (the physical world)
   e.g. reason (a) is a guiding light (x).

I may be able to show in the course of these studies that all metaphor in which objects of wholly different orders are compared is reducible to this second class.

The Roman rhetorician Quintilian[3] clearly distinguishes synecdoche from metaphor, and deals suggestively with the rôle of metaphor in oratorical style, but he does not bring us nearer to the inner nature of metaphor. As we have no intention of treating the matter historically we may at once pass to moderns.

[1] Chap. XXI.
[2] *Rhetoric*, III, xi.
[3] *Institutes of Oratory*, Bk. viii, chap. vi. Cicero's definition of metaphor as *similitudinis ad verbum unum contracta brevitas* does not seem very helpful.

THE NATURE OF METAPHOR

Benjamin Keach, in his formidable work *Tropologia or a Key to Open Scripture Metaphors*, first published in 1779 but several times republished,[1] throws but little light on the nature of metaphor. " As to its definition," he says, " it is said to be a trope when a word is translated from its proper and genuine signification to another less proper. . . . There are other definitions," he adds, " but all to this sense." One would expect more from a treatise on the figurative language of the Bible. Further on in the course of his work he reaches the words of the institution of the Blessed Eucharist, and he argues thus :

> Either Christ spoke figuratively when He said, " This is My body," or He did not. And that the words cannot be taken in a proper sense is evident ; for it is impossible for words to express anything more plainly than that by " this " is meant the bread. It is said that " Christ took bread and brake it, and gave it " and said, " Take, eat, this is My body " ; where " this " necessarily relates to that which Christ took, brake, and gave. . . . Now, can anyone be so ignorant and foolish, to believe it is Christ's proper and real body which the Holy Ghost calleth so often bread.[2]

In reality " this " is indeterminate : it is the substitute of a gesture. It is as though Christ said : " That which I now hold in My hands is My body." Is this a metaphor ? Regarding the question from a purely literary point of view it certainly cannot be said that the form of the phrase demands that it be understood as a figure. Its true interpretation must be determined according to sound hermeneutical principles.[3]

---

[1] My edition, a demy 8vo vol. of 1,007 pages, was printed at the Bonmahon Press, Co. Waterford, a proselytizing institution, in 1858.

[2] Op. cit., p. 632. The author also refers to 1 Cor. xi, 26 ; John vi, 51 ; 1 Cor. x, 16, where the Eucharist is referred to as the bread.

[3] See Cardinal Wiseman's *Lectures on the Eucharist*, in which these principles are admirably applied.

THEORY

Professor Eduard König of Bonn, writing on the Style of Scripture in Dr. Hastings' *Dictionary of the Bible*,[1] without expressly defining metaphor, says that its source is " a vivid simultaneous contemplation of the main elements in two notions ". " For instance," he continues, " the notions of joy and of light are naturally combined, because both exercise a liberative and elevating influence upon the health of men." And he adds : " Metaphor springs from the putting together of comparable instances of the material and visible and of the ideal spheres." This is not unlike the description given by an American writer, Hudson Maxim. " Metaphor is an attempt to express in terms of experience thoughts lying beyond experience."[2] While the first sentence from Professor König differs but little from M. Michel Bréal's description : " The instantaneous perception of a likeness between two objects or two acts."[3] The writer of the article " Metaphor " in Hastings' *Dictionary of the Apostolic Church* thus defines, or rather describes, this figure : " A metaphor is a blossom of one tree on the branch of another," which seems an instance of *ignotum per ignotius*, the application being far from clear. But he proceeds, " It is a figure of speech by which a word or phrase is lifted to a meaning to which it is not literally entitled." " Lifted " is another metaphor, and not a very apt one, for may they not be also " lowered " ? Again, " A simple metaphor expresses the resemblance (or

---

[1] Extra volume, p. 162. Professor König has published an important work on the subject of the style of Scripture—*Stilistik, Rhetorik, und Poetik in Bezug auf die Biblische Litteratur komparativisch Dargestellt*, 1900.
Vigouroux's *Dictionnaire de la Bible* contains no article dealing *ex professo* with the figurative language of the Bible.
[2] *The Science of Poetry and the Philosophy of Language*, New York, 1910. But the idea illustrated by metaphor is not necessarily beyond experience, nor does it necessarily belong to the " ideal sphere ". To speak of the leg of a table is to use a metaphor.
[3] *La Sémantique*.

identity) between two dissimilar objects or ideas by applying to one a term which can literally designate only the other, as, ' this is My body.' " Apart from the impropriety of the example cited, may we not ask whether it is correct to say that metaphor " expresses " resemblance ; and, if this word is here (incorrectly) used in the sense of " implies ", how can any figure of speech imply " identity " between two dissimilar objects ? In the example cited there is no naming of two distinct objects. The Divine Speaker states identity between an object to which the word " this " points, viz. the transubstantiated " bread " before Him and His Sacred Body. He does not say : " My body is bread," nor " Bread is My body ", but this object (in appearance bread) is (because this instant it becomes) My body. At all events, if this be not the true meaning of these hallowed words, the incorrectness of it must be proved from some source other than the laws of figurative language.

Let us next turn for light to writers on rhetoric and literary style. " Our mind," says M. Gustave Lanson,[1] " perceiving on a sudden a common quality in two different objects, or creating between them a relation which assimilates them to one another, names one of them by a term which suits, or belongs to, the other. It makes a metaphor." How the quality can be common, especially when the objects belong to different spheres, or how the mind can create a relation which did not previously exist, M. Lanson does not explain, nor ought such explanation be expected of a writer on literary theory. Professor Genung[2] merely states that in metaphor " instead of comparing one thing with another we identify the two by taking the name or assuming the attribute of the one for the other ", and Messrs. Seeley

[1] *Principes de Composition et de Style*, Paris, 1897.
[2] *Practical Elements of Rhetoric*, Boston, 1900.

47

and Abbott [1] that metaphor is " a transference of the relation between one set of objects to another for the purpose of brief explanation ". Professor Earle defines Metaphor as " a figure of speech whereby the word which properly belongs to one set of phenomena is transferred to another, not arbitrarily, but in accordance with some natural and obvious analogy ".[2] These are average samples of the definitions to be met with in similar works. We have no better definition to offer but may be able to throw further light upon the thing defined.

II

With a view to understanding more clearly the nature of metaphor, it will be helpful to analyse it into its component elements. Let us begin with a metaphor of the simplest kind : " You must try to root out your faults one by one." Leaving to those competent to judge it the feasibility of this piece of advice, let us examine the imagery it contains. This is represented by a single expression : " to root out." Yet the sentence may be analysed as follows :—

(1) A main idea " faults " (*a*), which is the real subject of the discourse.

(2) A concrete image (*x*) unexpressed but implied, viz. " weeds."

(3) A perceived resemblance or analogy between (*a*) and (*x*) implying in this case the further metaphor that the soul is a garden. This point of resemblance may be called the point or the scope of the comparison involved in the metaphor.

(4) The momentary and tacit identification of (*a*) with (*x*) in such a way that language properly applicable only to (*x*) may be used of (*a*).

Sometimes (1) is unexpressed—" Rid your soul of

[1] *English Lessons for English People*, London, 1890.
[2] *English Prose : Its Elements, History, and Usage*, London, 1890, p. 239.

all its weeds." Sometimes (2) is not merely implied but expressed—" Root out those *weeds* of the soul, your faults." [1] But always a metaphorical expression may be analysed into the same components.

The phrase chosen as an example is, indeed, now so hackneyed that it is used without consciousness of its metaphorical import. It is practically a fossil metaphor. The poet is a rejuvenator of language. Thus Tennyson :

> Full seldom does a man repent, or use
> Both grace and will to pluck the vicious quitch
> Of blood and custom wholly out of him,
> And make all clean and plant himself afresh.

Here the main idea (inherited and acquired vices or faults) and the imported image (quitch or couch-grass thought of as a weed) are both expressed. The point of the comparison, i.e. that wherein vices and weeds resemble one another, is plain enough—both are found where they are not wanted and ought not to be.

We have now four convenient terms which may be used in the rest of the discussion—" main idea or object," " imported image," " scope," " tacit identification."

We shall presently, when dealing with the rôle or function of metaphor, discuss the manner in which it affects speech, its literary and rhetorical qualities. There is, however, one characteristic of metaphor which is part of its nature and may fittingly be discussed here. I refer to its tendency to obscurity. Skilfully handled it may, as we shall see, cast a vivid flash of light upon a subject, but, unlike simile, its natural tendency seems to be to darken rather than to clarify thought. This obscurity arises principally

---

[1] In simile both (1) and (2) are expressed, and it is explicitly stated that (*a*) resembles (*x*). " His soul was like a star and dwelt apart." Element (4) does not belong to simile.

from the fact that in metaphor two notions are, as
it were, superposed, an adventitious and imported
image coming vividly before our mental vision,
while the notion which is the real subject of the
discourse momentarily fades into the background,
and is seen only through the image. Nay, for the
moment there is often complete fusion [1] between
main notion and imported image, so that the discourse
may continue for a time in terms of the image, while
all the while it is the main notion, though never
named, that is being spoken of. Thus Ruskin (in
denunciatory vein):—

> You will see that most men's minds are indeed little better
> than rough heath wildernesses, neglected and stubborn, partly
> barren, partly overgrown with pestilent brakes and venomous
> wind-sown herbage of evil surmise : that the first thing you
> have to do for them, and yourself, is eagerly and scornfully
> to set fire to this, burn all the jungle into wholesome ash-heaps
> and then plough and sow.

That is finely and strikingly expressed, and not more
obscure than the average metaphor. Yet, in spite,
even, of the explanatory words, " of evil surmise,"
which alone are non-metaphorical, one is left wondering
what precisely are the ideas behind the imagery,
what is represented by the " heath wildernesses ",
the " pestilent brakes ", the " ash-heaps ", what mental
process corresponds to setting fire to and burning.
Here are further and more unusual examples from
the prose of Francis Thompson :—

> In all their poetic smithy they (the " metaphysical " poets)
> had left never a place for a forge. They laid their fancies chill
> on the anvil.

[1] Using a different metaphor to express his meaning, Professor
Moulton says that in metaphor two ideas are *entangled* together,
sometimes so as to be scarcely distinguishable. But the degree of
closeness with which the two are associated varies greatly. *The
Literary Study of the Bible*, 1899, p. 408.

The coldest moon of an idea rises haloed through the vaporous imagination, the dimmest sparked chip of a conception blazes and scintillates in the subtile oxygen of his brain.

Thompson said of Shelley :—

Suspended in the dropping well of his imagination the commonest object becomes crusted with imagery.

So crusted, sometimes, that the object wholly disappears. Indeed, the imaginative writer is apt to deck his idea in trappings so gorgeous that our thought when not actually dazzled by the gems and the brocade, lingers curiously over the embroidery, admires the folds of the drapery, with scarce a thought for the figure behind. Thus a first cause of obscurity is the superposition upon the thought of an image which, though merely accessory in its function, may well catch the imagination and hold the attention to the detriment of the idea it is meant to picture forth.

A second cause of obscurity and uncertainty arises often from the writer's or speaker's choice of images. He may draw upon experiences peculiar to himself, or at least not shared by the reader or hearer, images drawn from his country, which is not ours, or from the technicalities of his calling. The seafaring man will garnish his discourse with the language of ships and the sea. The writer of a particular period will reflect in his writings the life of his times. Amos, the Shepherd, will speak of the desert and of flocks ; Paul of Tarsus will describe Christian life in terms of the arena. Long ago St. Augustine dwelt upon this as a difficulty in the interpretation of Scripture.[1] A generation that has

---

[1] *De Doctrina Christiana*, Lib. ii, c. xvi, § 24. "Rerum autem ignorantia facit obscuras figuratas locutiones, cum ignoramus vel animantium vel lapidum vel herbarum naturas, aliarumve rerum quae plerumque in Scripturis similitudinis alicuius gratia ponuntur." And he instances so familiar a saying as that of Our Lord : "Be wise as serpents and simple as doves" (Matt. x, 16).

forgotten the properties of fabled basilisk and phœnix will fail to understand ideas conveyed through such imagery, just as non-classical scholars are bewildered by amaranth and Lethe, nectar and lotus, Gorgon's head and sword of Damocles. Moreover, at different periods and in different lands, popular fancy has attached different qualities to certain things. When, in familiar talk among us, a person is referred to as a goose, an ass, or a pig, we catch at once the force of the depreciatory epithets.[1] But in the East the ass is in honour, in Rome the geese were sacred, and very possibly the pig itself may at some period in history have been an object of religious worship, like the hawk and the crocodile of ancient Egypt, or the sacred monkeys of Hindustan.

But, even if the object chosen as an image be perfectly known, the obscurity and uncertainty may remain. For every concrete object, even the simplest, possesses a number of different qualities or properties —a ball is spherical, but it is also, and necessarily, either hard or soft, of this colour or of that, weighty or light, and so forth. Now, when a writer or speaker compares some idea or notion to a ball he does so, in all probability, because of its rounded completeness. But that is not necessarily so. He may very well be thinking, for instance, of the resilience of a tennis-ball or a hand-ball. The image before his mind may be that of any one of the great variety of objects which are termed balls. There are even balls which are not spherical. And the point of his comparison may lie in any of the qualities they possess. Consequently, even when both the main notion and the imported image are known, the *scope of the com-*

---

[1] When Christ referred to Herod as " that fox " (Luke xiii, 32) did His words imply precisely the same kind and measure of disparagement as they would in the mouth of a modern ? And what is the point of the same metaphor in Ezek. xiii, 4 : " Thy prophets, O Israel, were like foxes in the deserts ? "

parison may still remain uncertain or obscure. To instance St. Thomas's favourite example in the *Summa*,[1] we may use the concrete object " lion " as an image, now of majesty and speak of the " lion of the fold of Judah ", now of ferocity and speak of the devil " going about as a roaring lion seeking whom he may devour ". Let us take at random some modern examples :—

> There was no agent of destiny waiting to call him out of his well-worn groove into the pathless forests of experience.

A fine image, the general sense of which we grasp at once. Yet we are not told, and might not in plain speech be able to say, wherein precisely the routine of daily life resembles a groove, or experience a pathless forest. Again :—

> Even the genius and ardour of Dr. F. must fail to disinter the soft pearl of distinction from the heaped potsherds and broken brickbats of a violent and self-imposed originality of diction.— (Coventry Patmore.)

Once more :—

> Our eyes are lamps in which the oil of reason more or less brightly burns to illuminate the hard and commonplace road of life ; their (children's) eyes are charmed magic casements through which the moon of imagination pours, bathing the whole landscape in the light that never was on sea or land.

In a word, then, metaphor, instead of saying : " Richard is brave," says : " Richard is a lion," i.e. something which is brave but also many other things. True, when a metaphor is in frequent use custom commonly confines within definite bounds

---

[1] The formula of objection and answer is as follows : *Objection :* *a* in Scripture is said to be *x*. But every *x* is invariably *y*. Therefore *a* is *y*. *Answer :* (e.g. 3ª Pars Q.X. a. 10 ad 6ᵐ.) " In his quae metaphorice dicuntur non est accipere similitudinem quantum ad omnia " ; or " In metaphoricis locutionibus non oportet attendi similitudinem quantum ad omnia. Sic enim non esset similitudo sed rei veritas ".

the scope of the image.   When we speak of a snowy beard or a stony heart, few will miss the meaning, but in newly-coined metaphors the reader or hearer must trust to the context or to his own keenness of insight.   It is of the very nature of metaphor not to explain itself.   It will not state in express terms wherein lies the resemblance, real or fancied, between main idea and imported image.   And often to grasp its significance there is needed an imagination equal in intensity and vividness to that which first evoked it.

Still another cause of obscurity lies in the frame of mind, the psychological state, which most commonly gives rise to metaphor.   In daily speech we habitually use ready-made metaphors just as we use the existing words and phrases of our language ; both are the current coin of speech.   We speak of " overstepping the mark ", of " putting the cart before the horse ", of " being on, or off, the track ", of " beating about the bush ", and our daily talk is full of similar expressions.

Such use of language involves no peculiar psychological state, the mind makes no special effort.   What we are now considering is the mental process whereby *fresh* metaphors are created.   It is a curious one and if we can succeed in describing it with any approach to correctness we may find ourselves a stage nearer to understanding the nature of metaphor, as well as to ascertaining a further source of its obscurity. Metaphor, then, would seem to be, very commonly at least, the outcome of an emotional mood reacting as such a mood generally does, on the imagination.[1] Such a mood, when it achieves adequate expression, issues forth in poetry.   Now metaphor is the natural language of poetry.   The mind, possessed by the

[1] Th. Ribot, *Essai sur l'Imagination créatrice*, chap. ii, " Le facteur émotionnel."   The author shows the mutual relation between affective states and the creative or constructive imagination.

imaginative and emotional realization of some idea, ranges in search of images wherewith to picture it forth in an outward expression which shall be in keeping with the inward state, that is to say, not in terms of the intellect, but in terms of the imagination, in concrete pictures rather than in abstract propositions.[1] In this state of heightened emotion and imagination objects from different spheres or orders of being are brought within the sweep of one mental glance. They are seen in the light of the idea which for the moment possesses the mind. In this light differences are ignored, some point of resemblance stands out in relief and is seized upon, and realized so vividly that the two objects—the idea already in the mind and the newly-found image— appear for the moment identical, and can be spoken of as such without any consciousness of falsehood. Victor Hugo can call illusion a hind :—

> La biche illusion me mangeait dans le creux
> De la main ; tu l'as fait enfuir . . .

Shakespeare sees the abstract intention or purpose as a horse, a motive is a spur :—

> I have no spur
> To prick the sides of my intent . . .

One writer will suddenly see literature as " a compost of blocks or slabs laid down in segments with dabs of editorial cement to fill up the chinks ".[2] Another sees it as " a great mosaic in which the stones are words ".[3] Criticism, in a flash, becomes an eddy—" These facts produced an eddy of criticism,

---

[1] " The moment our discourse rises above the ground line of familiar facts and is inflamed by passion or exalted by thought, it clothes itself in images." Emerson, *Nature*.

[2] A. T. Quiller-Couch, *Literary Studies*. This is not given as the author's own way of regarding literature. It is that of a supposed class of persons.

[3] Maurice Francis Egan, *A Gentleman*.

which would of itself have borne up the poems by the violence with which it whirled them round and round."[1] Can any two notions be at first sight more unlike than a wheel and accuracy ? Yet a writer can say with reminiscence of the adage about butterflies : "We need not break conversational exaggeration on the wheel of exact inquiry." An idea truly, as well as delicately, expressed.

When an idea has taken strong possession of the mind, aroused the emotions, caught the imagination, analogies and resemblances start into view on all sides in the most unlooked for places. And a thought thus vehemently felt, particularly if scarce expressible in proper terms, is prone to break forth in images. It seeks expression in terms adequate not merely to the intellectual concept, but to one's emotional possession of it. Indeed, the primary aim in such moods is not clearness of logical statement, but force, vigour, intensity, so that the outward expression may bear some resemblance and proportion to the inner frame of mind. Examples may be found in abundance throughout literature, above all in poetry and oratory. Let me instance the following. St. Jude in his epistle thus expresses his abhorrence of the still half-pagan corruptors of early Christianity[2] :—

> These are they who are hidden rocks in your love feasts when they feast with you, shepherds that without fear feed themselves ; clouds without water, carried about by winds ; autumn trees without fruit, twice dead, plucked up by the roots ; wild waves of the sea foaming out their own shame ; wandering stars for whom the blackness of darkness hath been reserved for ever.

The singers of Israel, pouring out the fullness of their hearts in praise of Jahwe, seize upon every

[1] Coleridge, *Biographia Litteraria.*
[2] I quote from the A.V. as better expressing the imagery.

lovely and majestic image that comes within their ken. He is by turns a rock, a shield, a fortress, a horn (image of strength), light. Heaven is His throne, the earth His footstool, the vault of the sky His tent, He walks upon the wings of the winds. But, as might well be expected, it is above all in the works of the prophets that imagery abounds. Their intense consciousness of a divine commission to deliver a message and of the sublimity of that message expresses itself in image after image. This profusion of imagery culminates in the amazing phantasmagory of the Apocalypse of St. John.

In so far, then, as imagery is the outcome of emotion, it gives to the expression of thought colour, vigour, intensity, not logical clearness. The obscurity of imagery is generally recognized. " In metaphor the object spoken of disappears behind another which resembles it. Comparison illuminates discourse, metaphor darkens it."[1] " In the case of the simile the introducing word ' like ' or ' as ' puts the illustration in the clearest light, whereas in the metaphor the illustration is decidedly, if not deliberately, obscured."[2]

The obscurity, or alleged obscurity, of German philosophy has been attributed to the over metaphorical character of its terminology. " Compare," writes M. Arsène Darmesteter, " such picturesque and ' sensible ' words as Anschauung, Empfindung, Vorstellung, Begriff, to those abstract, bare terms of our language, intuition, perception, representation, idea, etc. [Note that all these words except the last, and there the difference is exceedingly slight, are the same in English.] In the one case terms repre-

---

[1] R. P. Prat, S.J. (author of the well-known work *La Théologie de Saint Paul*) in *Études*, 1913, tome 135, p. 109.

[2] J. G. Jennings, *Metaphor in Poetry*, p. 33. M. Gustave Lanson says the same more at length in *Principes de Composition et de Style*, pp. 213 sqq.

senting accurately pure abstractions ; in the other, metaphorical terms which affect the reader with particular sensations. On the one hand ideas ; on the other subjective and personal impressions. Here one has only to understand ; there one must translate and translate according to the peculiar idiosyncrasy of one's imagination, the outcome of heredity and antecedents." It is, as M. Darmesteter acknowledges in a footnote, to scholastic philosophy that French owes the clearness and precision of its philosophical language. Its terms are nearly all abstract and give no opening to those betrayals of thought to which metaphor may lead.

Yet it would be a mistake to regard metaphor as *necessarily* obscuring thought. It may be quite clear and even illuminating but only on two conditions— it must be easily resolvable into the underlying simile or comparison, and that simile or comparison must be obvious. Its proper function, however, is not logical illumination. What that function is we shall investigate expressly in a subsequent chapter.

Meanwhile, we must remind ourselves that our analysis has not yet laid bare the inner nature of metaphor. We have seen how by metaphor *identity* between two objects [1] may, without falsehood, be stated or taken for granted where only *analogy* exists. We have yet to inquire first by what process the mind makes this identification, and secondly wherein this analogy lies. Between objects belonging to wholly different spheres the material, for instance, and the spiritual, how can real resemblance exist ? And if the resemblance has no existence in reality but is wholly created by the mind, what becomes of the *truth* of metaphor ? The answer to that question involves certain further principles which we hope

[1] We shall see later if it be really between two *objects* that metaphor predicates identity.

to consider presently. Let us content ourselves meanwhile with the following suggestive page from a book that has but recently appeared [1] :—

> There is a certain mystery in the relation of mind and matter . . . We see a material table and we are conscious of the immaterial idea of " table " in our minds ; but for all the big words we use, we understand but little of the process that is the link between them. And not merely does our mind represent such an object, but matter in general is of still further aesthetic and ethical and intellectual significance for mind. The Roman basilica speaks to us of sure faith, the Gothic arch of soaring hope, in the Moorish architecture there is, surely, a touch of the unclean : in music, likewise, we discern the sublime and the meretricious. Matter is symbolic *to* mind, because it is symbolic *of* mind. Everywhere Almighty God expressed Himself in His works, never completely, for that is impossible, but with varying degrees of fullness ; and man also expresses himself through matter, not merely in his art, but in all his works, even in his handwriting, his own body, his very countenance.

[1] *First Notions of Holy Writ*, Cuthbert Lattey, S.J., Longmans, London, 1923.

CHAPTER III

The Nature of Metaphor (*continued*)

We have seen that every metaphor may be analysed into four elements : An idea or notion of some kind which is the main subject of the discourse, an image brought in to illustrate the main idea, a point in which the image resembles, or is analogous with, the main idea, and finally such momentary identification of the image with the main idea as permits us to speak of the latter in terms of the former. If I call fame (1) a spur (2) it is because its effect on men is similar to that of a spur on horses (3), and I can now speak of fame as " goading " men on to greatness (4). So much I have endeavoured to make clear in the course of the preceding chapter. But we have not yet reached the kernel of the problem. By what process can the mind not merely think together an idea and an image drawn from a wholly different order of things, but actually identify the two, fuse them into one ? I am well aware that to elucidate this question fully would be to throw a greater light on the working of the mind than this study can hope to throw on it. Yet we can at least throw a certain light on our subject by bringing to bear on it some of the accepted data of psychology. We can at least carry our investigation up to the edge of the darkness.

There are two mental processes the study of which will help us in our inquiry. They are the Association of Ideas and Thinking by Analogy.

What is called the association of ideas is a matter of the most familiar and everyday experience. Instances so abound that choice is difficult. Take, for example, conversation—" heart affluence in discursive talk." We know how, as we talk, one topic leads to another in, apparently, the most haphazard way, and how hard it is, even with the best of goodwill, to keep to any one subject. Memory wanders down inviting byways, and talk follows after. There are story tellers who must pause to run after every notion or recollected impression that presents itself. And every story told calls forth a " that reminds me " from one of the hearers. The connexion with the story just told may be evident only to himself. A chance remark has awakened in his mind some perhaps long dormant memory.

Again, how strangely certain places are haunted with memories. Twenty, thirty years may have gone by since last we found ourselves in this spot, and now its half-forgotten sights call up from the recesses of memory recollections of things experienced here, of joy or pain, of which this was long ago the scene. Sometimes a faint, floating perfume, a strain of some old air, suffice to bring the memories thronging back. The caw of distant crows may be linked with memories of spring days when we went picking cowslips in the fields ; the sound brings back, in a flash, forgotten scenes.

Indeed, association of ideas, or rather of mental states in general, is the basis of the whole process of recollection. If, for instance, I would recall my doings during the past few days I first call up certain outstanding circumstances. Certain other doings may, at first, refuse to rise into consciousness at the summons of the will. In order to recover these by means of those already recollected, I seek to establish some association. It may be a sequence in *time*—what did I do next . . . and next. Or the association may be one of *place* : I retrace in memory my footsteps backward through the places where

I have passed.[1]   Or one might seek some more rational link—cause and effect, motive, purpose, and so recall the momentarily lost recollections.   Learning by rote is an attempt to establish a fixed association between neighbouring sounds or ideas by mere repetition of them, always in the same order.   A piece of music is so learned.   Systematic memory training does not rely on mere repetition.   It seeks to discover or establish between notion and notion links other than those of mere contiguity and sequence.   The two may be related as cause and effect, genus and species, whole and part, and so forth.   Failing all these, intermediate links may be sought till we have formed a chain between these two ideas which we are seeking to connect, and so to remember together.   In general, kinship between two ideas or mental states renders them apt to call one another into consciousness. This law not only governs, as we have said, our processes of recollection, it is likewise the basis of what is known as the constructive or creative imagination.[2]

Indeed, some law of association would seem to rule the whole of our mental processes.   If an idea emerges into consciousness from its repository in the subconscious, that is because it is linked in some way with an idea already in consciousness.   We may be unable to discover the link.   Many a wandering thought floats unbidden into the mind, we know not whence.   Nevertheless it comes in obedience to law.

> It has been established [writes Sir William Hamilton] that thoughts are associated, that is, are able to evoke each other : 1°.   If coexistent or immediately successive in time; 2°.

---

[1] As St. Thomas says admirably, *reminiscendo venamur* (Commentary on Aristotle's *De Mem. et Reminisc.*, *Lectio V.*, Vives edition, vol. xxiv, p. 283, col. 1).   The whole process of reminiscence is here excellently described.

[2] Ribot, *L'Imagination créatrice*, Paris, 1921 (sixième ed.).

If their objects are adjoining in space; 3°. If they hold the dependence to each other of cause and effect, or of means and end, or of whole and part; 4°. If they stand in a relation either of contrast or similarity; 5°. If they are the operations of the same power; 6°. If their objects are the sign and the signified; or, 7°. Even if their objects are accidentally denoted by the same sound.[1]

As Aristotle had long ago observed,[2] all these laws of association are reducible to three yet more fundamental laws—Contiguity or Simultaneity in time and space, Resemblance or Affinity, and Contrariety. All now agree that the last-named really falls within the second law, and many philosophers have further sought to reduce all to a single principle[3] to which they have given various names.[4] It is natural and right that this attempt should have been made. It does not, however, seem to have been very successful.[5] The fact remains that on the one hand present mental states tend to awaken representations of their *like* in past life, and that on the other these reproduced representations usually call up at the

[1] *Lectures on Metaphysics*, 1865, vol. ii, p. 231. See also Myers, *Text-book of Experimental Psychology*, p. 151.

[2] *De Memoria et Reminiscentia*, c. ii, § 8. In his commentary on this passage St. Thomas Aquinas elucidates and carries forward the Philosopher's thought. (Loc. supra cit.)

[3] For Herbert Spencer the fundamental law is that of Resemblance; similarly Höffding. Others, as for example, Maas, the writer (James Ward) in the *Encyclopædia Britannica* (Art, Psychology), and Lahr, op. cit., tome i, p. 135, think the law of Contiguity the more fundamental of the two. The last-named formulates it thus: "Two ideas or impressions acquire a tendency to call one another up from the moment that, for any reason, they have once happened to occupy together the field of consciousness." This seems also to have been St. Augustine's view, *Confessions*, x, c. 19.

[4] Law of Frequency (James Mill), Law of Redintegration or Totality (Sir W. Hamilton in *Lectures on Metaphysics*, a view considerably modified later).

[5] Thus, after a careful analysis and criticism, Father Maher (*Psychology*, 4th ed., 1900, p. 187) concludes that similarity and contiguity "contain each a separate element of its own". This was Hamilton's later conclusion in his work *On Reid* (note D * * *) where he puts forward a more elaborate theory than in his earlier work. St. Thomas Aquinas, in his Commentary on Aristotle, loc. cit., maintains and develops the view of the Philosopher.

same time certain *unlike* elements which formerly coexisted along with them.[1] For practical purposes at least these two facts are quite distinct.[2]

Let us now see what light we may derive from these laws for the elucidation of our present subject. Suppose the mind in travail with a thought for which it is seeking expression. In its endeavour to express its thought, whether inwardly or outwardly, it casts about among its stored ideas and images for help to do so. If the thought to be expressed be simple or familiar, the mind, no doubt, will light at once upon the ready-made expression which, at least for ordinary purposes, is generally accepted as the equivalent of that thought. But either the thought may be unfamiliar or it may, owing perhaps to its abstract character, be difficult to convey at once adequately and intelligibly to another mind, or, again, the thinker may be dissatisfied with any expression of his thought which shall be but a bare equivalent, a scientific, or so to speak, algebraical equivalent thereof : he would fain put into the expression some element of colour, warmth, force, beauty, pathos, or passion which no bare equivalent could convey.

Thus circumstanced the mind turns aside from any merely *equivalent* expression of its thought and ranges through its ideas and images, seeking *adequate* expression. The search may last but a fraction of a second, though it take many minutes to describe. As it were in answer to an unspoken query, " To what shall I liken my thought ? " a multitude of ideas and of images may start up into consciousness in obedience to the laws of association. Here the law of contiguity avails us little. No doubt there

[1] Maher, *Psychology*, p. 187.
[2] See James Sully, *Outlines of Psychology* (1884), pp. 235 sqq., and especially pp. 267–8. E. Rabier, *Psychologie*, c. 18.

will arise many an idea and image associated with this thought merely in space and time. But they arise only to be set aside : they are not *like* our thought, they cannot avail to give it expression. But the second law comes into play. There emerge into consciousness ideas and images *akin* to my thought, like it by some aspect of their being, reflecting some facet of it. Yes, my thought is like this . . . and this. Two concepts of the mind which, a moment before, seemed a world apart, are suddenly brought together, seen in some hitherto unsuspected connexion. The newcomer is seized upon to add force or colour or beauty or even mere intelligibility to the thought which at the moment occupies the centre of the field of consciousness and is seeking to express itself.

Children and primitive people, in order to describe the unfamiliar, will seize upon a merely outward and secondary aspect of some familiar object. A child will call the moon and stars a mother and her children ; an Australian aboriginal will describe a book as a mussel, because it opens at the sides like the valves of a shell. But it is quite the same instinct which makes us speak of a ship as " ploughing " through the waves and leaving a " furrow " in its wake. It was much the same instinct, too, which led primitive men to project human personality into animals and plants and even inanimate nature. Thus were born the myths. Men described what they could not fully grasp or understand in terms of their own familiar feelings and desires. And as the mood of the poet is akin to the mind of the child, to the mind of unspoiled, fresh-eyed, primitive man, he, too, spontaneously puts forth his thought clothed in images. Moreover, as the poetic mood is one of heightened imagination and feelings, the poet's thought has a glow and an intensity which seems to call up, upon every side, images that reflect it. And in that strange crucible of the mind image and thought are straightway welded into one.

When the link between image and thought has been perceived, the mind may say, my thought is *like* this . . . or this, a potato or a constellation. Already the bounds of truth and verisimilitude seem sufficiently strained. But, once the mind is all aglow with its thought and realizes its evoked imagery with vividness, it may go still further and declare, " My idea *is* a potato—or a constellation." " Music is both *sunshine* and *irrigation* to the mind." " My soul is a garden." " Reputation is but a farthing candle of wavering and uncertain flame." Life is anon a river, and again a journey, or else a stormy ocean, or, once more,

> A tale, told by an idiot, full of sound and fury, signifying nothing.

We are still, however, faced with the double problem of *how* the mind can thus think, and how, thus thinking, it can remain within the bounds of truth. The solution must, I suggest, be sought in a study of the mental process of thinking by analogy. And here it becomes necessary to expound somewhat the nature of analogy.[1] For the average man, perhaps, analogy is just another word for resemblance. Yet the two concepts do not coincide. Let us bring out the difference by example. Two equiangular triangles are like : we do not call them analogous. Neither do we say of a portrait and its enlargement that the two are analogous, yet they are undoubtedly not only like, but exactly proportional to one another. Two people of our acquaintance have the same way of talking, of gesticulating, or of dressing. We say

[1] In this portion of my study I am much indebted to *Analogie et Symbolisme* by Maurice Debaisieux, Paris, 1921.

they are very like each other, but we do not say they are analogous. On the other hand, in biology two organs, an organ of the human frame and an organ of one of the lower animals, are said to be analogous, though there may be no outward resemblance whatever. The hand, the wing, and the fin are analogous, and so are gills and lungs.[1] In spite of extreme dissimilarity there is a recognized analogy between sound and light, and an analogy that is at least serviceable between water and electricity. And there are analogies in mathematics where resemblance would be a meaningless term.[2]

We may now endeavour to formulate more precisely the difference thus illustrated. Two objects *resemble* one another when they both participate in the same form or the same quality. Two faces, for instance, may be alike in profile, in complexion, in expression, in the shape of some feature. The mind ignores for the moment the many differences that exist—" That child," it says, " is the very image of its mother." On the contrary, when the mind perceives an *analogy* it is not concerned with such resemblances, however real ; it recognizes differences but fixes on the relations that link one object with the other, or each with yet other objects.[3] An analogy

[1] In physiology or biology a morphological resemblance or likeness in *form* or structure is termed homology : the term analogy is applied to similarity or identity of *function*. Cf. F. le Dantec, " Homologie et Analogie " : *Revue Philosophique*, May, 1900.

[2] Thus Mgr. Elie Blanc, in his *Dictionnaire universel de la pensée*, vol. ii, col. 94, defines analogy, somewhat vaguely it must be confessed, " A relation which does not imply similitude, still less equality, but which allows of reasoning by comparison."

[3] M. Debaisieux writes : " L'Analogie est essentiellement une égalité, ou tout au moins une *similitude de rapports* entre des choses qui par ailleurs peuvent être extrêmement différentes . . . en sorte que l'analogie apparaît comme susceptible d'une infinité de degrés, depuis la diversité de rapports à un même terme . . . jusqu' à des ressemblances intrinsèques très profondes, très accusées . . . Ce qui détermine l'analogie et la distingue décidément de la ressemblance, c'est la direction de l'esprit dans la considération des choses ; quand l'esprit se porte sur les rapports intrinsèques de qualité ou de forme en

is always translatable into the form of a proportion,
thus:—The lungs are to the breathing of an animal
living in air what the gills are to the breathing of
an animal living in water. Or again, sound is
analogous to light because, like light, it is propagated
by vibrations, though in a different medium.

Now the use of metaphor is, implicitly, a reasoning
by analogy. It implies a likeness, or even an equation,
of relations between two objects of thought which
otherwise may be wholly different. Let us illustrate
concretely this very abstract statement. "Religion
was to Napoleon a useful vaccine against social
distempers." Here the analogy of proportion is
obvious enough:—

Religion : social evils : : vaccine : bodily maladies.

It is scarcely less obvious in this more elaborate
example : "Descartes commenced his investigations
into the nature of the soul by assuming the certainty
of his own existence. Standing upon this adamantine
foothold he sought around him for ground equally
firm which should support his first step in the quagmire
of metaphysics." Which may be analysed thus:—
The certain truth that I exist : subsequent research
in metaphysics: : a firm foothold at the edge of a bog:
the passage across it. Or, to take a Scriptural
example, Our Lord's metaphor: "I am the vine,
you the branches," is resolvable into—

Christ : souls of men : : a vine : its branches.

To say this, is not, of course, to *explain* the metaphor
(for a vine has more than one relation to its branches):
it is merely to restate it in clearer terms. I think
it is not too much to say that every metaphor may

négligeant les différences, il conclut à une ressemblance ; quand il
néglige, au contraire, ces ressemblances . . . pour traiter les choses
comme différentes et ne considérer en elles que leurs relations com-
munes entre elles ou à d'autres termes, il fait une analogie " (op. cit.,
p. 29).

be thus restated. It will be easy for the reader to test this conclusion for himself.

Such a conclusion will seem obvious enough once it has been stated. But it has some important bearings which are not always sufficiently adverted to. In the first place such an analysis enables us to see wherein precisely lies the *truth* of metaphor. From certain descriptions of metaphor one would gather that it is an observed resemblance which the mind turns arbitrarily into an identity, or which, at all events, is stated as an identity. Whence it might be inferred that there is *necessarily* some imperfection in the truthfulness of all metaphorical statement. For it would seem to involve confusion between resemblance and identity and a perception of an object of thought so blurred that that object may be momentarily confounded with another and wholly different object of thought. *Fame*, it would seem, is called a *spur*, merely because the mind, in its confused conception of the two notions, fails to observe the essential differences that exist between them. And so, when the Great Teacher spoke of a narrow gate and a strait way, of the salt of the earth and the light of the world, of shepherds and of sheepfolds, He spoke in language that was picturesque and charming, but not *strictly* true. For did it not fall short of truth by as much as the earthly image fell short of the heavenly idea it was meant to body forth ?

But in all this there is surely a misconception. In reality the mind is not simply comparing " fame " with the concrete object " spur ", and then proceeding to confound the two. What the mind perceives is a resemblance of relations so close as to be practically an equality.[1] Thus:—spur : horse = fame : soul.

[1] Speaking of the analogy of proportion (of which metaphor is a species), a writer in *Etudes* (1907, tome 112, p. 344, in footnote) says :

Fame has the same effect on the human soul as a spur has on a horse: it acts as a stimulus. This can be represented by symbols thus:—$a : b = $ (or::) $x : y$. A statement true in the strictest sense of the word may be made in such a form, and that though the notions represented by a, b, on the one hand and x, y, on the other, may belong to wholly different orders of being. In mathematics, it is true, these symbols represent *quantities*, but besides the fact that these quantities may be of wholly different kinds (a, b, may be numbers ; x, y, weights, measures, money, etc.), the formula in any case states no resemblance between a and x, but, let us repeat, merely an equality of *relations*. And that is precisely what is done in a metaphorical statement. May we not conclude that metaphor *may* state a truth with what is practically mathematical exactness ? Metaphorical statement is, in fact, capable of quite the same degrees of accuracy or inaccuracy as any literal statement. When Christ said, " I am the light of the world," " I am the door of the sheepfold," He spoke in metaphor ; yet he uttered truth, not vague, nor merely approximate truth, but truth of mathematical exactitude.[1] And on the other hand a statement so entirely free from figure as " he is a man of excellent qualities " may in varying degrees approach to, or recede from, the truth, according to the person spoken of. It may be unmerited flattery or a damning with faint praise.

The truth, therefore, of a given metaphor depends upon the truth of an implied equation, an equation not between two objects belonging to different spheres of being (life and a river, for instance, or moral

" On n'affirme aucune similitude, aucune correspondance individuelle des termes d'un rapport à ceux de l'autre. Ce qui est établi c'est uniquement la similitude des rapports eux mêmes."

[1] I do not say that our understanding of His meaning has necessarily the same exactitude.

degradation and mire), but between two relations, or, to use a mathematical term, two *ratios*. The mind perceives an analogy between these two relations, and uses one as an illustration of the other. But may we not carry our analysis a stage further and inquire into the nature of this perceived analogy that is at the back of metaphor. For analogy is of many kinds.[1] To rehearse their various definitions and above all to discuss their terminology (as to which there is great diversity among writers[2]) would lead us far afield and might not be of very great profit. Accordingly we must confine ourselves to the particular species of analogy to which metaphor belongs.[3] Strictly speaking, then, metaphor consists not merely, as does all analogy, in a proportion (an equation of simple ratios), but in a proportion between proportions.[4]

This further analysis may be deemed a needless refinement, a mere scholastic subtlety ; but its justification lies in the part played by analogy in some of the gravest problems of theology concerning the divine nature and attributes.[5] Nor is the matter quite so complicated as might at first sight appear. Let us take a familiar example. " You are the light of the world." If we analyse this we find that an analogy is drawn between the effect of the Apostles'

---

[1] I refer to analogy in expression or, to use a Scholastic term, in predication. For the moment we are not concerned with analogy in things (ontological) or with analogy as a process of reasoning (logical).

[2] Analogy of intrinsic and extrinsic attribution, of proportionality, etc., are only a few out of many terms used.

[3] The simplest and most appropriate term for this kind of analogy would seem to be *analogy of proportion*.

[4] Thus Suarez in his Metaphysics : " Quia haec est proportio inter duas habitudines [i.e. ratios], ideo solet proportio proportionum seu proportionalitas appellari." (*Disp.* xxviii, § 3, n. 4.)

[5] " L'analogie est un des procédés les plus fréquents de la connaissance, du langage, ou du raisonnement théologiques." *Dictionnaire de Théologie Catholique* (1909), t. i, p. 1142. See also the entire treatise *De Analogica nostra Cognitione et Praedicatione Dei*, by Joseph Bittremieux, Louvain, 1913.

preaching on the minds of men and the effect of light upon surrounding objects. The Apostles as preachers cause enlightenment : light causes enlightenment. But two different species of enlightenment, the one physical, the other intellectual and spiritual ; and two correspondingly different kinds of causality (physical and moral) are involved. This may be expressed in the form of two proportions, thus :—

(1) The Apostles as preachers of Christianity (a): the "enlightenment"[1] of men's minds and hearts (b) : : cause (c) : effect (e).

(2) Light (x) : the lighting up of surrounding objects (y) : : cause (c^1) : effect (e^1).

Now the mind sees in a flash that as light has in the physical world a vivifying, brightening, joy-giving effect, dispelling darkness and gloom—religion, the Christian religion, has in the spiritual world effects that are analogous—quickening the spiritual life, bringing a sense of joy, dispelling error and ignorance (ever thought of as darkness) and so forth. Accordingly it brings together, equates, the two proportions, and we get a proportion of proportions[2] :—

$$\frac{\dfrac{a}{x}}{\dfrac{c}{c^1}} = \frac{\dfrac{b}{y}}{\dfrac{e}{e^1}}$$

That is to say, light and the Apostles as preachers of the Christian religion are related to one another,

---

[1] This term has, of course, a metaphorical origin, though usage has dulled our sense of the metaphor underlying it.
[2] Debaisieux, op. cit., p. 34.

analogous to one another, as causes ; just as physical
and moral enlightenment are related to one another,
analogous to one another, as effects.   Henceforward
we may speak of the Apostles as lights, and of the
effect of their preaching upon the world in terms
of light.[1]

The use of metaphor, then, involves no sacrifice
of truth.   But I think we may go further and say that
it may express a portion, or at least an aspect, of the
truth which would not otherwise find expression.
By means of it (and of other figures of speech) an
imaginative and emotional element which is really
in the mood is put into the expression of that mood.[2]
Without this element the expression would be
inadequate, that is, less completely expressive of the
object of thought as affected by the mood or frame
of mind, and so less completely true.   When it is
said, " If thy right hand scandalize thee, cut it off ;
if thy right eye scandalize thee, pluck it out," is not
the truth, and Christ's feeling about that truth,
more fully conveyed than were one to say, " If you
find that something very dear to you becomes to you
an occasion of sin you are bound to get rid of it " ?
This is but one aspect of the great fact that often
the poetical expression of truth reaches nearer to the
heart of things, above all reaches nearer to the heart
of man, than any philosophical or scientific statement
thereof.   In the light of that fact we wonder less
that so great a portion of the divine message to man-

---

[1] The present writer is conscious of the debatable nature of this
portion of his study, and would welcome helpful criticism.
[2] " The difference," says Coleridge, in his *Biographia Literaria*, " is
great and evident between words used as the arbitrary marks of
thought, our smooth market-coin of intercourse, with the image and
superscription worn out by currency, and those which convey pictures,
either borrowed from one outward object to enliven and particularize
some other, or used allegorically [? metaphorically] *to body forth the
inward state of the person speaking* ; or such as are at least the exponents
of his peculiar turn, and unusual extent, of faculty."

73

kind should have been conveyed in poetry.[1] And
the study of the rôle and function of metaphor (the
very language of poetry) in the expression of thought
becomes a matter of no small interest.

[1] Setting aside the purely narrative portions, by far the greater part of the Old Testament is actually poetry, and though but a small portion of the New Testament is poetry, still, at least the Gospels and the Apocalypse abound with poetic imagery and poetic expression of thought.

CHAPTER IV

The Functions of Metaphor

WE have next to inquire into the rôle which metaphor plays in the expression of thought. One might be tempted to deem it little better than an aberration of thought and a mere excrescence, or at best an ornament, of speech ; in any case a deviation from wholesome honest directness in both thought and speech. We hope to show that such a conception of its functions would be a mistake. Latin literature was sparing of figures and certainly not prodigal of metaphor. Yet Quintillian was quite alive to its value. In his *Institutes of Oratory* [1] he distinguishes three main reasons for its use in literature, namely (1) necessity, (2) the gaining of increased significance and force, and (3) ornament. This is helpful as far as it goes and points the way for the fuller analysis which I shall presently attempt. A modern writer sums up the value of imagery in literature by saying that it presents truth more *concisely, vividly, memorably,* and *emotionally* than literal statement. [2] Such effects of metaphor, and others to which we shall point, are but consequences of a single fact—metaphor presents to the mind a *picture*. [3] It will be helpful, nevertheless, to study these consequences severally.

[1] Book viii, chap. vi.

[2] Margaret Wilkinson, *New Voices*, 1919. If, says M. Michel Bréal, the sole function of language were to speak to the intellect, the most ordinary, well-known words would be the best. But language does not address itself to the reason only : it aims at *moving, persuading, pleasing.* And so we see new images ever springing up for things as old as the world. *La Semantique*, 1921, p. 288.

[3] More than one writer has remarked the affinities between metaphor and *painting*. Thus John S. Hart in *Rhetoric* : " Metaphor, indeed, of all the figures comes nearest to painting, enabling us to clothe at will the most abstract ideas with life, form, colour, and motion." But cf. Burke, *The Sublime and Beautiful.*

THEORY

I

It would seem that the original and primary function of metaphor and kindred images is to express some idea not adequately expressible otherwise—at least to the speaker's knowledge. On this function I have already dwelt in speaking of the genesis of metaphor. Language, even after long ages of development, remains an essentially inadequate instrument for the expression of mind. Much more inadequate must it have been in its earlier stages. We have seen that the problem of expressing in speech immaterial mental concepts was solved by borrowing language which originally expressed simple physical actions and material objects. This borrowing, this transference of the meaning of words is metaphor. We have, after Max Müller, called it *radical* metaphor. It has given us an entire vocabulary of words from which all metaphorical connotation has long since faded. In the course of the development of language, expression has thus been provided for our chief ideas and mental phenomena. Yet the process still goes on. For, owing on the one hand to an ever finer and more searching analysis of mental states and on the other to the growth of knowledge, we are ever adding to our store of ideas, and consequently ever in need of fresh terms for their expression. The existing powers of expression must be increased either by the invention of entirely new words or by the transference of old words to new meanings. Now, as M. Darmesteter says :—

> Of all the processes employed by language to extend the meanings of words it is metaphor that plays the most important rôle. Not content with substituting for dry abstraction, for the bare statement of fact, the colour and brilliancy of imagery, it enables language to express abstract ideas.[1]

[1] *La Vie des Mots*, p. 84. Similarly Max Müller, *The Science of Thought*, p. 485 : " More important than any of the contrivances for

THE FUNCTIONS OF METAPHOR

The simplest words describing elementary physical actions or processes or objects have given rise to whole tribes of words denoting mental acts or states or spiritual ideas. The working out of this constitutes the main theme of a work already more than once referred to, *Figurative Language, its Origin and Constitution*, by L. H. Grindon. Two examples taken from that work will serve to illustrate our present point. The first is the simple word *to see*. This is applied, in the first instance, to the observation of material objects by the eye. But it seems quite natural to use it in expressing a very different though analogous act, the comprehension of immaterial notions by the mind—" I *see* your drift ", " I *see* how this is going to end ", " Video meliora proboque ; deteriora sequor ". This, however, is but a beginning. From this simple word springs a numerous progeny, some of whose members retain the double meaning, material and spiritual, of their progenitor, while others have wholly lost the former. In English, for example, there is insight and foresight and over-sight. The Latin equivalent of see, *video*, has given us a host of useful words. We have from it, through the French, *view*, which is equally used in material or literal and spiritual or metaphorical senses. Also through the French we have purvey and survey, purview and review and interview. This last, strange to say, has been borrowed back in its English form by the French. From *pro-video* we have Providence, provision, provident, and also prudent. Other derivatives are supervise, advise, and revise, advice and evidence. Let our next example be flow, or rather *fl* and its associates *pl, bl, pr, fr, br*. Whatever be the original Aryan equivalent, we have the

the increase of words which we have hitherto examined is the influence of what commonly goes by the name of Metaphor. M., in one sense of the word, is to language what rain and sunshine are to the harvest. It multiplies each grain a hundred and a thousand fold."

77

Sanskrit plu, which means to float or swim ; the Greek φλεω, φλυω, πλω, πλεω, πλυω, etc. ; the Latin flo, fleo, fluo ; the Anglo-Saxon fleotan, fleogan, flowan, blawan ; and at last the familiar words float, fly, flow, blow. The original meaning of these *fl* words was motion. " As with all other words," says our author, " while the circumstance of material or physical movement was thus provided with a designation, these *fl* words became at the same moment, by virtue of the natural harmonies of things, appellations for every variety of emotional and intellectual ' movement '. Every derivative of *fl*, directly it was framed took its place in the language of metaphor."[1] He then pursues the word from the parent root through all the ramifications. In daily speech we employ such phrases as flow of feeling, flow of fancy, flow of ideas, of language, sentiment, good spirits. So it is with other primitive forms such as *flee*, *fly*, *flit*, or *float*. The Latin equivalents of these have given us numberless words to express spiritual realities. " Affluent " still describes a physical object, but " affluence " has a purely abstract significance. And so with influence, while influx keeps both its senses. Compare confluence, effluence, superfluous. It is unnecessary for our purpose to work out all the derivatives of such cognate words as *pleo*, to fill, *fleo*, to weep, *flos*, a flower, and many others. It is enough to remark that not only were such words given at once a metaphorical sense in addition to their literal meaning, but that, in many cases, we are still quite conscious of both senses. In other words, they are still " live " metaphors, and the process of transfer from one sense to the other is still going on.

Metaphor then is a necessity not only, as we have seen, in the earlier stages of the growth of language

[1] p. 120.

but even in the latest. M. Gustave Lanson does not exaggerate in saying that without metaphor it is impossible to speak or to write.

It would be easy to draw numerous examples of this from popular speech, with its traditional element of proverbs and sayings and its fresh elements of slang. Both these elements largely consist of imagery. Quite abstract ideas are conveyed by picturesque phrases— any port in a storm, at the parting of the ways, putting the cart before the horse, make hay while the sun shines, drawing a red herring across the track, a rolling stone gathers no moss, to be hand in glove with, to feather one's nest, the thin end of the wedge, to put one's foot in it, a bird in the hand, and the like.[1]

To literary style metaphor may render a service similar to that which it renders to colloquial speech : it may be a perennial source of vividness and freshness. Words are ever growing old. Little by little the colour and the life fades out of them. They cease to be pictures and become mere signs and tokens of ideas or of objects.

> Language [it has been well said [2]] begins in poetry and ends in algebraical symbols. . . . The word candour first meant something shining white, the sunlight of the soul ; horror was having the hair stand on end ; emolument once gave the picture of the mill and the ground wheat ; tribunal was once the place where sat the officer of the tribe.[3]

Such words no longer call up a picture. And so it is with the vast majority of words in common use. Little by little they have lost their picturing power, their

[1] I deal with this point more fully in the chapter on Metaphor in Common Speech.

[2] F. P. Donnelly, S.J., *The Art of Interesting*.

[3] Similarly *irritate* originally suggested the snarling of a dog ; *exaggerate*, a heaping up ; *scrutiny*, a careful search among broken pieces (Lat. *scruta*) ; *dilapidated*, stones in a wall fallen loose ; *result*, something that bounds back ; *error*, a wandering astray, and so on. See *English Words and their Background*, by G. H. McKnight, New York, 1923.

vividness, their freshness. By the use of new metaphors or the infusion of new life into old ones, this vividness and freshness may be restored to language. "To cherish a grievance," "to fix one's gaze," "to break a record" were once picturesque expressions. Use has staled them. To restore their freshness writers have replaced them by "to *nurse* a grievance", "to *rivet* one's gaze", "to *smash* all records". These, too, are fast growing stale.

The skilful use of imagery is assuredly not the whole art of writing. It is nevertheless a vital element in style. La Bruyère summed up the power of expression as "knowing how to define well *and to paint well*", that is to say the power on the one hand to give perfectly clear and accurate expression to the thought and on the other to embody it in a picture, to speak at once to mind and imagination, to combine colour and line in perfect synthesis. As a more recent French writer well says : "La science d'écrire ne consiste pas toute dans l'image ; mais la magie du style, sa couleur, son éclat, son effet, sa vie sont certainement dans l'image."[1] Colour, effectiveness, life, freshness—these are qualities that imagery lends to style. There must come to many would-be writers in these days of ours moments of discouragement in which it seems to them that not only has everything been said in some way, but that the time has long gone by when anything can be said in new ways. Language has been worn down by use and by abuse till it has lost its edge. All that may once have made the charm of style has grown colourless and withered. Every turn of speech has become, from constant iteration "weary, stale, flat, and unprofitable". One is tempted to give up writing altogether or to take refuge in mannerism, preciosity, or violence of effect. It is a mistake. True, the

[1] Antoine Albalat, *L'Art d'Écrire*, dixième édition, 1904.

present-day European languages are as fixed and as stable as language can be : we can no longer allow ourselves the glorious licence of the Elizabethans. But there remains, besides the incalculable element of personality, a perennial well-spring of freshness in imagery, inexhaustible sources of which are at hand on all sides.

Speaking in general, figure is, as Professor Earle has well expressed it, "the most potent, the most prolific, and the most legitimate source of Novelty ".[1] Only the master writers may safely coin new words. And even they may do so only within narrow limits. But any writer may draw upon the world of imagery and may illustrate his writings with ever new analogies of nature and human life. For the store is at hand and it is inexhaustible.

II

Thus imagery enables us to express certain ideas for which there exists no literal term that is their precise equivalent. It gives freshness and novelty to the expression of ideas. But even when our ideas can, without figure, be equivalently and even adequately expressed, yet in the process of bringing home these ideas to other minds figures render to speech a further service. In the use of our faculties of knowing we are creatures of sense.

> This world is the nurse of all we know
> This world is the mother of all we feel . . .

The data of the senses are the primary material of all knowledge : without such data the immaterial principle within us cannot function.[2] A living man

---

[1] *English Prose*, p. 234.

[2] Not, of course, that our higher faculties of apprehension and reasoning do not transcend the data of sensation, but that cognition begins in sensation and mind-processes involve brain (i.e. organic) processes.

bereft of all possibilities of sensation is conceivable, but he would be wholly unable to know or to think. It is needless to insist further on a truth admitted by most schools of thought, and already sufficiently alluded to.

But the application of it to our present point is of no small importance. Abstract terms, as we have said, have gradually been created for most of our habitual ideas, and the use of such abstract terms is, speaking generally, sufficient for conveying these ideas. But if we would lay hold of the reader's or hearer's whole mind and bring him not merely to understand with the point of the intellect but to *realize* and bring home to himself our thought,[1] something more is needed. We must appeal to the imagination, i.e. the purely reproductive imagination, the mind's eye of popular speech, the *phantasia* of scholastic philosophy. Consequently you must give him not abstract terms but concrete, not general terms but particular and individual (all images are particular and individual) ; you must speak to him in pictures. Hence the need of illustration when dealing with subjects recondite, abstract, or unfamiliar. As the pictures or illustrations in a book, were they the merest schematic diagrams, speak to the intellect through the eye, so imagery brings ideas home to the mind through the imagination. And ideas so brought home lay hold of the mind in a way that abstract statement seldom succeeds in doing. It should be here recalled that the purpose of language is not simply to convey ideas but to arouse in reader or hearer a feeling of attraction or repulsion in regard to them.

The greater effectiveness to this end of concrete and particular, as compared with abstract and general, statement may be illustrated from the works of almost any good writer. Examples abound in the pages of

[1] I recall here Newman's distinction between *notional* and *real* assent.

Macaulay. To emphasize the contrast let us set out abstract and concrete expressions of the same idea in parallel columns :—

Abstract.	*Concrete.*
The men of fashion were little disposed to obey the moral teaching of the Church but were ready to fight *to the uttermost* for her *temporalities* and her *ritual*.	Little as the men of mirth and fashion were disposed to shape their lives according to her precepts, they were yet ready to fight *knee deep in blood* for *her cathedrals and palaces*, for every *line of her rubrics and every shred of her vestments.*
They justly said that one-half of what His Majesty spent on *unworthy objects* would relieve hundreds of old Cavaliers who after *many sacrifices* for his father were now in *extreme want*.	They justly said that one-half of what His Majesty spent on *favourites and buffoons* would gladden the hearts of hundreds of old Cavaliers who, *after cutting down their oaks and melting their plate* to help his father, now *wandered about in threadbare suits* and *did not know where to turn for a meal.*

In the following passage the same idea is stated first in concrete then in abstract form :—

As long as there was a man left in Prussia that man might carry a musket ; as long as there was a horse left that horse might draw artillery. The coin was debased, the civil functionaries were left unpaid ; in some provinces civil government altogether ceased to exist. But there was still rye bread and potatoes ; there was still lead and gunpowder [concrete] ; and, while the means of sustaining and destroying life [abstract] remained, Frederick was determined to fight it out to the very last.

I give one more example, this time from a very different writer. It will be noticed how the abstract statements are brought home to the imagination by means of imagery.

83

˪ The purity of Christ was purity which had known evil and overcome it, which had passed through the dusty ways of men and received no speck upon its white robes. A tempest of trial had only driven it, like the snow on Alpine summits, into more dazzling spotlessness.[1]

In his *Philosophy of Style* Herbert Spencer attributes the superiority of specific over generic words to the economy of the reader's or hearer's mental energy gained by the use of the former. If one is told that a certain man " fought like an animal " the mind seeks for an image corresponding to " animal ". But all images are particular, they represent individuals not classes. So whatever image the mind pitches upon will represent " animal " but vaguely. The statement will be accepted and understood but not vizualized and realized. To say he fought " like a wild beast " calls up a more vivid image. But it is not till one names the particular wild beast which this fighting man resembles, that you begin to see the fight in your mind's eye. " He fought like a tiger—like a wild cat—like a mad dog." There at last you have a picture. So, to cite Spencer's own example, the statement that " When the manners, customs, and amusements of a nation are cruel and barbarous the regulations of their penal code will be severe " will by most readers be accepted without examination as a current platitude. Not so this equivalent statement : " When men delight in battles, bull-fights, and combats of gladiators they will punish by hanging, burning, and the rack."

Now imagery is one form, the principal form, indeed, of concrete statement. Metaphor, simile, and to a less extent metonymy and synecdoche give pictures instead of propositions. They reach the mind, but they reach it by way of the imagination.

Clearly then imagery is invaluable to literature for all

[1] Stopford Brooke, *Christ in Modern Life.*

84

purposes of description. It is the writer's task so
to paint the real or imaginary objects of his thought
as to make them real to the reader, that is, such that
the reader's imagination can grasp them vividly and
bring them home to himself. It is above all when such
objects are to the reader remote and unfamiliar that
imagery comes to his assistance. Milton describing
the armour of Satan compares his spear to the tallest
Norwegian pine, his shield to the moon seen through
a telescope. The spears of the angelic host wave
as thick as wind-swept fields of corn. To a landsman
the unfamiliar sea can best be made real by comparisons—a vessel ploughs a furrow through it, its sound
is like thunder or like trampling steeds, its waves
charge, the sun glinting on its ripples strews it with
diamonds, the dykes of foam are " like broken walls
on fields of black rye ",[1] the advancing and retreating
waves, as they spread over sand and pebbles, edge
the sea with lace. Often metaphor gives us in a flash
a picture which could else be called up before the mind's
eye only by the laborious enumeration of details.[2]

> It may [says George Brimley in one of his essays] be regarded
> as a natural shorthand which substitutes well-known things
> for the unknown qualities of whatever has to be described
> and which therefore gives the general impression of the things,
> without necessitating the task of minute description.

" The most meagre description of Napoleon and
Washington," says Sidney Lanier, " will have
instantly acquired . . . a force and a beauty unattain-
able by any amount of detail, when the writer finishes
it with : Napoleon was lightning, Washington was
sunlight."

[1] Fiona McLeod.
[2] By a single figurative expression with which ideas of well-known
quality and value are connected . . . something can be shortly and
graphically expressed which, without figure, would require a much
more extensive description." Wendt, *The Teaching of Jesus* (trans.
Wilson), vol. i, p. 143.

Further examples abound. Carlyle, in his *Frederick the Great*, when describing Silesia brings it within his reader's ken by simple pictures:—

> This Giant Mountain Range . . . shapes itself *like a bill-hook* ! Handle and hook together may be some 200 miles in length. . . . Like *the palm of the left hand* well stretched out with the Riesengebirge for thumb . . .

and so forth. De Quincey illustrates admirably certain points in his description of Ceylon by comparing it with a peach. In the following passage a homely image is made to say as much as could be said by explanatory matter many times as long :—

> The electors of to-day know where the shoe pinches, which is what the old drawing-room electors never had the chance of knowing ; and it is a very important piece of knowledge. But though they feel the pinching, which the old electors did not, they do not necessarily know more of the why and the wherefore of it. All the gain is in their greater, their personal, eagerness to stop the pinching ; not in any greater knowledge of how to do it. And the eagerness may induce them to do it by methods which ruin the shoe or even injure the foot.[1]

Another writer thus concludes an argument against the excessive use of the strike weapon:—

> There is small hope of getting the boat safely to shore so long as we insist on our right to drill holes in the timbers to spite another section of the crew.[2]

As this function of illustrating an idea, of aiding the understanding of it, belongs more properly to simile than to metaphor, we shall deal with it more fully under the former head.

The peculiar effect of metaphor is thus to make intellectual ideas in some sort visible to the eye, by giving them colour and substance and sensible qualities.

[1] *Times Literary Supplement*, 3rd January, 1924.
[2] *Irish Statesman*, 24th May, 1924.

THE FUNCTIONS OF METAPHOR

Not literature only but philosophy, the physical sciences, even theology itself, must needs at times have recourse to comparisons, similes, and metaphors, if they would bring the abstract and the spiritual within the ken of minds unaccustomed to abstract thought and unfamiliar with the spiritual world. Max Müller's essay " On the Stratification of Language " is a good example of imagery from a concrete science, geology, used to elucidate the abstruse theories of linguistics. The science of the mind is forced to speak in language originally borrowed from the operations of the body and still reminiscent of its origin. To describe phenomena that lie beyond the ken of our perceptions it has recourse to the phenomena of the visible world.

> Thought [says M. Rabier, illustrating a point upon which we have dwelt in a preceding chapter], thought is like a kite held to earth by a string ; without this string, instead of rising it falls to the ground ; but though held by this string it freely moves about and hovers in the sky.

So thought cannot exist without an accompanying image, yet acts independently thereof. The image is the condition, not the controlling force, of its exercise.

Moral and religious ideas, highly suprasensuous as they are, are grasped, or at all events realized, with difficulty. If sublime truths would find an easy way into simple minds they must utter themselves in simple imagery. When St. Francis de Sales writes of the spiritual life, his writing is full of homely images— the birds and their ways, the properties of plants, children at their games. The sermons of the Curé of Ars are full of the like familiar imagery. And the Master Himself taught the deep things of God by the lilies and the vine, the birds of the air, and the springing corn.

III

Ideas are not the whole of what we wish to express by speech. A side of our personality other than the intellectual constantly seeks expression, the emotional side, the side of feeling.[1] Now figures of all kinds are a normal vehicle for the expression of emotion. As a rule the strictly literal statement conveys the idea, the intellectual concept, only, and not the feeling bound up with the idea in the speaker's mind. No doubt one may *explain* one's feeling, describe it in suitable but literal terms. But by figure may be conveyed at once the idea and one's feeling about it. " The companions in arms of Richard I were not simply stating their *conception* that he was a brave man when they called him Cœur de Lion : they were trying to express the *feeling* that his valour stirred in them, not to say what they *thought* but what they *felt* about him." [2] Furthermore, it may be said that at times through metaphor alone can a given emotion find adequate and, so to speak, *precise* expression. One seeks an epithet to convey the emotional tinge of one's idea, its intellectual and emotional savour, its peculiar quality, and very often an epithet is not to be found. " For most of the things," says Mr. Middleton Murry, " whose quality a writer wishes to convey there are no precise epithets, simply because he is always engaged in discovering their qualities, and, like the chemist, has to invent names for the qualities he discovers." For this he instinctively has recourse to comparisons. " Try to be precise," continues the same writer, " and you are bound to

[1] "Exception faite des langages techniques et notamment du langage scientifique, qui est par définition en dehors de la vie, l'expression d'une idée n'est jamais exempte d'une nuance de sentiment." Vendryes : *Le Langage*, p. 163.
[2] E. Greening Lamborn, *The Rudiments of Criticism*, 1921, p. 91. " In its origin," this author says elsewhere, " every metaphor is . . . an attempt to express an emotion within by an image or picture of something external."

be metaphorical ; you simply cannot help establishing affinities between all the provinces of the animate and inanimate world : for the volatile essence you are trying to fix is quality, and in that effort you will inevitably find yourself ransacking heaven and earth for a similitude."[1] A writer in the Literary Supplement of *The Times* for 14th October, 1926, contends that the highest function of imagery is "to define indefinable spiritual qualities ".

Hence it is that the same idea may be translated by a variety of figures each conveying a different *nuance* of feeling, a different subjective attitude towards the idea in question. The imported image will be so chosen as to give a humorous, pathetic, ironical, or contemptuous turn to the idea. And much of the writer's or orator's art consists in the choice of imagery in keeping with the emotion of the moment. When the thought is of things familiar the imagery is homely, when the thought soars the imagery is dignified and lofty. Yet skilfully used even the simplest imagery may picture forth thoughts the most sublime.

It will be interesting to adduce here some examples of the use of imagery to enhance emotional effects. The sun is an image which lends a certain grandeur to the idea which it is used to illustrate. " The condemnation of Socrates took him away in his full grandeur and glory like the setting of a tropical sun." Tennyson, wishing us not merely to understand but to feel moved by the splendid calm of the Princess in the midst of the disaster to her college, speaks of her thus :—

> Fix'd like a beacon-tower above the waves
> Of tempest, when the crimson-rolling eye
> Glares ruin, and the wild birds on the light
> Dash themselves dead. . . .

[1] *The Problem of Style*, p. 83, London, 1925. " Metaphor," he says elsewhere, " is the unique expression of a writer's individual vision " (p. 13).

THEORY

The following from Byron invites sympathy for the extreme abandonment and friendlessness of the speaker:

> I am as a weed
> Flung from the rock, on ocean's foam to sail
> Wher'er the surge may sweep, the tempest's breath prevail.

Campbell's simile in the *Battle of the Baltic* may have grown hackneyed, but it was finely chosen to mark the solemn hush on the eve of battle.

> There was silence deep as death. . . .

I know few passages that convey an emotion so powerfully as Coleridge's description of a ruined friendship:—

> Alas they had been friends in youth ;
> But whispering tongues can poison truth,
> And constancy lives in realms above ;
> And life is thorny and age is vain
> And to be wroth with one we love
> Doth work like madness on the brain . . .
> They parted ne'er to meet again !
> But never either found another
> To free the hollow heart from paining.
> They stood aloof, the scars remaining,
> Like cliffs that have been rent asunder ;
> A dreary sea now flows between,
> But neither heat, nor frost, nor thunder,
> Shall wholly do away, I ween,
> The marks of that which once hath been.

The more emotion grows upon a man the more his speech, if he make any effort to express his emotion, abóunds in figures—exclamation, interrogation, anacoluthon, apostrophe, hyperbole (yes certainly, hyperbole !), simile, metaphor. His language is what we sometimes euphemistically describe as " picturesque ". Feelings swamp ideas and language is used to express, not the reality of things but the state of one's emotions.[1] And when the purpose of

---

[1] Gustave Lanson, *Principes de Composition et de Style.*

a piece of writing is to portray a frame of mind, a mood, imagery is the natural form of expression. " Metaphors," says Sidney Lanier, " come of love rather than of thought. Love, i.e. the underlying principle of all emotion." [1]

And herein precisely lies a manifest danger of figurative language. As it is normally the outcome of an emotional state, so it tends to produce in reader or hearer a corresponding emotional state. And an emotional state is not always the best disposition for clear thinking and calm reasoning. Rather is it a foe to calmness, impatient of any deliberate weighing of pros and cons. And so a man comes to take his feelings for premisses, and to let passion draw the conclusion.

IV

Distinct from the intellectual value and the emotional value of metaphor is its function in giving æsthetic pleasure. We delight in a beautiful picture even when it neither conveys an intellectual idea nor stirs any emotion other than pleasure. What precisely is the origin of the pleasure we take in the pictures of metaphor and simile, as distinct from unfigurative word-pictures ? I think that, over and above the delight in a picture, there is the little shock of surprise caused by the unexpected *rapprochement* of two notions that seemed, a moment before, unconnected and remote from one another. The noticing of likenesses (need I refer to babies ?) would seem an ever-fresh source of pleasure—we call comparisons odious but love them none the less. And when the likeness is perceived in the midst of unlikeness, perhaps even despite obvious and preponderating unlikeness, the pleasure is proportionately greater.

[1] *Music and Poetry.* " No form of language is so adapted to the expression of idealized passion as metaphor." F. I. Carpenter, *Metaphor and Simile in the Minor Elizabethan Drama*, Chicago, 1895.

Now, as we have seen, true metaphor implies the bringing together of two notions which not only are unlike but belong to different spheres of being. The unlikeness of the "imported image" to the "main idea" ought therefore to be obvious and preponderating. Accordingly, when imagination nevertheless discovers a hidden analogy between the two, the discovery comes upon us with a pleasant shock of surprise.[1] Perhaps we had never thought of experience and the lights in the stern of a ship as in any way connected and related. Coleridge writes :—

"Human experience, like the stern-lights of a ship at sea, illumines only the path we have passed over," and we suddenly perceive a delightful analogy. The likeness between skating and a delicate discussion may not strike us till we read—"The usual deputation of Nonconformists followed and the audience watched with keen interest the very dexterous way in which the Dissenting spokesman and the Bishop successfully skated over thin ice."

Can a thing so abstract as a resolution, and a thing so material as a cloud be likened to one another? Tennyson writes—

> For, when the blood ran lustier in him again,
> Full often the bright image of one face
> Making a treacherous quiet in his heart
> Dispersed his resolution like a cloud.

All metaphor that is fresh has something of this unlooked for bringing together of unlikes. Hence the importance of freshness in metaphor if attention is to be stimulated. The stale and the familiar awakens no surprise.

Sometimes the pleasure we experience from metaphor comes not so much from agreeable surprise

[1] See supra, pp. 65–6.

as from the recognition of the aptness of the comparison or its ingeniousness. Many of the similes and metaphors in Pope have this quality. They are neat, well-turned, clever, felicitous, rather than imaginative or emotional.

> Man like the generous vine supported lives;
> The strength he gains is from the embrace he gives.

> On life's vast ocean diversely we sail,
> Reason the card but passion is the gale.

> Words are like leaves and where they most abound
> Much fruit of sense beneath is rarely found.

> Envy will merit as a shade pursue,
> But like a shadow proves the substance true.[1]

Or this from a recent book—" Newman's mind was like a mezzo-tint in its delicate half-tones ; Manning's like a woodcut in its sharp outlines." Or once more —" Tennyson clove the mark at which he aimed, but Browning's arrow, like that of the archer of ancient story, sped, in an arc of light, beyond the ken of the gazers, to be lost in the overarching heaven." [2]

V

Metaphor, then, besides enriching our resources for the expression of thought, introduces into language the elements of *concreteness*, of *feeling*, and of *æsthetic pleasure*. Now when expression is given to what is called the poetic spirit, precisely these elements spontaneously appear in speech. For poetry is the language of *imagination* (expressing itself concretely in pictures) and of *emotion*. Its aim is the achievement of *beauty* in thought and word. The tendency of poetry to put its ideas into imaginative pictures must be manifest to any reader of poetry. To the poet life becomes a journey or a river or a

---

[1] See further Bain, *Composition and Rhetoric*, vol. i, pp. 144-6, 161.
[2] W. M. Dixon, *A Tennyson Primer*.

garden, joy after sorrow is the sky after storm, the future is the dim horizon of the wayfarer, grief the murky clouds that hide the sun.

These are figures common to innumerable poets, and their frequency is testimony to the common impulse in poetic natures. "Thus in reading poetry one of the first necessities is to visualize, to see clearly every picture as it is presented by the poet. Without visualizing the poet's words the reader in no sense has before him that which the poet had at the time of writing. Nor can he in any full sense share his emotion."[1]

No less manifest is the preference shown by poets for *emotional* forms of expression. Reasoning, logical statement, precise definition chill the fervid mind and exclude the emotions ; pictures, on the contrary, warm the heart. So for this reason also poets delight in pictures. Plain prose might state in carefully accurate and balanced phrase the benefit that death confers on us by enabling us to know truth in all its purity and integrity. In one marvellous image the poet touches the depths of feeling:—

> Life, like a dome of many-coloured glass
> Stains the white radiance of eternity
> Until Death shatters it to fragments.

So had St. Paul said, in a different image: "For now we see in a mirror darkly, but then face to face." [2]

There is one form of metaphor which lends itself peculiarly to the expression of emotion—personification. It is evident that by its means all inanimate nature can as it were become suffused with human feelings, till it seems to share the poet's ecstasy or melancholy, and provide a setting for all his changing moods.[3]

[1] J. G. Jennings, Metaphor in Poetry, p. 82.
[2] First Epistle to the Corinthians, ch. xiii, v. 2.
[3] "Une description n'est belle que si le paysage qu'elle représente est, pour ainsi dire, imprégné d'âme. La nature est un prodigieux miroir où la sensibilité humaine se réflète." Sully-Prudhomme.

THE FUNCTIONS OF METAPHOR

The achievement of concrete and emotional expression is far from being the only service rendered by imagery to poetry. It is of the nature of poetry to shun the trite, the commonplace, the well-worn phrases of daily speech, at least in their conventional setting. We have already pointed out that metaphor renders just this service to language in general— it renews and refreshes our powers of expression.

Of poetry in particular, in this connexion, a recent writer has said : " The poet, since he is constantly seeing new resemblances and uncovering new objects of ideas which, because they are new, lack words to express them, is constantly forced to make such extensions [of language]. By using figures he gains greatly in power of expression ; indeed he is enabled to express ideas which would otherwise remain inexpressible. The poets, therefore, are the great builders of language."[1]

It is therefore but natural that poetry, in *turning away*[2] from the commonplace and the conventional, should often find themselves at a loss for expression, should have recourse to imagery, and should clothe therein its thoughts and fancies. Imagery is of course not the sole resource of poetry in thus securing aloofness from vulgarity. There is also poetic diction —the word of antique flavour, the turn of expression as yet unhackneyed, unprofaned, the epithet exhaling already a poetic perfume. But imagery remains poetry's most unfailing treasure-house.

Further, imagery, helps poetry towards the end at which it aims in common with all the other arts, the achievement of beauty. Poetry deals with the same objects of thought as philosophy, theology, or science. But it differs in the expression of its

[1] F. C. Prescott, *The Poet's Mind*, 1922.
[2] A turning away is the root meaning of the word trope, a generic term for figures of speech.

95

ideas about them, not only because, as we have seen, that expression is emotional and imaginative, but because it seeks to be beautiful. The poet sees man, life, nature, God in beauty and strives to put into sorry words the loveliness of his vision. With the texture of his thought about these objects he may by means of metaphor interweave all manner of beautiful images. They seem, they are all in a sense, extraneous to the thought. But imaginative insight discovers affinities hidden to the most of men and weaves these various thoughts and images into a perfect harmony. " Nature," says Emerson, " offers all her creatures to the poet as a picture language." And he if will can choose the loveliest to embody his poetic thoughts and dreams. Every reader of poetry will know Shelley's *Skylark* and it would be difficult to find a more apt illustration of our present point. The poet to describe the skylark's song pours forth one exquisite simile after another. Each does little to explain to us the nature of that melody but all combine to make us realize it in beauty. And thus the poet's purpose is achieved.

Perhaps we may claim for imagery a still further function in poetry. Pure prose, the prose of science, business, matter of fact, presents ideas and facts detached, as far as may be, from all extraneous connotations which might distract the intellect. To present them thus is in some sort to segregate them from real life, to take them out of their actual setting and fit them into the categories of the mind. And for the purely intellectual expression of ideas words are pure symbols. The tendency is towards the algebraical formula. Poetry on the contrary rejoices in multitudinous connotations, in infinite suggestiveness. It chooses words that have emotional significance, words to which memories cling, around which fancy can play. Moreover, far from segregating ideas, it would on the contrary place them against a changing, beautiful, varied background. The theme of a poem might often be stated in one brief sentence of prose. But the poet, by means of imagery, blends in with the expression of his thought something of the significance, beauty, majesty, and mystery of the great world.[1] The average prose writer will say " insular and mountainous situations have always been favourable to the political independence of small states." Wordsworth says :—

> Two voices are there ; one is of the sea,
> One of the mountains ; each a mighty voice :
> In both from age to age thou didst rejoice,
> They were thy chosen music, Liberty.

Mutability, the title of another of Wordsworth's sonnets, might suggest to a philosopher reflections on the ultimate causes of change and decay, to a scientist the physical and chemical causes of disintegration. The poet's thought is set in a picture of all earth and the heavens.

> From low to high doth dissolution climb,
> And sink from high to low, along a scale
> Of awful notes, whose concord shall not fail ;
> A musical but melancholy chime,
> Which they can hear who meddle not with crime,
> Nor avarice, nor over-anxious care.
> Truth fails not ; but her outward forms that bear
> The longest date do melt like frosty rime,
> That in the morning whitened hill and plain
> And is no more ; drop like the tower sublime
> Of yesterday, which royally did wear
> His crown of weeds, but could not even sustain
> Some casual shout that broke the silent air
> Or the unimaginable touch of Time.

---

[1] Metaphor is the supreme agent by which disparate and hitherto unconnected things are brought together in poetry for the sake of the effects upon attitude and impulse which spring from them . . . Metaphor is a semi-surreptitious method by which a greater variety of elements can be wrought into the fabric of the experience." I. A. Richards, *Principles of Literary Criticism*, 1925, p. 241.

THEORY

It is by means of metaphor that all these beautiful images are interwoven with the main theme. In like manner the sustained similes in Homer and Dante and, may we add, Isaias, do not so much illustrate and elucidate the narrative as give it a majestic background, a noble setting amid God's creation. In Shakespeare's *Macbeth* and *King Lear* tragic deeds and passions are set against a background of time, place, and weather which harmonizes with the mood. So in *In Memoriam* the poet's ideas and moods are set over against an ever-changing panorama now of nature, now of history, and now of philosophic world-thought. Such a background stands to the theme of a poem somewhat as the harmonies and variations to a simple air in music, as when a folk song is made the theme of a sonata.[1]

The present writer has elsewhere ventured to define poetry as the " art which expresses in metrical and otherwise fitting or congruous language, self, life, nature, God, and all their interactions seen in beauty and realized or apprehended in a mood of emotional and imaginative exaltation ".[2] If this definition, in spite of its clumsiness, be accepted as substantially correct, then it will scarcely be too much to say that there is no element in language which better expresses the poetic spirit than metaphor and kindred imagery. " Imaging," said Dryden long ago, " is in itself the very height and life of poetry." " Metaphor," says the writer whom we have already[3] quoted more than once, " is not the

[1] "Very much of the poetic lies in the vivid perceiving of relations between the world of matter and the thoughts or feelings of the mind." Macbeth: *Might and Mirth of Literature*, p. 188.

[2] *The Realm of Poetry*, London, Harrap, 1921, p. 71.

[3] An American writer, Hiram Maxim, goes so far as to say, "Metaphor is the soul of poetry " (*The Science of Poetry and the Philosophy of Language*). "Poetry," says another American writer, " is a tropical zone of metaphor." H. W. Wells, *Poetic Imagery*, New York, 1924.

spirit of poetry itself but it is the very atmosphere of the land in which that spirit breathes and roams."[1] And he rightly says elsewhere [2] that " some grasp of the meaning and function of metaphor is essential, if not for the understanding, at least for anything approaching a real appreciation of poetic art." A French writer on Psychology goes so far as to say " There is no poetry in the direct expression of an idea, the poetry is in the figurative, symbolical, metaphorical expression ".[3]   If this be an overstatement it at least goes to show how closely wedded to the poetic spirit is this element of poetic form.   Such a modern poem as Francis Thompson's *Hound of Heaven* springs to the mind as a supreme instance of the manner in which metaphor often becomes for poets the very warp and woof of poetic expression.   I prefer to quote a simpler example and that from a very ancient poet, the author of the twenty-second Psalm [4]:—

The Lord is my Shepherd, I shall not want.
He maketh me to lie down in pastures of tender grass,
He leads me beside waters of rest.
He restores my soul.
He guides me in the paths of uprightness for His name's sake.
Yea, though I walk through the valley of the shadow of death
    I will fear no evil.
For Thou art with me : Thy rod and Thy staff, they comfort me.
Thou spreadest a table before me in the presence of mine
    enemies.
Thou hast anointed my head with oil : my cup flows over.
Naught but goodness and loving-kindness shall follow me all
    the days of my life.
And I will dwell in the house of the Lord for length of days.

---

[1] J. G. Jennings, *Metaphor in Poetry*, p. 17.
[2] Ibid., p. 83.
[3] Elie Rabier, *Psychologie*, p. 64.   Cf. Alfred Biese, *Das Metaphorische in der dichterischen Phantasie*, Berlin, 1889, p. 4.   F. I. Carpenter, p. xv.
[4] Father M'Swiney's translation.   Ps. xxiii in the Hebrew.

THEORY

The difference between the function of imagery in poetry and in pure prose has been well expressed as follows :—" The poetic image has an emotional and richly imaginative value, leaving its subject nobler, more delightful, or more abhorred. The image of science, on the other hand, appeals to the calculating and descriptive faculty, leaving its subject more vivid, more memorable, more accurately perceived." [1]   Yet all that we have said of poetry applies in due proportion to prose also.   " Metaphor," says Earle, " is common to Poetry and Prose, because it is the prime agent of progressive thought growing by experience and the comparison of experiences, a process from which is derived the nutriment of all literature and of all science."   For, apart from mere business or pure science, prose that would be an expression of human personality cannot remain wholly alien to the spirit of poetry.   And according as it draws near, whether through the emotions or through the imagination, to the expression of that spirit, so will the rôle of imagery gain an ever greater importance. The writings of all the great masters of prose are witnesses.

[1] W. H. Wells, *Poetic Imagery*, New York, 1924.

CHAPTER V

The Sources of Imagery

From our study of the functions of imagery in thought and language the conclusion seems to emerge that imagery plays in both one and the other a part of no small importance. If this conclusion be admitted it may be well to study next how the riches of imagery may be put to amplest use in picturing forth thought, and in endowing speech with emotional, imaginative, and æsthetic qualities.

I

In themselves the stores of imagery are inexhaustible. As we have seen, metaphor is the expression of a perceived analogy between objects belonging to different spheres of being. Now, between these different spheres there are a myriad interrelations, and the number of analogies that the mind of man can perceive is beyond all reckoning. Still vaster the number that it can fancy.

> To attempt [says M. Lanson] to classify the metaphors in use would be to enumerate all the relations perceived in the universe by the mind of man[1]—to attempt to catalogue all possible metaphors would be as chimerical as to attempt to draw up a list of the future discoveries of humanity. Everything is connected with everything else, anything can be compared with anything else; in an instant, a relation hitherto unperceived is adverted to, and forthwith starts into existence, at least in the mind that perceives it.[2]

[1] Similarly Michel Bréal, " Ce chapitre de la métaphore est infini. Il n'est rapport réel ou ressemblance fugitive qui n'ait fourni son contingent " : *Essai de Sémantique*, 5th ed., 1921, p. 288.
[2] *Nihil est in rerum natura unde simile duci non possit.*—Cicero, *De Oratore*, Bk. iii. " The Sources of similitudes are coextensive with the world of knowledge."—Bain, *Rhetoric and Composition*, pt. i, p. 152.

Yes, *tout tient à tout*—that is the sum of the matter, and the root reason for it is the simple fact that the Author of all is One. The Universe, therefore, is a boundless storehouse of imagery.

> If all that poetry has dreamed [wrote Oliver Wendell Holmes] all that maddening narcotics have driven through the brains of men, or smothered passion nursed in the fancies of women— if every human feeling that sighs or smiles or shrieks or groans, should bring all their innumerable images, the epic which held them all, though its letters filled the zodiac, would be but a cupful to the ocean of similitudes and analogies that rolls through the universe.

And, however turgid in style such a passage may be, it does not overestimate the wealth that lies at the command of the literary artist. The painter has his score or so of pigments. Doubtless he can blend them into a wonderful variety of tints and shades. The musician can combine the few notes of his instrument into a still more marvellous variety of melody and harmony. But painter and musician are straitly limited by their medium. Still more narrowly limited are the sculptor and the architect. Not so the literary artist, the writer or the speaker. Of all the vast complexity of things there is scarcely an object or a relation that may not serve him as a medium of expression. His imagination can reach forth to the ends of the earth and gather in the wherewithal to clothe his thoughts, not decently only, but fittingly and beautifully.

External nature is of course the chief treasure house of imagery. Not a sight, nor a sound, nor a movement in the world of nature but may be pressed into the service of expression—the endless variety of weather, the changes of day and night, sunset and dawn, the succession of the seasons, all the elements of landscape, mountain and vale, woodland and meadow, river and sea and sky. All these

may serve, have served a thousand times, to picture
forth man's inmost thoughts, and to furnish him the
means to make palpable and intelligible that inward
world which eye cannot look upon nor finger touch.
It is an idea that keeps ever recurring in the writings
of Emerson that it was for this that nature primarily
was made, that it is the chief function of the world
of things to minister to the world of thought. "The
use of natural history is to give us aid in supernatural [1]
history: the use of the outer creation to give us
language for the beings and changes of the inward
creation." [2]   Nay, " every natural fact is a symbol
of some spiritual fact. Every appearance of nature
corresponds to some state of the mind and that state
of the mind can best be described by presenting
that natural appearance as its picture." This is but
harking back to a very old thought indeed, on which
we hope to dwell more fully later. There is nothing
in nature too insignificant to serve as the image of
some idea. A swarm of gnats on a summer's evening
may serve as an image of the lives of men. The
Hebrew sage bade us learn wisdom from the ants.[3]
And a greater than he taught us wisdom through the
lilies and the birds. From the characteristics and
ways of animals we borrow expression for our soul
states. We describe, whether in praise or disparagement, the temperaments of human beings in terms of
some real or supposed qualities of theirs. He that
was very God walking the earth as Man accepted
to be called a Lamb and the Spirit of God took upon
Him the name of the Dove. A writer complains
that poets have failed to use for imagery a tithe of

[1] Emerson has no idea of the supernatural in the Catholic theological
sense. He means merely " suprasensible ", belonging to the world
of ideas.

[2] So, too, Carlyle, " All visible things are emblems. What thou
seest is not there on its own account. Matter only exists to represent
some idea and body it forth."—*Sartor Resartus*.

[3] Prov. vi, 6.

the wealth that lies within their reach in the animal world.

> Taking the bird-world alone [he says] . . . there are known to science more than three thousand species of birds. But poetry takes ken of a bare hundred, and of these a third are so casually mentioned that, virtually, they are useless to the text, and so far as they contribute any special significance, force, or beauty, almost any other birds might have taken their places.[1]

As for the vegetable world it is enough to recall that upwards of a hundred thousand species of plants are known to science. Flowers, above all, have at all times served the poets for beautiful symbolism and imagery. "Every plant that grows," says a writer on our present subject,[2] "corresponds laterally with something in human nature," and so can be used as a metaphor or a symbol of human affairs.

Inanimate nature is no less full of images and symbols of the unseen—"sermons in stones, books in the running brook." Our changeful moods are as those of the sea and sky. Joy and knowledge are light, ignorance and despondency darkness.

> This fair earth is recognized to be a mighty parable. Its manifold forms and hues are the outer folds, the waving skirts and fringes, of that garment of light in which the Invisible has robed His mysterious loveliness. There is not a leaf, nor a flower, nor a dewdrop but bears His image. . . . The whole face of nature, to him, who can read it aright, is covered with celestial types and hieroglyphics, marked, like the dialplate of a watch, with significant intimations of the objects and processes of the world unseen.[3]

The mineral world affords a rich mine for illustration and imagery. John the Seer in the Apocalypse had used the precious stones as symbols of things

[1] Phil Robinson, *The Poet's Birds*.
[2] L. H. Grindon, *Figurative Language*, London, 1879, p. 249, where the subject is admirably worked out.
[3] Hugh Macmillan, *Bible Teachings in Nature*.

divine. The qualities of the various metals have long been applied to the qualities of the spirit—an *iron* will, true as *steel*, the *leaden* hours, *golden* opinions, a *mercurial* temperament. And so of other common substances—wood, glass, rubber, stone, clay, sand, wool, as well as the old-time " elements " fire and water and earth and air. We can scarcely name one of these substances without figurative associations starting at once into memory. And no doubt, the countless other substances known to chemical science will furnish ever fresh sources of imagery according as they become widely enough known for imagery drawn from them to be intelligible.

Were it possible to exhaust the imagery of external nature one might yet fall back upon those modifications and manipulations of nature which are the product of man's hand and brain—his sciences, arts, pursuits, and pastimes. All of these have enriched language permanently with terms transferred from their original and technical sense to new and more human usages, not merely fresh colloquial terms for things already named, but terms that express some newly observed trait of human nature, some more subtly analysed shade of emotion.

Seafaring, for instance, has ever been a rich source of imagery, and terms borrowed from the language of ships and the sea are found embedded in well-nigh every tongue. The word *arrive* once meant to reach the shore, to *accost* had a similar origin. The Latin verb *portare*, from which we have so many derivatives in English, meant " to bring to port ". *Opportune* and *importunate* once suggested the notion of an easy or a difficult landing. And so of that other most ancient occupation of man—the chase. Language is filled with fossil metaphors that once were technical hunting terms. Such are pounce, crestfallen, at bay, in abeyance, toils, cajole, decoy,

—words which we use without any feeling of their origin. Others still bear with them the flavour of their original meaning—on the wrong scent, breaking cover, in full cry, and so on. We recall what noble use Francis Thompson makes in the *Hound of Heaven* of this imagery of the chase. And Janet Erskine Stuart, as Mother-General of the Society of the Sacred Heart, illustrated her lectures to her nuns with metaphors drawn from her old hunting days. " We are not riding out for exercise," she would say, " we are hunting for sport's sake ; hence these fences, bullfinches, five-barred gates, and even occasional rolls in the mud are all part of the day's sport," or again, " Don't pull so hard at the bit, you wrench every muscle in my hand trying to rein you in." [1]

If we think of the most familiar industries, what a wealth of imagery they have furnished from the beginning for the illustration of thought. There is the primitive tending of flocks with its pastoral imagery. Hebrew literature from Genesis to the Apocalypse abounds in it. There is agriculture with its processes of ploughing and sowing, reaping, and harvesting. Building furnishes abundant imagery—foundations, walls, roof, floors, windows, battlements, doors, all have been used to body forth religious and philosophical ideas, as well as those of daily life. Trade gives us images of buying and selling, profit and loss, bargain and barter. Mining and quarrying have given us many a striking image. And so with all processes of manufacture, especially the most primitive—the making of wine and bread and cloth, the moulding of clay, the carving of wood and stone, the smelting and working of iron and bronze and the precious metals.

War with all its horror and its pageantry has

[1] *Life and Letters of Janet Erskine Stuart*, by Maud Monahan. Longmans, 1922, p. 75 sqq., where many other examples are quoted.

furnished us with imagery for many a struggle fought
out with other than material weapons.   Armies and
battles, helmet and sword, spear and shield, general-
ship and serried phalanx, all have their counterpart
in the world of ideas.   Rifle, shell, and machine-gun,
camouflage and poisoned gas, and all the other horrors
of modern warfare, will furnish and are already
furnishing imagery to modern literature.   And so
with civil government, beginning with the glory
and pomp of kingship:—

> Mont Blanc is a *monarch* of mountains,
>   They *crowned* him long ago
> On a *throne* of rocks, in a *robe* of clouds,
>   With a *diadem* of snow.

So, too, with all the other functionaries of the
State, from Emperor to petty official.   Again, there
are the instruments of government—councils and
parliaments, and the rest ;   and the forms and
machinery of civil rule and of the administration
of law.   And if the profession of the law has given
us imagery so has the great profession of healing.
The language of physical disease and well-being
has been transferred to that of the soul.   " Physician,
heal thyself ! "
The language of travel has furnished endless
images by which we may speak of journeys in regions
other than the surface of our earth.   The very word
" progress " is a metaphor.   We speak as often in
metaphor as in literal fact of roads and paths, uphill
and downhill, bridges and mountain passes, halting
places and stages, ports and harbours, milestones
and stepping-stones.   Equally fertile as a source of
imagery is the household with all its occupations and
contents, domestic furniture, implements, and utensils
of all kinds.   The loftiest thoughts may be brought
home (significant word !) to the mind and heart by the

humblest of these objects, used as imagery. Christ Himself spoke of candlesticks and beds, cupboards and loaves and brooms. Similarly recreations, sports, and pastimes have enriched language with new ways of expressing ideas. The theatre has been made an image of human life, and it is said that every situation in Whist has been used as a figure.

Then, we have the language of the arts and crafts to draw upon—music (as yet but little used), painting, sculpture, metallurgy, and the rest. The " art of life " is a familiar term to-day, and in a very beautiful little book with that title all life has been described in terms of Art.[1]

A most prolific source of imagery, and one that we have scarcely begun to exploit is furnished by the sciences. Gradually the technical language of the sciences is being transferred to the use of common speech. We have long ago borrowed from Arithmetic such terms as addition, multiplication, subtraction, fractions, proportion, direct and inverse. Geometry and Algebra too have furnished their contribution, though a small one. The language of the mechanical and natural sciences has been borrowed to describe the processes of the world of mind. We speak of inertia, momentum, velocity, acceleration, cohesion, adhesion, repulsion, equilibrium, reaction, polarization, tension, clockwork, gravity, distillation, evaporation, magnetism, compass, refraction, radiation, strata. As the bounds of knowledge widen, and as the elements of the various sciences become the common possession of educated people, the possibilities for the making of images grow ever greater. Already in quite familiar speech we can use in figurative senses such once technical terms as a " short-circuit ", to " switch-on ", a " live wire ".

[1] *The Art of Life,* by Frederick C. Kolbe, a South African priest.

THE SOURCES OF IMAGERY

Sources of imagery scarcely less rich will be found in the numberless arts and crafts of our complicated modern life—photography, printing, engraving, wireless transmission, the cinema, motor engineering, and the like.

In spite of the extent to which these sources of imagery have been exploited already, endless possibilities of fresh imagery yet remain, and every new progress of science increases them.[1] Indeed, apart from such possibilities, all the works of the scientists, of a Buffon or a Linnaeus, would be, for a mind like Emerson's or Carlyle's, primarily interested in the spiritual, merely dry catalogues of facts. But in view of these possibilities, the most trivial of these facts takes on a new significance—the habit of a plant, the organs or work or noise of an insect, might be applied to the illustration of " a fact in intellectual philosophy ", or in some other way associated to human nature. So regarded it became full of interest.

There is, however, an important limitation to the use of imagery whether drawn from the sciences or from any other source. It is the limits of the knowledge possessed by reader or hearer. In order to fulfil any of its functions an image must first be intelligible. Else it can neither aid thought nor stir emotion. Music is a case in point. The poet is quite intelligible when he says :

> How light the touches are that kiss
> The music from the *chords* of life.

Or

> And I—my *harp* would *prelude* woe—
> I cannot all command the *strings* :
> The glory of the sum of things
> Will flash along the *chords* and go.

[1] " Material for Parable lies unnoticed and unused on the field of recent science in inexhaustible profusion." Henry Drummond, *Natural Law in the Spiritual World.*

THEORY

Or once more—

> Love took up the harp of life, and smote on
>   all the chords with might;
> Smote the chord of self, that, trembling,
>   pass'd in music out of sight.

We have grown familiar even with such expressions as "set in a *minor key*", "a *staccato* utterance", "a *crescendo* of disapproval". But one would soon find oneself outside the ken of the average reader were one to speak of arpeggio and pizzicato, adagio, and allegro, chromatic and diatonic,[1] and even bars and rests, crochets and quavers, breves and semibreves. *A fortiori* is this true of those sciences which are of a highly specialized nature, and whose technicalities are the secret of the initiated.

Nevertheless, it is not without reason that the author of that curious book *The Might and Mirth of Literature*[2] declared it arithmetically impossible that true genius could ever find its materials run out. There is in such a reflection no slight comfort for the writer or the speaker. No doubt the resources of language—literal current speech, are great and manifold. Yet there are times when they seem to fail us. We find no fit expression for our thought, or only such expression as is too worn and threadbare to clothe it as we desire. It may be that the thought or feeling or fancy seeking utterance is of such as "break though language and escape". Or it may be that we have but a feeble grasp upon the word-treasures of the tongue we speak. Be that as it may, aid may be sought in the resources of the world of imagery. By such aid frail fancies, subtle shades of

---

[1] I have since come upon this very word in De Quincey, "Ceylon is a panorganon for modulating through the whole diatonic scale of climate."

[2] John Walker Vilant Macbeth. The book, which was published in America in 1876, and is now hard to procure, is an elaborate treatise on figures of speech.

thought, feelings that seem unutterable may find expression. With such aid the writer or speaker may afford to set aside the well-worn conventional phrase, the stale epithet, the flowers of speech that once were an adornment and are but faded finery now, like costumes from some great city theatre, long discarded and flaunted only by strolling players.

II

But it is not enough that the stores be there: one must have the faculty to use them. The ether held, a thousand years ago, as vast a store of that mysterious fluid electricity as it holds to-day. But men had not learned to harness it to their purposes. It is but indifferent comfort to be aware that the resources of imagery are of endless richness and variety, if we are powerless to draw upon them. But how is the ability to do so to be gained? It is simple to suggest practice, but practice is merely the exercising of something already there: it contributes nothing new to our equipment. It gives facility, not fresh knowledge. True, there is much in the realm of imagery that any man can draw upon who has a head with eyes in it.

> The poorest experience [says Emerson] is rich enough for all the purposes of expressing thought. Why covet a knowledge of new facts? Day and night, house and garden, a few books, a few actions, serve as well as would all trades and all spectacles.

In this, however, I may be pardoned for thinking there is some overstatement, and I would venture to counter it with this passage from the philosopher Hobbes:—

> From knowing much proceedeth the admirable variety and novelty of metaphors and similitudes which are not possible to be lightened on in the compass of a narrow knowledge. And the want whereof compelleth a writer to expressions that are either defaced by time or sullied with vulgar and long use.

For if one is to write or speak in a manner above the merest commonplace, if, in other words, one is to write what has any fair claim to the attention of readers, or to speak with any hope of impressing hearers, one must bring to the task something more than just the equipment of " any man ".

We thus find ourselves confronted with the general question of the cultural preparation for literary work. That is, however, too considerable a matter to be dealt with here. We must confine ourselves to that aspect of cultural preparation which is concerned with imagery. Thus limited, the problem is, how to become familiar with the world of imagery, how to gain the skill to draw upon its riches for the expression of ideas, fancies, and emotions. In the first place let it be said that such preparation is not merely a matter of school-work. Nay, rather it is when school days have ended that self-culture of this kind may be said properly to begin. Yet, unless in school days the road has been at least pointed out, and some impulse to travel it communicated to the learner, the journey towards culture is scarcely likely to begin at all.

If one is to acquire any considerable command over the resources of imagery one of the first requisites would seem to be the cultivation of our powers of observation. The faculties must be alert, that is, first aware of, and then, if possible, interested in, what comes within their ken. Indeed, one must be interested in certain objects in order to be even aware of them, to be consciously alive to their existence. To the farmer cattle, crops, varieties of soil, and the like are primary objects of interest. His mind is habitually alert to such things, they catch his attention and arouse his powers of observation. The images of these things are garnered in memory. But to the rest of the world he may be all but blind. The artist seizes upon the picturesque, his eye almost spontaneously appraises tint and shade, he sees what other men do not see—violet in the shadows and blue reflections of the sky in grazing cattle. His memory stores up forms and shapes of beauty. But of many other things he may be wholly unobservant. The most of men retain little of the stream of sensation that pours through their faculties of perception. Here and there something will strike them and leave a clear-cut impression, but for the most part all is vague and blurred. Their eyes look without seeing, they fail to observe.[1]

But the faculty of observation may be deliberately cultivated. We have the power, among the many things we *see*, to select that which we shall *observe*. That power may grow by exercise. And opportunities for such exercise lie around us on all sides, offer themselves well-nigh at every moment.

> The more [says an excellent writer on the art of writing] the more the brain stores up the images of things seen, the richer is the stock upon which our mind can work. It behoves us, therefore, constantly to add to the store of sense-images in the memory. To this end the outward senses, the sight and hearing in particular, must be trained to observe keenly the objects and phenomena that come within their reach.

But ever behind those outward senses, the mind active, curious, discriminative, must be at work watching men and things, gathering from them materials for its own enrichment. "A mind thus intense, investigatory—amounts to a tremendous loadstone in the midst of a full-stocked creation— full stocked with the materials of thought." Speaking more especially of the observation of outward nature,

---

[1] I find the substance of the foregoing paragraph excellently expressed in Mr. J. Middleton Murry's recent book *The Problem of Style*, London, 1925, p. 92 sq.

THEORY

Victor de Laprade says in a passage which I venture with diffidence to translate :—

> The poetic style presupposes the most delicate acquisitions of the senses and of the imagination: it presupposes an intimate and constant intercommunication between the soul and the outer world. It is in the loving observation and contemplation of nature that the mind enriches itself with the images, the colours, the harmonies necessary for the poetic style. It is necessarily from nature, from the spectacle of sky and sea and forest and their living denizens that the poet draws the similes, metaphors, descriptive epithets, figures of all kinds which give life to his style. *Pour écrire en poète, pour peindre, il ne suffit pas d'avoir pensé, il faut avoir vu.*[1]

Besides this alertness of observation, there is needed in one whose calling it is to write and speak, be he journalist, statesman, or even preacher, a sort of catholicity of interests. For the farmer or the soldier or the merchant it is enough, in a sense, that he be fully trained in all that concerns his craft.[2] Other interests he may pursue, but only by way of pastime or distraction. But it is of the greatest advantage to the writer or speaker that his faculties be trained to as great a keenness of observation in many directions as they are capable of attaining, that he be alert to a great variety of interests, that he aim at knowing, according to the adage, not only " everything about something ", viz. the particular department of literature or life that he may have chosen as his own, but " something about everything ". For there is no aspect of nature or of life or of human nature that falls outside the scope of literature, there is no class of fact and no department of knowledge that may not lend its treasures to enrich style. Moreover, unless one be a specialist, writing or lecturing for specialists, or a literary dilettante writing to please oneself,

[1] V. de Laprade, *Le Sentiment de la Nature.*
[2] Of course an education that is not narrowly technical, but liberal, is of advantage in almost any walk of life.

the audience addressed consists of all sorts and conditions of men. To meet all sorts and conditions of taste and temperament it is highly advantageous to be equipped with a wealth and variety of illustration.

But in suggesting that catholicity of observation and of interests is of advantage to the writer and speaker, I do not mean to suggest it as desirable that our soul windows should lie open to every wind that blows, agape to the dust and the smoke as well as to the wholesome air. I mean that the mind should be keenly alive to what is apt for its purposes in many and various scenes and actions and spheres of thought, that it should accustom itself to go treasure-hunting for its images along many a divergent path. One might recommend, though perhaps not without reservations, the example of a man of letters thus set forth by an American writer :—

> He habitually fed himself with any kind of knowledge that was at hand. If books were at his elbow, he read them; if pictures, engravings, gems, were within reach, he studied them ; if nature was within walking distance he watched nature, if men were about him he learned the secrets of their temperaments, tastes, and skills ; if he travelled by stage he sat with the driver and learned all about the route, the country, the people, and the art of his companion,[1] and so forth.

Coleridge quite late in life attended lectures on Geology in order to add to his power of making new metaphors and similes.

And all such acquisitions may be put to good uses in literature as well as in life. We have all in the course of our early education learned much that served, no doubt, to train our minds, but which we shall never have the opportunity of following up and grasping thoroughly. We thus acquired what was little better than a smattering of many subjects. Is all this merely " learned lumber " ? For the writer

[1] Mabie, *Essays on Books and Culture.*

and speaker it is not so. Latent in memory he bears a wealth of illustration which he may at will arouse into living images.

In a word the wider and more catholic is a man's culture even from early years the greater his command over the resources of the world of imagery.

NOTE TO CHAPTER V (PART I)

Mr. T. Hilding Svartengren, of Lund, Sweden, in his remarkable work *Intensifying Similes in English*, Lund, 1918, essays a classification of similes according to their sources, that is to say, the provinces and departments of life and nature from which they are drawn.

These provinces and departments are :—
God, Heaven, Hell, the Devil.
Other aspects of man's religious life.
Death.
The Bible, Worship.
Classes, professions, trades.
Human beings, sexes, ages, family relations.
Nationalities.
Human body, parts, and functions.
Diseases.
Smoke, perfumes, meals, food, and drink.
Coins, clothes.
Learning, books, government, banking.
Art, music, play.
Implements, tools, weapons.
Vessels, receptacles.
Buildings, furniture.
Raw materials.
Precious stones, minerals, metals.
Street and road.
Seafaring.

THE SOURCES OF IMAGERY

Abstract ideas, human actions, words.
Domestic animals.
Other animals (mammals).
Birds, fish, insects.
Plants.
Earth, sea, land, water.
Sky, air, celestial bodies, seasons.

Such a list, if it have no other use, may serve as a sort of literary examination of conscience with a view to filling up the lacunæ of one's reading and observation.

CHAPTER VI

SIMILE

THE readiest means of illustrating an object or an action or even an idea is by representing it as *like* something more familiar. When the two objects so likened to each other belong to the same order of being we have merely a comparison ; when they belong to different orders of being we have the figure known as simile. It is the likeness or analogy perceived amid essential unlikeness that makes the figure.[1] Thus the familiar line

Blue were her eyes as the fairy flax

is, strictly speaking, a comparison only and not a simile, for the two objects compared, however different, are both material, and the quality in which they resemble one another viz. blueness, is literally in both.[2] There is therefore no figure. Nor is there in Tennyson's fine comparison for the dark eyelashes of a girl—

Black as ashbuds in the front of March.

Yet the author of that excellent little book *The Rudiments of Criticism* speaks of it as " this beautiful simile ". The same must be said of most of the familiar sayings of everyday speech—cold as ice, white as snow, black as a sloe, brown as a berry.

[1] Genung, *Practical Rhetoric*, p. 89: " In order that Resemblances may be figurative the things compared must differ in kind." Bain, *Rhetoric and Composition*, 1893, vol. i, p. 138.

[2] The word blue is used in a curious variety of transferred senses— in the blues, a blue look-out, a true blue, blue blood, a blue funk, once in a blue moon, etc. Cf. the *yellow* press, the *red* peril, a *brown* study, aller au diable *vert*, the *green*-eyed monster.

SIMILE

It is, however, difficult to maintain this strict distinction in practice. For example, French writers, for the most part, seem scarcely conscious of it, using, as they do, the word *comparaison* for simile and comparison alike. In Willstack's *Dictionary of Similes* [1] the author acknowledges that his book contains many examples which are rather comparisons than similes strictly so called, but he adds, not without reason : " The reader will find, I trust, the few comparisons in the dictionary quite as welcome as the out-and-out similes." The author of an important work on Simile [2] which we shall have occasion to refer to more than once, acknowledges the difficulty, in many cases, of drawing a distinction between a literal comparison and a simile. He appears to think that it depends largely on the context. In point of fact simile and mere comparison are the same in form, being expressed by terms such as " like " or " as " or some equivalent. Their functions likewise are, as we shall see, quite similar. Nevertheless the distinction is a real one and worthy of note.

I

Simile and metaphor are often distinguished by saying that the former is an explicit comparison introduced by the word " as " or " like ",[3] while the

---

[1] London, Harrap, 1917.

[2] *Intensifying Similes in English*, T. Hilding Svartengren (University of Lund, Sweden, printed by Aktinebolaget Skånska Centraltryckeriet).

[3] Formal words of this kind are not necessary to the nature of the Simile. What is essential is that both sides of the comparison be distinctly expressed. The following is a simile :—

> He who ascends to mountain tops shall find
> The loftiest peaks most wrapped in clouds and snow ;
> He who surpasses or subdues mankind
> Must look down on the hate of those below.

Simile may likewise be stated as a negative or in degrees of comparison.

latter is an implicit comparison, all *terms* of comparison being omitted. In reality such a distinction is at best superficial : the difference, both from a literary and from a psychological point of view, lies deeper. In the first place metaphor has a higher poetic quality. Emotion so fuses thought and image that they appear as one and we have metaphor : simile deliberately holds them apart and views them separately. The formal nature of the introductory " as " or " like " brings a pause, a slackening, and a certain coldness.[1] We lose the force and rapidity of metaphor. Hence for rhetorical purposes, too, the superiority of metaphor : orators prefer it to a simile. It has been remarked that in all Demosthenes a simile is scarcely to be found.[2] " Simile," says Professor Genung, " being the great illustrative figure, is especially adapted to promote clearness of thought and expression ; not so well adapted to force and passion.[3] Hence it is more naturally used in the less emotional kinds of discourse." It is hardly enough to say, with Aristotle,[4] that the simile is less pleasing than metaphor, because more at length. Carlyle, for instance, writes in metaphor for whole paragraphs

> that she may feel
> How sharper than a serpent's tooth it is
> To have a thankless child.
> > *King Lear*, ii, 4.

> The sea enraged is not half so deaf,
> Lions more confident, mountains and rocks
> More free from motion ; no, nor death himself
> In mortal fury half so peremptory,
> As we to keep this city.
> > *King John*, ii, 2.

[1] Goldsmith, if it be Goldsmith, perhaps overstates the case in saying, " the language of passion will not admit simile which is always the result of study and deliberation."

[2] Macbeth, *The Might and Mirth of Literature*, p. 186.

[3] " Rooted grief, deep anguish, terror, remorse, despair, and all the severe dispiriting passions are declared enemies, perhaps not to figurative language in general, but undoubtedly to the pomp and solemnity of comparison." Lord Kames, op. cit., p. 322.

[4] *Rhet.*, iii, 10.

at a time. And the similes in Homer are scarcely the less pleasing because so long drawn out. It is the formalness, the deliberateness, the pause, the explicitness that makes the simile in itself less poetic. " Similes," says Professor Earle, " are sought out for the sake of ornament, but Metaphor is a resource of expression that starts up instinctively by affinity with the process of sincere meditation." Moreover, the imaginative stimulus of simile is also *ceteris paribus*, less than that of metaphor. " He fought like a lion " is a weaker image than " he was a lion in the fight " because it involves two distinct pictures and divides the attention. It is curious, then, to note that in the opinion of certain writers [1] simile " stands on a higher plane of poetic development than metaphor ". The reason assigned is that " Much more art, more balance is needed to pause in the current of poetry and hold two objects apart, then returning to the main subject and proceeding quietly with the interrupted narration. This demands a higher faculty, a more analytic, self-contained faculty ". The most, I think, that can be shown is that simile, to justify its place in poetry, makes greater demands than does metaphor on a writer's ingenuity. Metaphor is more *naturally* poetic.

II

But what simile loses in suggestiveness it gains in *clearness*. This is well expressed in the following passage. " While simile (*la comparaison*) leaves to words their own meaning, metaphor gives them a figurative meaning ; in simile two similar objects are compared ; in the metaphor the object spoken of disappears behind an object that is similar to it. Simile lights up discourse, metaphor darkens it, unless the likeness on which it is based be very obvious; the simile

[1] Professor Gummere, *Manual of Poetics*, p. 107, Boston, 1886.

is instructive, the metaphor *piquant*; simile brings to bear on one object the light of another object that is naturally luminous, metaphor arouses curiosity, makes the eye more attentive, increases the sharpness of the glance."[1] Professor Ed. König in his article on the Style of Scripture in Hastings's *Dictionary of the Bible* (Extra vol., p. 162) says : " None of the above phenomena (viz. Zeugma, Chiasmus and certain peculiarities of Hebrew style), as they are psychologically explicable, diminish the perspicuity of the style of Scripture, and there are a number of devices whereby its clearness is *increased*. The first place amongst these is held by the Simile." But the superior clearness of simile can only be maintained in the most general way. It does not follow that any and every simile is clear, clearer than any and every metaphor. There are metaphors which everybody understands, whether because they are so familiar or because the tacit comparison they imply is obvious to all. On the other hand a simile may be quite obscure. It is enough that the object or idea which it is meant to light up be very imperfectly known or not directly perceptible. No simile will fully explain the nature of colour to a blind man. And all the beautiful similes in Shelley's *The Skylark* will convey but the vaguest impression of the bird's singing to one who has never heard it.

Nevertheless what has been said above regarding the usefulness of imagery for the elucidation and exposition of the abstract and abstruse applies with special force to simile, precisely because of its quality of superior clearness. Writers dealing with recondite or with spiritual subjects have ever felt this, especially when their purpose was not merely to record their views or to communicate them to a select circle of

[1] " Nature et but des paraboles évangeliques," an article by Père Ferdinand Prat, S.J., in *Études*, t. 35, p. 199, 1913.

SIMILE

kindred spirits, but to reach the ordinary mind. The
early Christian writers valued, as they well might,
such an instrument of exposition. In forty-six sermons
of St. Basil some 582 similes have been counted and
in St. Augustine's *Sermones ad populum* some 858.
Both writers, it is true, had been trained in the schools
of rhetoric : Augustine was even a professor of
rhetoric. But these were men too earnest and sincere
to sprinkle their writings with the mere ornaments
of the professional sophist. Simile was for them a
means of reaching men's souls as it had been for their
Master.

Writers of the didactic order naturally seize upon
simile for its expository qualities. Pope, whom we
may take as a typical didactic poet, used it with point
and brilliance. These few examples may serve as
illustration :—

> Man like the generous vine supported lives :
> The strength he gains is from the embrace he gives.
> 'Tis education forms the common mind
> Just as the twig is bent the tree's inclined.
>
>   *   *   *
>
> And hence one master passion in the breast,
> Like Aaron's serpent swallows up the rest.
>
>   *   *   *
>
> As fruits, ungrateful to the planter's care,
> On savage stocks inserted learn to bear,
> The surest virtues thus from passions shoot,
> Wild Nature's vigour working at the root.
>
>   *   *   *
>
> All forms that perish other forms supply,
> (By turns we catch the vital breath, and die)
> Like bubbles in the sea of matter borne,
> They rise, they break, and to that sea return.
>
>   *   *   *
>
> Self-love but serves the virtuous mind to wake,
> As the small pebble stirs the peaceful lake ;
> The centre moved, a circle straight succeeds,
> Another still and still another spreads ;
> Friend, parent, neighbour, first it will embrace ;
> His country next ; and next all human race.

This is a prosaic, rather than a poetic, use of simile, but it serves well the purpose of the didactic writer. All expository writing is to some extent didactic and quite naturally resorts to comparisons and similes.

III

It may, however, be said in general that simile is used as often as not because of qualities other than clearness and for purposes other than exposition or explanation. Like metaphor it is a product rather of the imagination than of the logical faculty. Like metaphor, too, it frequently does more than make an unimpassioned objective statement : it indicates a certain subjective attitude towards the object it is intended to illustrate. This attitude or frame of mind dictates the choice of the image and the image shosen places the object in an aspect that is humorous, catirical, disparaging, sublime by turns.[1] Thus Shakespeare makes us laugh at Falstaff walking before his page—

Like a sow that has overwhelmed all her litter but one.

And Dickens in the following simile sadly detracts from the dignity of Mr. Pickwick : " The unwonted lines which momentary passion had ruled in Mr. Pickwick's clear and open brow gradually melted away, as his young friend spoke, like the marks of a black lead pencil beneath the softening influence of India rubber." Ruskin is intentionally disparaging in the remark : " We have got into the way, among other modern wretchednesses, of trying to make windows of leaf diapers, and of strips of twisted red and yellow bands, looking like the patterns of current jelly on the top of Christmas cakes." And a like frame

[1] This may be termed the *associative* use of simile, its function being to suggest the hidden character of the object described, by associating with it some other object having the connotation we desire to convey.

of mind is evident in the following similes from
A. C. Benson : " There is a club I sometimes visit
where he sits like a moulting condor in a corner " . . .
" with a big head of a uniform dull tint, as if it were
carved out of a not very successfully boiled chicken."
" I love to hear other people's views and to contrast
my own with them. I do not wish to lie, like a merchant
vessel near a pirate ship, and to be fired into at intervals
until I surrender. Neither do I wish to do all the
firing myself." Or take Moore's answer to the
question, " Why is Lord Castlereagh like a pump ? "

> Because it is a slender thing of wood
> That up and down its awkward arm doth sway
> And coolly spout and spout and spout away
> In one weak, washy, everlasting flood.

Milton, on the other hand, lends, in the following
passage, a certain sublimity to Satan, the real hero
of *Paradise Lost* :—

> On the other side Satan, alarmed,
> Collecting all his might, dilated stood
> *Like Teneriffe or Atlas,* unremoved :
> His stature reached the sky, and on his crest
> Sat Horror plumed."

Elsewhere Satan is like a tower, his shield like the
moon, his spear like the tallest Norway pine. Menaced
by Death, the Fiend

> . . . like a comet burned
> That fires the length of Ophiucus huge
> In the Arctic sky, and from his horrid hair
> Shakes pestilence and war.

By contrast Milton compares the defeated rebel
hosts to a flock of goats driven headlong, just as Homer
had compared the Trojans shouting in battle to the
noise of cranes or to the bleating of a flock of sheep.

But, as simile is a form of imagery, its main function
is pictorial. It calls up before the mind's eye a
picture which may or may not make clearer the object

which it is intended to illustrate, but at all events makes its own impression on the imagination. Often it has an attractiveness and beauty of its own. Take this from Browning :—

> Over the waters in the vaporous west
> The sun goes down as in a sphere of gold.
> Behind the outstretched city, which between,
> With all that length of domes and minarets,
> Athwart the splendour black and crooked runs
> *Like a Turk verse along a scimitar.*

Compare the following from Coppée :—

> Dans ce beau pays blanc le Danube s'étale,
> Couleur d'acier, et coupe en deux la région
> *Comme un sabre jeté sur la peau d'un lion.*

And this from Shelley :—

> Deep her eyes as are
> Two openings of unfathomable night
> Seen through a tempest's cloven roof.

The suite of similes in Wordsworth's *To a Daisy* is decorative rather than descriptive.

Such imagery beautifies and ennobles speech, as Johnson rightly says simile ought to do. An ill-chosen image, on the other hand, may lower its tone. A classic example is this from Butler's *Hudibras* :—

> Like a lobster boiled the morn
> From black to red began to turn.

Prose, too, without gaining clearness, may gain picturesqueness and interest from such similes as the following from a recent work,[1] " The history of philosophy is like a procession of evening clouds, many-hued and impermanent."

" Never had there been such a time (the age of Spanish and Portuguese discoveries) in Europe. High romance on canvas wings skimmed the ocean as swallows skim a pond."

[1] *Ignatius Loyola.* By Henry Dwight Sedgwick, 1924.

SIMILE

" Words," writes Mr. L. Pearsall Smith, " are like sea-shells, they have their voices and are full of old echoes."

Or again, " Newman's mind was like a mezzotint in its delicate half tones ; Manning's like a woodcut in its sharp outlines."[1] Joseph Conrad was a master of the descriptive simile. Indeed, his use of it in his earlier novels was excessive—some sixty may be counted in the first six chapters of one of them. He grew more discriminating with time.

I cannot at all agree with M. Svartengren[2] that " modern descriptive prose such as we have it in newspapers and in technical and scientific works has altogether discarded this figure of speech ". True, prose that is strictly technical equally eschews all figures of speech. But prose is seldom strictly technical for long. It is bound to relapse into human-ness, and in doing so to take up again so indispensably human an instrument of expression as is comparison and simile. Writers, for instance, on the science of mind are bound to use simile and even metaphor. Writers, such as Max Müller and Arsène Darmesteter, on the science of language, have likewise frequent recourse to metaphor and simile. How much more journalists and popular writers in general. When, however, the author adds, " but if we go to the imaginative language whether it be highly literary and poetical, or colloquial, we are certain to meet with simile again," it is easy to give one's assent. The mind needs often to think in pictures and in pictures express its thoughts.

It has been contended,[3] not without reason, that, as picture-language, simile has a certain advantage over metaphor. For, as the imported image is kept

---

[1] *Roman Converts.* By Arnold Lunn, 1925.
[2] Op. cit., p. 462.
[3] Moulton, *The Modern Study of Literature*, p. 403.

quite distinct from the idea to be illustrated, it may more easily be worked into a complete and detailed picture. Herein, incidentally, lies the superiority of parable (which is but developed simile) over allegory which is developed metaphor. The former can easily be worked into a coherent and intrinsically probable story, the latter only with difficulty. These elaborate pictures are suited to the stately march of epic poetry. They abound in Homer, Virgil, Dante, Milton. Shakespeare has them occasionally,[1] we find them in Matthew Arnold's *Sohrab and Rustum*, and in Tennyson's *Idylls of the King*. And often the picture seems so to have captivated the poet's imagination as to make him half forget that it is, after all, but an illustration of the idea which he is striving to express.

There are passages in literature in which the similes follow one another like threaded pearls, as in Shelley's *The Skylark* or in the following :—

> Men, in whose words, to be read with many a heaving
> Of the heart, is a power like wind and rain ;
> Whose thoughts, like bars of sunshine in shut rooms,
> 'Mid gloom all glory, win the world to light,
> Who make their very follies like their souls,
> And like the young moon with a ragged edge,
> Still in their imperfection, beautiful ;
> Whose weaknesses are lovely as their strengths,
> Like the white nebulous matter between stars,
> Which, if not light, at least is likest light ;
> Men whose great thoughts possess us like a passion
> Through every limb, and the whole heart ; whose words
> Haunt us as eagles haunt the mountain air ;
> Whose names are ever on the world's great tongue
> Like sound upon the falling of a force ;
> Whose words, if winged, are with angel's wings,
> Who play upon the heart as on a harp,
> And make our eyes bright as we speak of them.[2]

---

[1] There is, for instance, the simile about the bees in the beginning of *Henry V.*

[2] A fine example is the passage in *Troilus and Cressida*, iii, 3, 144.

SIMILE

IV

Besides its literary and artistic functions simile has other uses. The average man sprinkles his talk with comparisons, because the readiest way of bringing out his ideas is to liken them to something else more familiar to his hearer. Many people acquire a habit of punctuating their talk with the word " like " in the form of an expletive, or of adding it as a sort of tag to all sorts of expressions. Scores of similes have become the current coin of speech. Originally accepted by the public as *ben trovato* they have long lost their savour and grown hackneyed. Yet they continue in use. Among the eighteenth century poems of John Gay there is to be found an amusing copy of verses which he has entitled ironically *A Song of New Similes*. Here are some of the stanzas :—

My passion is as mustard strong
  I sit all sober sad,
Drunk as a piper all day long
  Or like a March hare mad.

Round as a hoop the bumpers flow
  I drink, yet can't forget her,
For though as drunk as David's sow,
  I love her still the better.

Pert as a pear-monger I'd be
  If Molly were but kind ;
Cool as a cucumber could see
  The rest of womankind.

Like a stuck pig I gaping stare,
  And eye her o'er and o'er.
Lean as a rake with sighs and care
  Sleek as a mouse before,

Plump as a partridge was I known
  And soft as silk my skin.
My cheeks as fat as butter grown
  But as a groat now thin.

THEORY

I melancholy as a cat
    Am kept awake to weep;
But she insensible of that
    Sound as a top can sleep.

Hard is her heart as flint or stone
    She laughs to see me pale;
And merry as a grig is grown.
    As brisk as bottled ale.

And so it goes on—busy as a bee, sound as a bell, brown as a berry, sharp as a needle, etc., etc.—most of them still as commonly used as ever.

It is curious to note the persistence of these popular comparisons, and, more curious still, the persistence of many of them in spite of the fact that everybody has forgotten what they really mean. How many of those who use such comparisons can tell the point of " mad as a March hare ", or " mad as a hatter " (perhaps Alice might inform us !), " as proud as Punch ", " as deaf as a post ", " dead as a door nail ", " sleeping as sound as a top ", to say nothing of " as deep as Garrick (or Garry or Garlick) ", " as cunning as Crowder (or as a crowder) " ?

One likes to garnish one's talk with a flavour of proverbial wisdom, and in all languages proverbs are wont to take the form of simile. We may readily see this if we open that collection of apophthegms in the Bible known as the Book of Proverbs :—

Well-ordered words are as a honeycomb; sweet to the soul and health to the bones.
He that trusteth to lies feedeth the winds.
The tongue of the just is as choice silver,
As vinegar to the teeth and smoke to the eyes so is the sluggard to them that sent him.
A golden ring in a swine's snout, a woman fair and foolish.

And we may find the like turns of thought and phrase in the proverbs of all countries but above all among Celtic peoples.

SIMILE

Quite commonly the use of popular similes lends an element of humour to conversation. There are people, like the immortal Sam Weller, who have a gift for unexpected or grotesque comparisons. But even the man in the street will refer to a restless person as "like a hen on a hot griddle" or to an irritable one as "like a bear with a sore leg [or lug]" or "as cross as a bag of cats". An awkward person is "like a bull in a china shop", an industrious one is "as busy as a bee". A person in stupid amazement is described as "like a stuck pig". Going somewhat further afield one hears occasionally droll comparisons such as "much cry for little wool like shearing a pig", "to stare like a choked throstle [thrush]", "as hungry as a June crow", "as lonely as a milestone", "as dark as a boot", to look like a bit of chewed twine or like a wet rag or like a drowned rat. Somebody with dishevelled hair is like a bewitched barley stack and another dressed up smartly is as fine as a new-scraped carrot. And so on endlessly.

It will be noticed that alliteration plays a noteworthy part in the choice of popular comparisons—dry as dust, bold as brass, smooth as satin, dull as ditchwater, busy as a bee, plain as a pikestaff, hungry as a hawk, fit as a fiddle, and so on.[1]

By way of résumé we may say that simile has a three-fold function which we may name, roughly, intellectual emotional, and aesthetic.[2] In description, narrative, and exposition, its natural rôle is to aid understanding by imparting clearness, simplicity, and, if possible, impressiveness also, to discourse. Here literal comparison is commonly just as effective as simile. Under

---

[1] In *Lean's Collectanea*, vol. ii, pt. ii, pp. 899–939, will be found an extended list of such alliterative expressions.

[2] Professor Grenville Kleiser classifies the uses of simile under four heads : (1) Purely descriptive ; (2) Associative ; (3) Ornamental only ; (4) To give an effect of proverbial wisdom. *Similes and their Use*, Funk & Wagnells, New York, 1925.

this heading may be ranged the colloquial comparisons and similes just referred to. However trite they may have grown with time they once contributed at least impressiveness by arresting attention and stamping themselves on memory. In poetry and oratory, on the other hand, the appeal of simile is mainly to the feelings. Used in this way it heightens or intensifies the emotional effect, raising the tone of a passage towards the sublime, or imparting pathos, or giving it a humorous turn. Thirdly there is, as in metaphor, the aesthetic appeal. Its source is our delight in a picture, a picture which may neither make the thought clearer nor stir emotion, but is loved for itself. But often there is derivable from simile a different and a subtler pleasure, that of the perception of likeness between objects that differ widely, that may even seem at first glance to have nothing in common. Such a discovery gives a shock of agreeable surprise.

CHAPTER VII

MINOR FORMS OF IMAGERY

§ I :   PERSONIFICATION

IT is a strange though familiar phenomenon of human nature that our inward life tends to project itself upon our surroundings, thence to be reflected back as though it came from without. Our sorrows sadden the landscape and this sadness intensifies our own. Joy makes sunshine within and straightway the world without is bathed with light. " Love," says Shakespeare, " adds a precious seeing to the eye,"[1] makes it see the world in a new light, as though the world itself were transfigured. We paint nature in the hues of our emotions so that the outer world seems to change in sympathy with our changing moods. " Nature," says Emerson, " always wears the colours of the spirit." In Milton's words we

> Work our flattered fancy to belief
> That Heaven and Earth are coloured with our woe.

A man may of course grow callous to such impressions or he may free himself from them by deliberate effort. But the tendency of human nature is ever to project the subjective (mind and emotion) upon the objective[2] until the two can scarcely be disentangled. For the " idealist " philosopher the explanation is simple. The outer world is a creation of our own consciousness ; it has no other existence. Coleridge

[1] *Love's Labour Lost.*
[2] I crave pardon for employing terms which Ruskin described with characteristic vehemence as " two of the most objectionable words that were ever coined by the troublesomeness of Metaphysicians."

133

seems to give poetic expression to this theory in the lines :

> O Lady we receive but what we give
> And in our life alone doth nature live,
> Ours is her wedding garment, ours her shroud,
>   And would we aught behold of higher worth
> Than that inanimate cold world allowed,
> To the poor loveless ever-anxious crowd,
>   Ah, from the soul itself must issue forth
> A light, a glory, a fair luminous cloud
>   Enveloping the earth,
> And from the soul itself must there be sent
>   A sweet and potent voice of its own birth
> Of all sweet sounds the life and element.

We need not pause to refute the theory. Enough that the poet's lines express a truth of observation which needs no such theory to account for it. All of us, no doubt, in moments of unwonted emotion, have passed through such experiences as we find recorded by the poets. Our moods alter the world for us.

> Thy braes were bonny, Yarrow Stream,
>   When first on them I met my lover :
> Thy braes how dreary, Yarrow Stream,
>   When now thy waves his body cover.

Tennyson, especially in *In Memoriam* and *Maud*, dwells often on this theme :—

> With weary steps I wander on
>   Tho' always under altered skies
>   The purple from the distance dies,
> My prospect and horizon gone.
> No joy the flowing season gives
>   The herald melodies of Spring . . .

Again—

> A happy lover who has come
>   To look on her that loves him well
>   Who 'lights and rings the gateway bell
> And learns her gone and far from house,
> He saddens all the magic light
>   Dies off at once from bower and hall
>   And all the place is dark and all
> The chambers emptied of delight.

PERSONIFICATION

Very similar in its significance is the passage in the *Confessions of St. Augustine*[1] in which he describes his feelings on the death of one of his friends :—

> With this affliction my whole heart was darkened, and whatsover I beheld had the face of death. My country became a punishment to me ; my father's house was extreme misery, and all that which I was wont to share with him was converted into a vast kind of torment, now that I was without him. In every place mine eyes would look for him but found him not, and I hated all things because they told me no news of him . . .

The mind, when a prey to certain emotions, if denied consolation and sympathy from human beings, will seek it even from inanimate things and fancy that these things respond. Thus Tasso :—

> Ho visto al pianto mio
> Responder per pietate i sassi e l'onde,
> E sospirar le fronde.

So Moschus, lamenting the death of Bion, had fancied the birds, the fountains, the trees lamenting with him.

"It is," writes the Rev. Basil Maturin, "a strange thing when we come to analyse it, that so much light and shade, so many lines and curves, so much inanimate matter, should be able in such an extraordinary way to reflect the mind of man, that we even transfer to it our own moral ides and struggles. Who has not felt that not only can the skies and the earth and the winds rejoice with us in our joys and sorrow with our sorrows, but that they echo our stormy passions, and reflect our wrath and rebellion and cruelty, and melt with us into tears of penitence and sing with us our *Te Deums* ?"[2]

Not only do we colour nature in accord with our emotions. We are prone to carry the illusion further, and to suppose in inanimate objects the presence of

[1] Book iv, chap. 4, § 3.
[2] B. H. Maturin, *Self Knowledge and Self Discipline*, p. 54.

human traits and feelings, nay, even intelligence and will. This is personification.[1] It has many degrees and even kinds, all of them owing their origin to certain characteristics of human nature, and all of them, no doubt, as old as humanity itself. We may perhaps distinguish two main types—the naturalistic animistic type which reached its highest expression in Greek mythology and poetry, and the abstract qualitative type which was characteristic of the Roman people. We may first consider the latter, but briefly, for it has but an indirect relation to our present subject.

The Roman spirit valued above all things those moral qualities and civic virtues which it conceived of as useful to the State. But it was as hard for the Roman as it is for the average modern mind to grasp, still more to worship, pure abstractions. It was natural then to clothe them in the tangible form of human personality, and thereby give to them a touch of warmth and life. Thus, *Sapientia* and *Scientia* and *Pax* and *Prudentia* and the rest figure in Latin poetry.

> Pudor et Iustitiae Soror
> Incorrupta Fides nudaque Veritas.

We meet likewise with personifications of Time and Nature and Death and the like :—

> Pallida mors
> Aequo pulsat pede pauperum tabernas
> Regumque turres . . .

Still better known is the description of Fama in the fourth book of the *Aeneid*.

This personification of abstractions runs through literature. It was peculiarly characteristic of the " Augustan " school in England.[2] Pope and Johnson

[1] Often termed *Prosopopœa*.

[2] " Poverty of significance and of poetic emotion is the characteristic of mere capital-letter personification, and this precisely is what distinguishes the manner of the English ' classical ' period from that of the Elizabethan period." F. I. Carpenter, *Metaphor and Simile in the Minor Elizabethan Drama*, p. 192.

and Gray and James Thomson sprinkle their verse with capitalized abstractions, together with all the worn-out paraphernalia of a dead paganism. Byron often echoes them, for Pope was his model in poetry.

> Smiles on past Misfortune's brow
> Soft Reflection's hand can trace . . .

writes Gray, and again

> Bright Rapture calls and soaring as she sings,
> Waves in the eye of Heav'n her many-colour'd wings.

But very different poets—Shakespeare and Milton, Shelley and Tennyson—achieve noble effects with personified emotions of man and powers of nature. One might instance from Shakespeare the apostrophe to Sleep in the beginning of the Third Act of *King Henry IV*, Part II, and the description of Slander in *Cymbeline* (Act iii, Scene 4). But many others might be cited.[1] In *L'Allegro* and *Il Penseroso* we meet with sublime though shadowy beings—Melancholy, Darkness, Care, Liberty, Night, Morn, Sleep. *Adonais* abounds with ethereal creations of the poet's thought :

> Desires and Adorations,
> Wingéd Persuasions and veiled Destinies,
> Splendours and Glooms and glimmering Incarnations
> Of hopes and fears, and twilight Fantasies . . .

In *In Memoriam* we meet with Love and Death, Chance and Time and Sorrow. Wordsworth's *Ode to Duty* is a piece of sustained personification of this kind.

Finally, here is an interesting example in modern prose [2] :—

> Never was there a more beautiful subject, and none therefore exposed to a greater variety of disasters. They come flocking

---

[1] Numerous examples from the Elizabethans will be found in Wells, *Poetic Imagery*, p. 162 sq.
[2] The *Times Literary Supplement*, 23rd December, 1920.

to mind even as Mr. Beerbohm takes his way smiling through their midst. Reason tempts him to follow her austere maze. The spirit of English prose begs him to turn his sentences smoother and smoother still. Vanity hints that the first person singular would sound nicely here. Sarcasm proffers her sword. Sentiment has her basket of rose-leaves. Common sense pleads that she can cover a bald patch as well as another. Convention and good manners smile and show false teeth. All these temptations are offered.

Sculptors and painters have striven to give visible form to these abstractions, but their efforts have resulted only in the creation of symbolic figures, not pictorial images of the things they represent. They belong to imagery only as symbolism does, not as metaphor. The poets cannot thereby give us even a picture. To attribute sex and personal attributes to Love and Joy and Melancholy and Duty is not to give any fresh foothold to the imagination. These abstractions remain abstractions, though it please us to fancy them as persons. It is otherwise with the second type of personification.[1]

The primitive Greek and, no doubt, all of primitive mankind that was without knowledge of the one God, felt vaguely in the world around him the presence of Mind : he dimly perceived in nature an order, a harmony, a beauty which seemed to witness to a Presence, a Soul akin to the soul of man. In days to come Greek philosophy would give to this harmonizing, rational Soul of the universe, the name of Logos. But early man was not a philosopher, he could not grasp the cosmos as an ordered whole. It was natural then that he should people nature—sky and sea and

[1] It is worthy of note that mythology is not a personification of abstractions. " It is often said," writes G. K. Chesterton, " that pagan mythology was a personification of the powers of nature. The phrase is true in a sense, but it is very unsatisfactory ; because it implies that the forces are abstractions and the personification artificial. Myths are not allegories. Natural powers are not in this case abstractions. It is not as if there were a god of gravitation." *The Everlasting Man*, p. 115.

stream and hill and plain, with a multitude of beings, human, semi-human, superhuman, spirits and genii, nymphs and naiads, satyrs and river-gods. Accordingly, primitive divinities are powers of nature endowed with human features and human passions, Wodin and Thor, Manannan and Lugh, no less than Zeus and Vulcan and Pan. In these deities man worshipped, as we have said, the order, harmony, beauty of the universe. He likewise bowed himself in awe before manifestations of force and energy which he could not master or control, and which he ascribed to the workings of unseen powers.

There is another characteristic of human nature which has ever led men to see personality in outward things. It is this, that man's first interest is man himself. What concerns himself, his existence, his well-being, his fate, surpasses for him in interest and significance all other things—till a Power that is above him lifts him above himself. And so he is quick to discern in external nature all that bears any semblance of the human form, all that bears any analogy to human moods,[1] all that harmonizes with the workings of the mind of man.[2] So eager is he to recognize a kinship in nature that his fancy will seize upon fleeting resemblances that have in the reality of things but the slenderest foundation. Trees have feet and body and arms, cowslips " hang the pensive head ".

In particular it is difficult to resist the conviction— and we who believe in God need not resist it—that nature's movements and manifestations of power have behind them will and purpose. It was natural to personify the winds ; the Greeks and Romans did so : Longfellow has cast into poetic form in *Hiawatha*

[1] " La nature," says a writer in the *Revue des Deux Mondes*, " est un prodigieux miroir où la sensibilité humaine se réflète."

[2] Yet I cannot but think it somewhat of an overstatement to say with the same writer " Une description n'est belle que si le paysage qu'elle représente est pour ainsi dire imprégné d'âme ".

the primitive beliefs of American Indians [1] ; modern romantic writers like Dickens or Victor Hugo can scarcely speak of the winds without making personal beings of them. And the sea—men in every age have spoken of it as a personal being of awful might and at times of awful malignity. Byron's *Address to the Ocean* voices the inarticulate awe of man from the beginning, though Byron may have felt but little of it himself. And so of other great phenomena of nature—night and storm and the seasons, the rising and the setting sun.

This tendency remained long after the mythopœic force was spent and man had lost belief in the gods. It is found in full force among the Hebrew people, who abhorred the gods of heathendom. It still prevails in modern poetry. For it is deep-rooted in our human nature.

The truth is that without this projection of human personality upon nature, natural objects can have significance and interest only for one side of our complex being—the intellectual, that is the philosophic and scientific side, or else that of practical utility. But there is another side, the emotional—that of the heart. The heart, too, seeks communion with nature. When emotion possesses us we can scarce reconcile ourselves to think of nature as cold, lifeless, insensible, unresponsive, a mass of inert matter, moved by mere chemical and mechanical forces. If we would but think of nature as impregnated with the divine, the thought would transfigure for us, and reconcile to us, the world.

> Earth's crammed with Heaven
> And every common bush afire with God.

But even believers in God's Presence, not indeed in

[1] We recall in that poem the personifications not only of the winds and other natural phenomena but those of Famine, Disease, Death, and many others.

moments of calm reason, but under stress of some emotion, crave from nature some subtle sympathy with human joy and woe, and are pained by the sense of her indifference. Sympathy is the appanage of persons, so the imagination endows nature with personality. When swayed by emotion one revolts against the thought that nature is compact of dead matter and the interplay of blind force—that mountains are but heaps of rock and earth, the wind only a current of air passing at a given velocity from an area of high, to an area of low pressure, that the sea is but a mighty mass of water, and the great rivers but large-sized drains. We continue to be awed in the presence of a towering mountain peak, we persist in thinking of the winds as sighing in melancholy or howling with rage, of the changing restless moods of the sea, of the lazy or hurrying river, now caressing its banks, now chafing with furious impatience within their narrow bounds. To the poets of all time such thoughts are habitual. The poetry of the Bible, that of prophet and psalmist above all, abounds with them.

> The waters beheld Thee, O God,
>   The waters beheld Thee and feared,
>   The deeps were dismayed . . .
> Let the rivers clap hands,
>   Let the hills rejoice
> Before the face of the Lord when He cometh . . .
> Fair bloom the desert pastures
>   And the hills are clad with gladness . . .
> The mountains saw Thee and were grieved . . .
>   The deep put forth its voice
>   The deep lifted up its hands . . .
> And the moon shall blush
> And the sun shall be ashamed.
> When the Lord of hosts shall reign in Sion . . .
> Give praise, O ye heavens,
> And rejoice, O earth,
>   Ye mountains give praise with exultation
> Because the Lord hath comforted His people . . .

The mountains and the hills shall sing praise before Thee
And all the trees of the land shall clap their hands . . .

For instances of the modern use of personification
I must content myself with but a few examples.
The following is from Shelley :—

> Morning sought
> Her eastern watch-tower, and her hair unbound,
> Wet with the tears that should adorn the ground
> Dimmed the aerial eyes that kindle day ;
> Afar the melancholy thunder moaned,
> Pale Ocean in unquiet slumber lay,
> And the wild winds flew around sobbing in their dismay.

Adonais has many other such passages. Again, once
more from Shelley, but in a different vein :—

> For winter came : the wind was his whip ;
> One choppy finger was on his lip :
> He had torn the cataracts from the hills,
> And they clanked at his girdle like manacles.

Here is a passage from Francis Thompson's *The
Hound of Heaven* :—

> I was heavy with the even
> When she lit her glimmering tapers
> Round the day's dead sanctities.
> I laughed in the morning's eyes.

> I triumphed and I saddened with all weather
> Heaven and I wept together
> And its sweet tears were mixed with mortal mine ;
> Against the red throb of its sun-set heart
> I laid my own to beat.

Shelley's *The Cloud, Ode to the West Wind,* and *The
Sensitive Plant* are familiar instances of the sustained
personification of natural objects or phenomena.
Among many examples in Keats may be recalled
the song of Sorrow in *Endymion* and the *Ode on
Melancholy*. Tennyson's *Maud*, which is a study in
emotions, is naturally full of personification. Even in
Browning we find passages such as this :

PERSONIFICATION

Oh how dark your villa was,
  Windows fast and obdurate !
How the garden grudged me grass
  Where I stood—the iron gate
Ground its teeth to let me pass.

One example may be cited from a contemporary poet :

But even now
As he sped on, forth Hermes stretched his wand
Beneath his passage and Earth answered him
With swelling heart : through every vein she sent
The awaited summons and all her children stirred.
The patient field sighed in its slumber ; oak
Was deepened into bronze, and sapling ash
Blackened the points on every smooth, gray stem ;
The chestnut boughs their oozy wealth upturned ;
Downward the alder dropped its frilly tails
Whilst beech, light held in realms of sleep, out-swelled
Slenderness of its auburn treasure-sheath.
Each bush a subtle thickening knew : the woods
Veiled their austerity in misty bloom.[1]

We might expect, too, to meet with personifications in writers of imaginative and impassioned prose. And in point of fact it appears in many passages of such writers as Burke, De Quincey, Carlyle, and Dickens.[2] Carlyle uses the figure in a way peculiar to himself. His imagination conjures up vast and vague abstractions—Dilettantism, Patrollotism, Dryasdust, or else the Destinies, the Necessities, the dumb Veracities, the Eternal Voices, Fact,[3] and so forth, and speaks of them as living personages.

It would seem, then, that personification is in the highest degree poetic. It appears to be the natural outcome of that mood of emotional and imaginative exaltation which gives birth to poetry. Nature seen in the glow of admiration, wonder, gladness, sorrow

[1] *The Spirit of Happiness*, by Lord Gorell, Fisher Unwin, 1925.
[2] The English language has with regard to personification this great advantage that it confines the masculine and feminine *genders* to persons.
[3] So many synonyms for the commonplace phrase " circumstances beyond our control ".

143

becomes suffused with humanness—if the word may pass. Is this to see it falsely ? Ruskin would answer, Yes. The feelings, he thinks, render us momentarily irrational. " All violent feelings produce in us a falseness in all our impressions of external things which I would generally characterize as the Pathetic Fallacy." Instancing Coleridge's lines :

> The one red leaf, the last of its clan,
> That dances as often as dance it can,

he goes on :—

> Coleridge has a morbid, that is to say a so far false idea about the leaf ; he fancies a life in it, and will, which there are not ; confuses its powerlessness with choice, its fading death with merriment, and the wind that shakes it with music.

We are not concerned to defend the poetic quality of lines which modern critics have admired, and in which Ruskin himself acknowledges some beauty. Doubtless Coleridge himself would not have appraised them otherwise than as a quaint conceit, a flight of fancy. But what is to be said of Ruskin's general principle ? The real nature of personification is that it is a species of metaphor,[1] a species in which what we have called the imported image is always human personality. It may therefore be analysed just in the same way as metaphor. Like metaphor it is based on an implied analogy, and its truth or falsehood depends upon the correctness of the analogy. To take a simple example, if we speak of a " frowning " mountain, the analogy may be stated in the form of a proportion, thus :—

> A frown : person : : a dark, overhanging appearance : mountain.

Now, this may be true or false, or it may have a certain degree of verisimilitude. It certainly is not *necessarily* false. There are the well-known lines from Kingsley :

[1] Aristotle, *Rhetoric*, iii, 11 ; Abbot and Seeley, *English Lessons for English People* ; Keach, *Tropologia*, Book i, chap. ix.

PERSONIFICATION

They rowed her in across the rolling foam,
The cruel, crawling foam.

On this Ruskin remarks : " The foam is not cruel,
neither does it crawl." To which answer might be
made in scholastic form—*literally* no (but are we to
suppose that the poet meant it literally ?), *figuratively*
yes, foam may be cruel [1] and may even crawl. For,
if this criticism were to stand, all metaphor would
be essentially false. " Ye are the salt of the earth "—
false it would seem, for the Apostles were certainly
not composed of that substance.

Believing personification, as being a view of nature
distorted under the influence of emotion, to be
essentially morbid and false, Ruskin naturally believed
that " the greatest poets do not often admit this kind
of falseness ", and that " it is only the second order
of poets who much delight in it ". For him there are
but two orders of poets : the Creative (Shakespeare,
Homer, Dante) and the Reflective, or Perceptive
(Wordsworth, Tennyson, Keats). To the writer
all such classifications of poets—as of saints—has
always seemed profitless, not to say meaningless.[2]
But let that pass. It is certain that Shakespeare
abounds in personification as in all other forms of
imagery. A recent critic says of him that " he seems
always to have thought in persons rather than in
things ".[3]

Almost always he speaks of the sea as a
person :—

The rude sea's enraged and foamy mouth
As good to chide the waves as speak them fair.

---

[1] Compare Milton : " I asked the waves and asked the *felon* winds."
[2] Not meaning for a moment to suggest that there is no difference
between poets great and little, nor yet that saint does not differ from
saint " as star differeth from star in glory ".
[3] E. A. Greening Lamborn, *The Rudiments of Criticism*, 1921,
p. 94.

And so of the sun :—

> Yet herein will I imitate the sun,
> Who doth permit the base contagious clouds
> To smother up its beauty from the world
> That, when he please again to be himself,
> Being wanted, he may be more wondered at . . .

or again—

> See, see, King Richard doth himself appear
> As doth the blushing discontented sun,
> From out the fiery portal of the east,
> When he perceives the envious clouds are bent
> To dim his glory.

And so of Sleep and Night, and many other inanimate things or forces of nature.

The poets use personification because it is a natural impulse of primitive man and children, and the true poetic spirit is primitive and childlike [1] ; because it is an outcome of emotion, and poetry is the imaginative expression of emotion. Moreover, emotion seeks sympathy and responsiveness, and seems at times to find both in " mute insensate things " rather than in man. That is perhaps the real secret of the poet's delight in Nature.

> Thanks to the human heart by which we live
> Thanks to its tenderness, its joys and fears,
> To me the meanest flower that blows can give
> Thoughts that do often lie too deep for tears.

Again, personification is " one of the poetic agencies for adding background to the scene, deepening it by the sense of all-pervading spirit, as metaphor proper deepens it by vistas of far-distant material beauty ".[2] Finally, it increases for the mind and heart of us the significance of things to think of them

---

[1] No doubt poets have often used it, as Spenser and Tennyson did, for conscious artistic effect. Others again have used it in playful vein.

[2] *Metaphor in Poetry*, by J. G. Jennings, London, n.d.

146

as purposeful beings like ourselves, to think of the wind as boisterous, blustering, playful, or enraged, to think of the savage ferocity of the sea in storm, of a bright spring morning as cheerful, of

> The holy time as quiet as a nun
> Breathless with adoration.

It might be thought that in this personification of nature there is a deeper significance yet, that it is a manifestation of the soul's inborn longing for God. Possibly it may be. But it should be remembered that it is one thing to think of various separate objects as endowed with personality ; it is quite a different thing to see all nature pervaded by one great Presence and Personality, to see it as a manifestation of its Maker :—

> That light whose smile kindles the Universe,
> That Beauty in which all things work and move,
> That Benediction which the eclipsing curse
> Of birth can quench not, that sustaining Love
> Which, through the web of being blindly wove
> By man and beast and earth and air and sea,
> Burns bright or dim as each are mirrors of
> The fire for which all thirst.

NOTE TO CHAPTER VII (PART I)

" FUNDAMENTAL " METAPHOR

MAX MÜLLER in *The Science of Thought*,[1] a later work than his *Science of Language*, attempts a radical classification of metaphor, dividing all metaphor into " fundamental " and " grammatical ". Fundamental metaphor is " the transference of our acts and states to the objects of nature " (p. 327). He contends that " there is no way of conceiving or naming anything objective except after the similitude of

[1] p. 495 sqq. Cf. Noiré, *Logos*, p. 258.

the subjective or of ourselves ". This is a disputable proposition, but at the moment I am merely recording a view. What is certainly true is that from the beginning man has spoken of animals as acting like ourselves, rejoicing, grieving, willing, resisting, and so forth. He may or may not have been aware that he was using these terms analogically, not, as the Schoolmen say, univocally, i.e. with precisely the same meaning as when using them of man's acts and states. Similarly in the case of inanimate nature, though by no means to the extent that Professor Max Müller seems to imply. It was convenient to use for the changes of inanimate things terms primarily applying to the actions of men or animals. The clouds *fly*, the river *runs*, the wind *sighs* or *howls*, the mountains *stand*, plants *die*, the sun *se lève* or *se couche* (terms used of getting up and going to bed), and so forth. Such a use of language is not necessarily an exemplification of the principle laid down by the Abbé Raynal[1] : " Savages wherever they see motion which they cannot account for, there they suppose a soul." No doubt tribes whose religion is of the animistic or of the fetishistic type " do ", as Max Müller says, " really believe sun, moon, and stars, earth, sea, and air to have understanding and active [he means immanent or self-originated] power " or more commonly they believe that spirits, not necessarily identified with these objects, dwell in them.

But how difficult it is to generalize on this subject may be judged from the example of the classical languages. These, no doubt, though not primitive languages at the stage at which they are known to us, must surely be derived from primitive languages. Now in Greek and Latin, as every schoolboy who has done composition ought to know, inanimate objects

[1] Quoted by Reid, *Essays on the Active Powers*, iv, chap. iii. See Mill, *Logic*, iii, 5, 2.

are spoken of as animate much less commonly than in the modern languages of Western Europe. Attic Greek prose, for instance, was much more sparing in the use of metaphor of that kind, in other words personification in various degrees, than is modern English prose.[1] " A most important characteristic of the classical languages," writes the same authority, " is the comparative absence of Personification and such-like linguistic contrivances attributing action to abstractions. . . . To the Greek observer the person alone is the agent." This remark applies, with limitations, to the personification of concrete but inanimate objects.

However that may be, Professor Max Müller's conception of Fundamental Metaphor seems clearly to fall under the head of Personification. It might be called primitive and instinctive, as opposed to deliberate and artistic, Personification.

§ 2 :   METONYMY AND SYNECDOCHE

THE forms of imagery which we have been studying hitherto are based, as we have seen, on analogy. A familiar concrete object is used to illustrate an unfamiliar or an abstract idea. The latter is likened to the former or even identified with it in virtue of a similar or identical relation which exists between each of them severally and two other objects. Vice, for instance, bears, in certain respects, the same relation to the soul as weeds to a garden. So we substitute the term weeds for vices and proceed to speak of vices in terms of weeds. In other words, we substitute for a given idea some term taken from a different sphere of things, because this term has a more direct appeal for imagination and emotion.

---

[1] See *Theory of Advanced Greek Prose Composition*, John Donovan, S.J., M.A., vol. ii, p. 308 sq., Oxford, 1922.

Now this substitution may be of a kind different from those hitherto studied. Instead of calling in an image from a wholly different sphere of things—the more different the better, we may take a notion more or less closely linked[1] with the idea we wish to express, and put it in place of that idea.

Here once more the principle of the association of ideas comes into play. When once the mind, consciously or subconsciously, has established between two mental states some association, the emergence of one of them into consciousness tends to cause the emergence of the other.[2] This law of the mind tends to become a law of language which might be formulated thus :—" Whenever two ideas are connected in such a way that the one cannot be thought of without the other, the name of the first can, when necessity arises, be transferred to the other."[3] Thus, whether or no so close a connexion exists in the objective order of things, the two notions have become so closely connected in the mind that their terms are practically interchangeable. I can say " the sword " for warfare because the sword is fixed in men's minds as the typical instrument of the fighter. Consequently, when I say " The pen is mightier than the sword " everybody understands that I am not comparing two material things, though a pen that would be a more formidable weapon than certain swords—toy swords, for instance—is at least conceivable. I am, of course, speaking of military power. And similarly in the phrase " to lay waste with fire and *sword* " I am describing devastation picturesquely by means of two typical means of destruction. In " I came not to bring peace but the *sword* " (Matt. x, 34) this last word stands for strife in general. Again, when

[1] Hence these have been called " Figures of Contiguity " as opposed to " Figures of Similarity ".
[2] See *Nature of Metaphor*, chap. ii.
[3] Geo. Wallis, *The Philosophy of Speech*, 1919, p. 55.

one says, " This quarrel can be decided only by *the sword*," one is not to be taken as excluding rifles and machine-guns but simply peaceful means. And when we wish to refer to actual swords we may again have recourse to a figure and speak of " a foeman worthy of one's *steel* ", or of one who—

> drew *his Toledo* and swore
> By the sword of a soldier to succour Portmore.

In the course of their passage from generation to generation words gather round them many associations. Some of these fade gradually away, others cling ever closer, and little by little colour the word with their own hue. Often the first meaning of the word drops out of remembrance and one of these associated meanings permanently takes its place. The history of the meanings of words[1] is full of the most curious substitutions. Here is one. The French word for the liver, *le foie*, is from the Latin word *ficatum* meaning " figged " or " stuffed with figs ". Why ? Because Roman gourmets were fond of *jecur ficatum*, liver stuffed with figs. *Ficatum* came to be the short for that delicacy, and finally came to mean not liver stuffed with figs but liver *tout court*. " Worry " and " anguish " are both from words originally meaning to choke or strangle. Much of the original meaning of the former survives in such an expression as " the dog is worrying the rat ", while the latter is traceable to the Latin *augustus*, narrow. The words denoting our modern " book " and " Bible " have very humble origins. The original of the German *buch* and English *book* meant simply a beech-tree and gradually came to be applied to its most important product. The original of the Latin *liber*, from which the French, Italian, Spanish, and Gaelic names are derived, meant

---

[1] This is the object of the science of semantics as distinguished from Philology which studies the *form* or words.

similarly the bark of a tree. The Greek *biblion*, from which comes Bible, was once the inner bark of the papyrus plant. " Code " comes from an old word (caudex) that meant a tree-trunk. What a multitude of associations have gathered round these words from the days of their remote origins ! [1]

If we wished to represent any given word by a general formula, we might take s for the sound element, d for the dominating element in the meaning, c for elements of meaning constantly associated as being parts of the object named by d or invariable accompaniments of it, and v for variable associated elements. Then the whole word would be represented by

$$s\ d\ (c.\ v.)$$

One of the elements represented by the symbols within brackets may, as we have seen, tend to take the place of d, as being more significant or more easy to grasp with the imagination, or in virtue of invariable association with d in current speech. [2] If the relations between the two notions thus interchanged be external, we have the figure *Metonymy*, if internal we have *Synecdoche*. The relations of these two figures to one another and to metaphor may be roughly illustrated by diagrams. Let the circle A represent the main idea that would be plainly expressed if no figure were used. Then b will stand for the notion that is brought in (imported) to take its place when a figure is employed.

[1] Many other examples will be found in Darmesteter, *La Vie des Mots* ; George H. McKnight, *English Words and their Background*, New York, 1923 ; Michel Bréal, *Essai de Sémantique*.
[2] McKnight, op. cit., p. 222.

METONYMY AND SYNECDOCHE

In Metaphor (Fig. 1) two circles intersect,[1] *A* and *b* appearing to the mind as identical in a certain respect. In Synecdoche (Fig. 2) a segment (*b*) of the main idea (*A*) is emphasized and in speech takes the place of *A*. Thus, " A fleet of twenty *sail* (i.e. ships) loomed up in the offing." In Metonymy the imported notion (*b*), though it may have various connexions with *A*, is not a part of it. " From the *cradle* to the *grave* (i.e. from birth to death). Let it be understood that these distinctions are approximate and that there is no rigidly definite line of demarcation between the three figures.

In the case of Metonymy and Synecdoche the two notions (*A* and *b*) may be linked in various ways, thus giving rise to varieties of each. Let us essay a classification of these varieties.[2]

METONYMY

Between two objects of thought there may exist, among other relations, those of :—

(1) *Cause and Effect,* and the cause in question may belong to any one of the various species of causality—efficient, instrumental, material, formal, final, exemplary. The first species of metonymy substitutes effect for cause or cause for effect. Examples :—You write a neat *hand*. Robed in the long *night* of her deep hair. Surrey to Wolsey, " Thou scarlet *sin*." (*Henry VIII*, Act iii, Sc. 2.)

We speak of reading *Cicero* when we mean his works, of *grey hairs* when we mean old age, we call a candle or a match a *light*.

" The *bright death* quivered at the victim's throat."
" O for a beaker full of the *warm South*."
" All *Arabia* breathes from yonder box."

---

[1] But the two are not, properly speaking, in the same plane.
[2] For various classifications see Keach, *Tropologia* ; Szekely, *Hermeneutica Biblica* ; Bain, *Rhetoric and Composition*.

THEORY

" He consulted *Baedeker*," meaning not the long-deceased person of that name, but one of his famous guide-books, and similarly, " Look up your Bradshaw." " They have Moses and the Prophets." Things are often described as possessing qualities of which they are the cause, or merely the accompaniment[1]—*pallida* mors, a *restless* pillow, *gaunt* famine, *slothful* couch, a *giddy* height—

" *drowsy* tinklings lull the distant folds."

" The *merry* bells ring round."

" Casting a dim *religious* light."

" Afar the *melancholy* thunder moaned."

Unless you mean my griefs and killing fears
Should stretch me out at your relentless feet.

Then there is the instrumental cause—

" Give every man thine *ear* but few thy *voice*."

Strange advice, surely, if it were literal and not figurative statement.

" C'est une de nos meilleures *plumes*," meaning writers.

" A smooth *tongue* wins favour."

" The *keys* of the kingdom of heaven,"

i.e. the power to open the gates, as one having authority—a metonymy added to a metaphor.

" There is *death* in the pot."

" Light has spread," wrote Kossuth, " and even *bayonets* think."

(2) *Container and Contents.*—" The whole *city* was in an uproar," we say, instead of " all the citizens or inhabitants ", for the notion of city is simple for the imagination to grasp. Again, " Can you drink the *Chalice* that I will drink ? "

---

[1] Macbeth, op. cit., chap. x, describes under the name " Trope " fourteen varieties of this figure of transferred adjective.

Here again there is a metaphor ("drink the chalice" meaning undergo the fate) combined with a metonymy (cup for what is contained in it). The power of the *purse*; he kept an excellent *cellar* and an elegant *wardrobe*; setting the *table* in a roar; the pick of the *basket*; from the *cradle* to the *grave*[1]; he was fond of the *bottle*; "amazement seized the rebel *thrones*." Such expressions become sheer nonsense the moment they are taken literally. Similarly, a defeat is spoken of as a fatal *field*. We speak of the *gallery*, the *pit*, the *boxes*, and the *stalls* for their occupants, and, carrying the figure further, seek to hit off the characteristics of certain sections of an audience by reference to the places they occupy. "Playing to the gallery" has come to connote cadging for popularity by cultivating the prejudices of some not very enlightened section of a given community.

Under this heading comes the use of a noun denoting the place for a noun denoting its inhabitants.

> For East is East and West is West
> And never the twain shall meet.

For once Downing Street has outwitted the Quai d'Orsay. In the Crusades Europe precipitated itself upon Asia. Roma locuta est, causa finita est. "Woe to thee Corozain, woe to thee Bethsaida: for if in Tyre and Sidon had been wrought the miracles that have been wrought in you, *they* had long ago done penance in sackcloth and ashes. But it shall be more tolerable for Tyre and Sidon in the day of judgment than for you."—Matt. xi, 21. Cf. with the favour of *Heaven*. "I have sinned against *Heaven* and before thee" (Luke xv, 18).

An article in *The Irish Ecclesiastical Record*, August,

---

[1] Mr. Shane Leslie varies this familiar expression thus: "Well had the voters voted, exhausting the poll of names from the cradle to the crutch, as the saying went," and again, "From the font to the funeral every vote was watched" (*Doomsland*).

1925, may be quoted in illustration of this form of metonymy. In studying the "semantic evolution" of the word λόγια the writer remarks that in general the written word may be regarded as the *containing* element, the mental or spoken word as the *contained*. By metonymy the mind is apt to see the same object in both forms, and, in speech as in thought to identify one with the other. He goes on to argue that the Logia of the Lord by a simple figure of speech came to mean God's word, the Scriptures simply. Then in course of time it came to mean discourses of the Lord as recorded in the Gospel, in other words Our Lord's Gospel teaching. This conclusion, if justified, is of importance to students of the Synoptic Question.

(3) *The Possessor and the Thing Possessed.*—Thus for simplicity's sake, no doubt, we speak of this general and that marching and counter-marching, winning victories and suffering defeats, when in reality we mean the armies or the divisions commanded by them. This is much less common in the reports of present-day warfare. In a somewhat different way we speak of rewarding *merit* and punishing *crime*.

(4) *An Office or Occupation and its Sign, Symbol, or Significant Accompaniment.*—It matters little that these latter are comparatively unimportant, sometimes merely imaginary, accompaniments of the offices in question. Usage has endowed them with definite associations. Moreover they are definite material objects and easily grasped by the imagination. Thus for the abstract royalty, kingship, we often write *crown* or *sceptre* or *throne*. "The loyal supporters of the *throne*," "*Le trône et l'autel*," "The *Cloister* and the *Hearth*." *Pro aris et focis*. In reference to the legal profession we speak of the *bench*, the *bar*, taking *silk*. In reference to the clergy *lawn sleeves*, the *mitre*. So the *press* for journalism, the *knife* for surgery.

" Caubeen and frieze trudged to Mass, Caroline hats and cheap tweeds to church " (Shane Leslie, *Doomsland*).

He has a practised gift for the oratory of the *platform*, with, perhaps, a suspicion of the *tub* (*Times Literary Supplement*, 9th April, 1925).

His banner led the *spears* no more amid the hills of Spain.

> Sceptre and crown must tumble down
> And in the dust be equal made
> With the poor crooked scythe and spade.

Under this heading come a vast number of current expressions—the *faggot*, the *block*, the *stake* for execution or for persecution, to bring under the *hammer*, to *toe the line*, *do manus vinctas*, on the *wrong scent*, to *take the plunge*, the *mailed fist* for the threat of force. Similarly such symbolical or otherwise significant actions as, " I *wash my hands* of it," to put one to the *blush*, *knitted brows*, *tongue in the cheek*, *turned up nose*, etc., etc.

In Holy Scripture there are many such passing references to symbolic actions, some of them no longer familiar—to bow the knee, to lift up the hand (swear), to kick up the dust of his feet, to give the hand (confederacy), to lay the hand upon the mouth (silence or inability to answer), to lift up the head (joy and hopefulness).

Perhaps we might refer to this figure the saying of Christ just before Gethsemane :—" But now he that hath a purse let him take it and likewise a scrip ; and he that hath not let him sell his coat and buy a sword " (Luke xxii, 36).

A striking example of the figure is to be found in the third book of Kings, xii, 10–14 (A.V. and R.V. 1 Kings).

" It is scarcely too much to affirm," says Mr. Macbeth, " that this one variety of this one class of figures deserves a long volume to itself, and would disclose a whole realm wealthy in many kinds of beauty." [1]

(5) *Any Subject and Various Adjuncts or Accompaniments.*—The village *green*, the *briny*, the *blue*, the *deep*. Similarly, *cockcrow* for morning, *sundown* for evening.

Mr. Macbeth, in the work from which I have already quoted more than once, specifies thirty-four different varieties of metonymy and rightly remarks that the close study of this figure is "fitted to give deep insight into the delicacy of language, that exhaustless marvel and proof of man's God-birth ".[2] We may add that no figure of speech is in more common use among all classes of people, uneducated as well as educated, as metonymy, though people are as little aware of the fact as was M. Jourdain of his accomplishments in prose.

Many of the varieties of metonymy cannot properly be classed as imagery, seeing that they lead not to the abstract by means of the concrete, but to the concrete by use of an abstract or general term. In this respect metonymy and metaphor are in inverse ratios, metaphor usually leading from concrete to abstract, rarely vice versa, metonymy frequently leading from abstract to concrete, comparatively seldom from concrete to abstract.

SYNECDOCHE

(1) The physical part for the whole and vice versa. The part chosen to stand for the whole is generally the portion of the object that most strikes the eye or else the portion that is most characteristic, or that makes the efficiency, of the object. " A *sail* ahoy ! " " Chasing the *red-coats* down the lane." " All *hands*

---

[1] Op. cit., p. 208.
[2] *Might and Mirth of Literature*, p. 202.

on deck." " How beautiful upon the mountains are the *feet* of them that bring good tidings." " *Flesh and blood* have not revealed it to you," i.e. the origin of the revelation is not merely human. A thousand *horse*, twenty *head* of cattle. In Scripture the *gates* often stand for the city, " thy seed shall possess the gates of their enemies " (Gen. xxii, 17). Tea now may mean not only a beverage but the meal at which the beverage is taken.

(2) *Genus and Species* (*Metaphysical Whole and Part*).—We say bread for the necessities of life. " Give us this day our daily *bread*." In the *sweat of thy brow* (metonymy) thou shalt eat *bread*" (Gen. iii, 19). A land flowing with *milk and honey*. Thou art my *bone* and my *flesh*, i.e. blood relations. *Panem et circenses*. *Cut-throat* may stand for murderer or assassin in general. Similarly as regards divisions of time, " A man of seventy *winters*," " a babe a double *April* old."

The process of specification may go further and a typical individual of the class be named :—" A Daniel come to judgment," " Some village Hampden," " Tom, Dick, and Harry," " a very Crœsus," " Smooth Jacob still robs homely Esau." Or, a typical action—" to cross the Rubicon," " to steer between Scylla and Charybdis," " a Judas kiss."

We sometimes find examples of the opposite process, genus substituted for species and abstract for concrete. Thus a vessel for a ship. This is exceptional and is generally due to either of two causes, viz.

(*a*) To the general name being suggestive or picturesque—*soldier* for general, the *workers* for the artizan class, an *action* for battle ; or,

(*b*) To the desire for euphemism, i.e. the suggestion of what for reasons of delicacy we avoid expressing more distinctly. Death, the devil, drunkenness, and insanity for instance are subjects regarding which euphemism is customary.

Again the abstract is sometimes used for the concrete on the principle that the point of importance is thereby isolated and so stands out in relief.

" There were gathered together *grace* and *female loveliness, wit* and *learning*."

" Blest that abode where *want* and *pain* repair."
" He was kindness itself."

" The frontiers of that extensive monarchy were guarded by *ancient renown* and *disciplined valour*."

(3) *The Material and the Thing Made of it.*—" A foeman worthy of his *steel*." *Gold* for money. " I will speak to my Lord, whereas I am *dust and ashes* " (Gen. xviii, 27 cf. iii, 19). Maledictus omnis qui pendet in *ligno* (Gal. iii, 13 cf. Acts v, 30 ; x, 39).

It will be seen at a glance that not all the varieties of these two figures can correctly be described as imagery. But the effect of most of them is to give the imagination a picture. This is, of course, fully true only so long as they are fresh. For the tendency of all such expressions is to harden, as it were, by use and become permanently imbedded in language. Indeed, " in everyday speech countless examples of fossil metonymy and synecdoche are embodied." [1]

What is the function of these figures ? What service do they render to language and to thought ? It may be said at once that they economize attention by fixing it upon the *serviceable* part of the idea to the exclusion of the rest. " Suchet's division mustered ten thousand *bayonets*."

> The gilded parapets were crowned
> With *faces* and the great tower filled with *eyes*
> Up to the summit, and the trumpets blew.

" Beware of *the bottle* " calls up a more vivid, because

[1] McKnight, op. cit.

more specific, image than "Beware of excessive drinking ". And by thus concentrating attention they help to heighten it. Their force lies in the more powerful effect, both as regards the understanding and the feelings, of the concrete and particular as compared with the general and the abstract. Food is general, bread is particular and more readily calls up a distinct object to the mind. So with "the games" as compared with amusement. So the popular demand took the form—

Panem et circenses !

Moreover, when they take the form of concrete imagery these figures are a direct stimulus to the imagination. They often lend forcefulness and suggestiveness to the style. But quite as often their only discernible effect is pleasing variety.

Additional Note

In a curious old pamphlet "printed for and sold by Samuel Fairbrother, Skinner's Row, Dublin", early in the eighteenth century—" *Troposchematologia, maximam partem ex indice rhetorico Farnabii deprompta,*" by the Rev. Thomas Stephen, I find the following set of verses embodying examples of the various kinds of metonymy and synecdoche [1] :—

Atque *Metonymia* imponit nova nomina rebus
Efficientis ; ut Inventoris ; *Marte, Lyaeo* ;
Authoris ; legetum *Juvenalis, Livius,* ingens
Aut instrumenti ; *gladius, lingua, arma, manusque*
Materiae ; *pinus, ferrum, aeris* acervus *arundo* :
Effecti ; *clades Lybiae,* Mors *frigida, pallet* ;
Subjecti ; *Curii, pateriae, Germania, rostra,*
Ucalegon, cor, os, patronus, Nox, Amarillis :
Adjuncti ; *fasces, scetus, aetas nulle, libelli.*

[1] I have not thought it well to correct the spelling and the misprints of these verses.

THEORY

Which is thus translated or rather paralleled in English—

A *Metonymie* does new Name impose
Th' Inventor's ; plump and ruddy *Bacchus* grows
Or th' Author's ; lofty *Statius, Virgil* read
                . . . defends his Head
Or the Matter whence 'tis moulded ; He shall kneel
An humble Suitor to thy conquering *Steel* :
Or th' effect ; *Pale* Famine and *cold* death
Attend on *Bloody* War's *infectious* Breath ;
The subject that contains ; we surfeited
On many *dishes* lately, now we're fed
With *England's* tears ; our *Pulpits* long exclaimed
Against those *Days*, yet ne'er a *Heart* was tamed :
Or th' Adjunct that attends ; now you may see
The *Mace* is coming ; what an *Age* are we !

Confundit totum cum parte *Synecdoche* Parti
Myrtoum, Auster, hyems, tectum, nuero Annibal Anglus
Totiụs. Orator color annus vixit Atrides.

Synecdoche. a thing compleat confounds
With part on't ; Th' oratour with Tropes abounds ;
Or take the Part for all, So many *Springs*
I've dwelt within this *Roof* Dear *soul*, she sings.

Such verses are, of course, little better than mnemonic doggerel. One is not a little surprised to find in genuine poetry mention of so highly technical a figure as Metonymy, yet here it is in Francis Thompson—

Thee God's great utterance bore,
O secret metaphor
    Of what
    Thou dream'st no jot !

Cosmic metonymy !
Weak word-unshuttering key.
    One
    Seal of Solomon.

Trope that itself not scans
Its huge significance
    Which tries
    Cherubic eyes.

PART II

APPLICATIONS

MORE exact and more logical titles for the first and second parts of this work would, perhaps, be " General " and " Special ", as, for example, we speak of General and Special Metaphysics. It would be the *Allgemeiner* and the *Besonderer Theil* so beloved of German savants. I have preferred the more familiar division—Theory and Applications. Not that the general principles set forth in the first part are in the second tested by application in practice, but that, having dealt with imagery in its general and theoretic aspects, we go on to consider various particular departments, with a view to seeing what part is, in practice and in application, played therein by metaphor, simile, and the rest. Having, in other words, broadly surveyed the world of imagery, we proceed to explore its several regions.

As these regions are of vast extent and not in all parts easily accessible, the treatment of the subject in this second part must needs be in outline only. I shall point out paths that others must more fully explore, setting up sign-posts at the entrance to them, giving some guidance as to the direction to be followed, and above all pointing out what has been recorded by previous explorers.

There is one region, and that, perhaps, the most extensive of all, the exploration of which has been reserved for a further volume, I mean literature. This has been done, not merely owing to exigencies

163

of space, but for the reason that I hope in the second volume to deal with parable and allegory, the former of which I should wish to treat in close association with one section of Imagery in Literature, viz. the Imagery of the Bible. Allegory, too, is a form of imagery that runs right through literature.

CHAPTER I

METAPHOR AND THE SCIENCE OF LANGUAGE

THERE is a curious analogy between the historical study of language and geology, the study of the earth's crust. As the crust of the earth is made up of stratum above stratum of various materials—rock, sand, gravel, shales, coal, chalk, and the rest, laid down at various epochs, so, as we look backwards into the past of one of our modern languages, we come upon layer beneath layer of various philological materials—words, phrases, grammatical forms added to, or lost by, the language at different periods of its history. When we compare the philological stratum of some period remote from our own with the language as it is to-day, we find therein certain elements which in the course of the intervening period have wholly perished, others which have persisted almost unaltered : but the greater number, we notice, have undergone a certain transformation, sometimes of the strangest kind. Thus, to exemplify the analogy in a general way, in studying the history of the English language we come upon a period when a stratum of Norman-French was laid down, upon another period, further back, when Christianity deposited a first stratum of Latin terms. Of course, philological strata are not nearly so definite and clear-cut as geological. For the most part the introduction of new elements can be better described as a gradual infiltration than as the deposit of a new layer. Yet in the main the analogy is striking and serviceable.

In applying this analogy to our present subject we may pursue it even further. Just as the fauna and flora of various geological epochs have survived in the shape of fossils embedded in the strata, so it is with imagery in language. Images are the flowers of language. But with use and wont they wither, harden, and, as time goes on, become embedded in speech, surviving as fossil imagery, the fossil poetry of language.[1]

We have already spoken, in a previous chapter,[2] of fossil metaphor, radical metaphor,[3] as Professor Max Müller prefers to call it. Much the same things may be said of other forms of imagery. Simile, for instance, has given to language countless epithets and adjectives, some retaining traces of their one-time freshness, many no longer even recognized as figurative. As samples of the former one might suggest feline manners, snaky tresses, dog-like fidelity, sheepish, waspish. The latter are no less abundant—dogged, furtive (thief-like) and stealthy (steal), stubborn (stumplike), civil (like a citizen), humble (from Latin *humus*, the earth), saucy (salty), cocksure, trivial (crossroads), capricious (*caper*, goat), cynical ($\kappa\upsilon\nu o s$ = dog), lynx-eyed, hare-brained. Personification, again, has permanently endowed certain inanimate things with sex—the moon, our country, the Church, and ships are feminine, the sun is male ; and it has given names implying personality to many a plant and flower. " Embodied in everyday speech," says a recent writer, " are countless examples of fossil metonymy and synecdoche of every kind."[4] The

[1] The above passage was written before Max Müller's essay on the strátification of Language (*Selecied Essays*, 1882, vol. i) came under my notice. There the parallel is much more fully worked out.
[2] Chap. II, p. 38.
[3] It would not, however, be strictly accurate to identify these two terms. In his work *The Science of Thought* (p. 486) he redefines radical metaphor as " the transference of one and the same root to different objects as when in Sanskrit both the sun and a hymn of praise are called arká from a root ærk, to shine, the one in the sense of what shines, the other in the sense of what makes shine or what blazes forth the glory of God ".
[4] Geo. H. McKnight, *English Words and their Background*, p. 233, New York, 1923.

word front originally meant "forehead" (Latin *frons*), a meaning it still retains in French, but came to be applied by synecdoche to the whole face, until by metaphor it was shifted to mean the façade of a house or of a stage and then the scene of war. The word "coin" comes from *cuneus*, a wedge (French *coin*), then a die for stamping. Then the name of the cause was given to the effect. The word "chafe" passed from its original meaning "to warm" (French chauffer) to express a method of producing warmth, viz. friction, and from that to express a state of impatience of which friction was a sign. "Fare" once meant a journey, as in "farewell" : it is now used for the price of a journey and even for the person conveyed at a price. The modern word "candidate" calls up no image reminiscent of the word (Latin *candidatus*, white-robed, in allusion to the costume worn by aspirants to office) from which it is derived. Nor does ambition remind us of a going about (Latin *ambire*) in search of votes. The Latin word *testum*, an earthen pot, gave to French and Italian the word *tête*,[1] *testa* (head) because of its shape and to English the word "test" because of its use for trying metals. What should we do without our "test-tube", and "acid test", and "putting to the test"?

To revert once more to the analogy from which we set out, just as the study of geology and of its sister-science, alæontology, opens up wonderful vistas of dead civilizations and forgotten conditions of society, so may the historical study of language. "The commonest words we use every day," says a recent writer,[2] "the souls of past races . . . stand around us, not dead, but frozen into their attitudes like the courtiers in the garden of the Sleeping Beauty." For

[1] Strictly speaking *tête* is from late Latin *testa*, but that also had the meanings earthen pot, then tile, shell, potsherd, skull. (Skeat.)
[2] *History in English Words*, by Owen Barfield, London, 1926.

the manners and conditions of an epoch are reflected in its current speech in various ways, and above all by way of imagery. Again, as M. Bréal remarks, when linguistics gives to the meanings of words a share of the attention it too exclusively devotes to their forms, it will be able to draw up for various languages curious and instructive lists showing the contingent of metaphors furnished by each class of citizens, each trade, etc.[1]   Thus it was the weaver who gave to Latin its words for to begin—*ordiri, exordium, primordial*. Ordiri meant originally to arrange the threads of the warp for the purpose of making a tissue.   No doubt, too, we might glean from a study of the metaphors of a given people some inkling of its genius.   " A people," says a writer, to whom I shall presently refer again, " impresses on its language its national character and the latter is to a great extent reflected in metaphors and comparisons which make so many hellenisms, latinisms, or gallicisms, that is to say, turns of speech borrowed immediately from its material life, its every-day occupations, its history and traditions." [2]   One must, however, beware of hasty generalizations. For many of these metaphors that secure a permanent foothold in language are merely the notions of Every-man and are very much the same in every language.

In a later portion of this work I hope to deal some-what fully with the imagery of the Bible. For my present purpose it will suffice to refer to the Bible as an illustration of the importance in linguistics of the study of imagery. As we shall see, the mere classification and analysis of the imagery of the Hebrew Bible as we have it to-day tells us much about the ancient Hebrew world and yields much light for the

[1] Twenty years ago a writer in the *Zeitschrift für Romanische Philogie* could say: " L'étude de la métaphore linguistique est à peine effleurée."   I do not think it has made very great strides since then.
[2] For an illustration of this see Note C to this chapter.

elucidation of the text. But with the progress of Assyriological studies it has become possible to carry the matter a stage further back. For in the family of languages Hebrew, as we find it in the Bible, was comparatively a newcomer. Embedded in it was much fossil imagery inherited from earlier tongues. And the study of this imagery in the light of those earlier tongues has yielded valuable data for the explanation of Hebrew words and ways of thought. A learned Dominican Père Dhorme has studied in this way the metaphorical use of the names of parts of the body in Hebrew and in Accadian, the Semitic language which was spoken by the dwellers along the Tigris and Euphrates and of which Babylonian and Assyrian were dialects.[1] A rather recondite study, one might say. Yet the results are of the greatest interest and value.

Père Dhorme began with these particular metaphors on the principle that in all languages the names of the various parts that go to make up the human body are transferred to animals, plants, inanimate objects and even abstractions. To-day we speak of the " leg " of a table and the " eye " of a needle. " L'homme, he says, " se projette ainsi au dehors exactement comme lorsqu'il prête ses sentiments ou ses émotions aux êtres qui l'entourent."

In the beginnings of language nature and the arts are animated and humanized and the organs of men and animals are attributed to things.[2] Once more to quote Père Dhorme, " The sky becomes animate, it possesses a heart, a face. Men see there horns which are those of the rising sun, a tongue of fire—

---

[1] *L'Emploi métaphorique des noms des parties du corps en hébreu et en akkadien*, Paris, Gabalda, 1923. For an illustration of the author's method and of the character of his conclusions see Note A at the end of this chapter.

[2] Op. cit., p. 161. As regards Greek one may consult a thesis by a lecturer of the University of Geneva published in 1875 : *De Vocabulis partium corporis in lingua graeca metaphorice dictis*.

the lightning. In the morning on awakening it opens the eyelids of the dawn,[1] and at night it enlightens mortals with ' the eye of the heavens and the earth '—the moon. The nether regions only show their breast or at times open their jaws to swallow human beings down into their belly. The waters have a breast [2] and a face. The sea hides marvels in its heart, it kisses the shore with its lips and sometimes thrusts its tongue far inland. The poet attributes to it white hair when he beholds the seething of its silver foam. The river has an eye which is its source ; it possesses a head, a neck, a mouth, and lips. And the earth ? It bares its breast ; we see its face and sometimes it opens its mouth. We may penetrate into it by the mouth of caves or the lips of wells. The mountain rears its head into the clouds and thrusts its feet into the earth. One may ascend it from the foot to the head, passing by the sides, shoulders, and neck." Again, "The plants in which life circulates will be for man as it were animals tethered to a fixed spot. They will have blood and fat, hair, a head, and a nose and limbs." And as with natural objects so with the products of man's arts and crafts. To name their various parts he transfers to them the names of his own limbs. Further, "the abstract world likewise borrows from the parts of the body names for ideas."

Many of the resemblances and analogies which have led to these metaphorical shifts of meaning are so obvious that such shifts were made by well-nigh every language in the course of its formation, and have become the common property of mankind.[3] Later generations may give more accurate and

---

[1] Cf. Milton, " Under the opening eyelids of the morn."
[2] Cf. Wordsworth, " This sea that bares her bosom to the moon."
[3] It has been pointed out that one of the most interesting branches of Semantics and one of the most useful to the etymologist deals with the study of parallel metaphors in different languages.

scientific names to things but the original popular designations subsist as part of the very warp and woof of language. We still speak of the "mouth" of a river, the "foot" of a mountain, the "heart" of the desert. In doing so we are scarcely conscious of speaking in metaphor. On the other hand, the genius of each particular people has passed into the language it created for itself. That language expresses its peculiar mentality, its outlook upon the world. Père Dhorme is able to state as one of the conclusions of his studies, "This comparison between Hebrew and Akkadian makes it possible for us to realize clearly how superior was the Hebrew imagination to that of the Babylonians and Assyrians, a positivistic and realist race." [1] And as this study reveals marked differences between these kindred peoples, it naturally reveals a still wider and deeper gulf of difference between them and peoples so widely sundered from them in time and so different in origin as are the Western Europeans of to-day. Incidentally Père Dhorme's study of metaphors throws fresh light on upwards of nine hundred passages of the Bible the thought and expression of which present difficulties to our modern and Western minds.

And as Semitic languages reflect Semitic civilization so the Western languages spoken to-day reflect the stages of civilization through which their makers have passed in the course of history.[2] "Like the shells which strew the sea-shore," says M. Bréal, "débris of animals that were once alive, some of them but yesterday, others centuries ago, languages are filled with the remains of modern or ancient ideas, some still living, others long forgotten. All the

---

[1] Op. cit., p. 3.
[2] See two fascinating chapters, "Words and Archæology" and "Words and Culture-History" in *English Words and their Background*, New York, 1923. Also the chapter entitled "Fossils" in *Words and their Ways in English Speech*, by Greenhough and Kittredge, 1902.

civilizations, all the customs, all the conquests, and all the dreams of mankind have left their traces, which by a little attention may be brought to light." Thus we have borrowed from the Romans many terms that once were the expression of their religion— auspicious, propitious, sinister, augur, contemplate. Spell, charm, enchantment, magic are used by moderns who have long outgrown the beliefs which gave rise to these words. Astrology has given us the words influence,[1] disaster, ill-starred. The science of Alchemy has long since fallen into disrepute, but it left us various words and phrases which are an addition to the common stock—alembic, crucible, together with many a poetic image.

And all our languages contain old names of obsolete weapons, memories of jousts and tourneys, old terms of venerie and falconry, now used for the most part in metaphorical senses. Many of our familiar words, again, are relics of old beliefs, not only in the sphere of religion but in that of science.[2] It was formerly supposed that the body was composed of solids, liquids, and aeriform substances. The belief in the aeriform substances called *spirits* survives in words that have now not a material but a moral or spiritual meaning. We speak of high spirits and low spirits, of animal spirits and keeping up one's spirits. The liquid elements were called *humours* and were supposed to be four in number : blood, phlegm, bile, and black bile. The *temperament* of a person (Latin *temperare* to mix) depended upon the mixture of these humours. And according as one or the other pre-dominated the temperament was *sanguine, phlegmatic, bilious,* or *melancholy.* Three of these survive as useful summaries of character or disposition. A

---

[1] Which curiously enough has come to us again in Italian guise and with a new meaning in the word *influenza.*
[2] McKnight, op. cit., p. 336.

well-balanced mixture (temperament) of these humours or elements was thought to be evidence of a well-balanced character—

> His life was gentle : and the elements
> So mixed in him that Nature might stand up
> And say to all the world, This was a man.

" Temper," " complexion," and " humour " also have their origin in these ancient notions of physiology. So have courage, cordial, spleen, and kidney.

We have said that the flowers of imagery fade in course of time and gradually fossilize. " En nostre commun langage," complains Montaigne, " il s'y rencontre des phrases excellentes et des métaphores desquelles la beauté flestrit de vieillesse et la couleur s'est ternie par maniement trop ordinaire." [1] The poetry of language is thereby a loser. But on the whole language gains in richness and expressiveness by the creation of imagery, however certain that imagery may be to lose its freshness eventually. For imagery is, as we have seen, for language one of the great factors of the enlargement of its word-store. The process is ever going on. " Candour," " ejaculation," " endorse " are now colourless words that suggest no picture. Yet it is not very long since the picture faded out of consciousness. Herrick could still speak of " the candour of Julia's teeth ", Bacon of " the ejaculations [flashings forth like darts] of the eye ", Milton of " elephants endorsed with towers ". The poetry has departed but there remain three useful words.

What happens is somewhat as follows. Weeds, since first there were gardens, must have been a familiar object to all gardeners and lovers of gardens. Somebody, with imagination more alert than the common or simply more absorbed in its object,

---

[1] *Essais*, iii, 5.

reflecting upon the effects of vice on the character, suddenly perceived an analogy between vices and weeds. Were they not both harmful intruders by all means to be got rid of ? So identical did the two notions appear in this respect that one could be spoken of in terms of the other. We must tear up our vices by the roots, we must eradicate them. Henceforth the words uproot, eradicate, and the like have a new meaning. They can signify the getting rid of some evil habit that had "taken root" in the character. In process of time those who use this word "eradicate" gradually cease to be conscious that they are speaking of roots and weeds. For long the image, or a faint wraith of it, hovers behind the word, but in the end "eradicate" comes to be a colourless term meaning "to abolish completely". Further examples will illustrate this process. The Latin word for a weighing scales is *libra*. Some writer or thinker seeking expression for his idea saw an analogy between the mental process of discussing the reasons and motives for and against a decision and the balancing of weights on either side of a pair of scales. Hence the word deliberate which now calls up no image of a balance. The image still lives faintly in the expression "to weigh the pros and cons". The word "ponder" (Latin *pondus*, weight) had a somewhat similar origin. So had the French word for "to think", penser (Latin *pendere*). One of the Latin words for "to think" *putare* (from which we have putative, impute, reputation, etc., etc.) meant originally the weighing and calculating of money.[1] Then (like aestimare, estime, esteem) it came to be used of mental reckoning up. The word reckon itself can be used alternately in

---

[1] It can be traced further back to a root *ρu* = clean, whence *putus* clean, and *purus*, clear. *Putus* gave *putare* to clean, then to clean or prune the vine (cf. amputate), to clean up accounts (*putare rationes*), and then to reckon.

its original material sense and as the description of a mental act quite unconnected with the counting of money or other objects. "Calculation" had its humble origin in a Latin word that simply meant a pebble. And so of hundreds of now indispensable words, made to express notions that had once no name of their own, not by the coining of a new combination of sounds, but by giving to an existing combination a new meaning. This function of metaphor has been fully recognized by such writers as Michel Bréal[1] and Arsène Darmesteter.[2] But, so far as I am aware, it has nowhere been more fully studied than in the work from which I have already so frequently quoted, *Figurative Language*, by L. H. Grindon. Not content with citing more or less random examples, he examines methodically most of the constituent elements of language. These, he holds, are no arbitrary creation of science, even primitive science. "Grammar exists in language because already in the system of the external or material world. Existence, quality, and number, the images and counterparts of sex and gender, the relations of time and space, possession, action, passivity, are all prefigured in it, and all enter into language, necessarily, because language appropriates for its glossary the objects with which they are identified. . . . In nature there is not only the whole *form*, but the entire *method* of language".[3] "Before a single vocable was constructed, the entire substance of language lay latent in nature".[4] Holding in a modified form the theory of the onomatopoeic origin of language, he first shows how root-words have their origin in the sounds of nature, applied by man to his own purposes. The sound once adopted and rendered articulate gave rise to an immense

---

[1] *Essai de Sémantique*, chap. xii.
[2] *La Vie des Mots*, pt. i, chap. ii, § vii.
[3] Ibid., p. 24.   [4] Ibid., p. 32.

progeny of words. Once admit a root "laq" leg, formed in imitation of the sound of animals lapping water—Hebrew "lāqaq" (used of the animals that licked up the blood of Achab, 3 Kings, A.V. and R.V. 2 Chron. xxii, 38), Greek and Latin "lego", to gather up, and you have a whole tribe of words, derivatives of this root : elect, select, collect, cull (through French "cueillir" = colligere), recollection, eligible, eclectic, elegant, lecture, lessons, intellect, intelligence, intelligible, delight, delectable, neglect, diligence. Thus one simple onomatopoeic base or root underlies scores of derivations, all of which preserve the primal idea in a metaphorical or figurative manner. The author works out in a series of delightful chapters the derivatives of such primitive words or rather sounds, as *mur*, *ab* or *pa*, *ma*, *our*, *st*, *fl*, *um* or *mu*.

Given the primitive roots, multitudes of new words may be formed by means of prefixes, affixes, or combinations of other already existing words, the meaning being often thereby rendered figurative. Prefixes and affixes merit the most careful study. For the most part they are in origin separate words, once independent nouns or verbs. Thus *mis*, seen in mislead, mistake, misjudge, seems traceable to the root word appearing in Latin as *mit*, or *mis* = to send. The preposition *per* is etymologically congenerate with πειρο to pierce. Hence numberless derivatives, mostly metaphorical—perfect, pervious, perplex, persecute, pervert. The preposition *trans* is from a verb existing in Sanskrit as *tara* = to step or place beyond. Metaphors innumerable exist in the compounds which begin with the Latin "ab", "ad", "ante", circum", "ex", "prae", "pro", "sub", "super", etc., or with the Greek "kata", "eu", "an" or "a", "anti", "apo", "dia", "meta", "para", "syn", or "sym", etc. These words call up in the memory hosts of other words made out of these.

Affixes are no less important. Their function is definite, their origin often historically ascertainable. Like the prefixes they originate in independent words, though usually worn down by time till the original form is scarcely recognizable. " The evidence," says Mr. Grindon, " is all in favour of their having been originally in all cases integral and organic realities, not simply marking inflexions, number, or gender, but introducing new and enlarged significations, often highly figurative or poetical." The adverbial termination -*ly* is a worn-down form of like which is traceable to the Moeso-Gothic *leik*, the human frame, in Anglo-Saxon *lic*, in German *leich*. The name of the body was made to serve for resemblance or verisimilitude. When we say that one thing is " like " another, we say, figuratively, that it has a similar kind of body, a similar configuration and appearance. Then the word passed on to designate resemblance in *spiritual* qualities, character, behaviour, etc. Thus we get a new light on many words—early is literally spring- or morning-like, quickly is lifelike, cf. the quick and the dead, a quickset hedge, and for the meaning compare " lively ".

Most of these words ending in -*like* and -*ly* are, or originally were, condensed similes, when applied to non-material things. Another very large group of condensed similes is made up of words ending in -*id*. Such are candid, acid, solid, frigid, tepid, turbid, arid, rapid, fervid. To speak of arguments as solid is implicitly to compare them to the firm earth (*solum*, soil) beneath one's feet. To say that someone's demeanour is frigid is to compare it to something frozen (Lat. *frigeo* = to freeze). Candid, though we are no longer conscious of the fact, implied candor, i.e. shining whiteness. Horrid implied hair standing on end. This termination *-id* (Lat. *-idus*) is itself a remnant of an ancient Aryan word seen in the Greek εἶδος and in the ancient verb ἴδω or εἴδω, to see.[1] It was natural to use the word εἶδος to signify likeness. We have it in the word idol from εἴδωλον, a representation and more particularly the likeness of a God.

Other terminations which give us condensed similes or metaphors are *-ic*, as in cynic, civic, heroic, classic, lyric, rustic, critic, barbaric, poetic, prosaic, prophetic, intrinsic, artistic, Catholic ; *-ent* or *-ant*, as in ardent, lenient, patient, pungent, dormant, jubilant, vigilant ; *-ness* (derived, strange as it may seem, from a word meaning nose[2]) as in boldness, politeness, suppleness, kindness, comeliness, forgiveness, fearlessness, etc., etc. ; and *-ship* (originally meaning shape, German *schaft*) as in friendship, fellowship, courtship, lordship, worship (worth-ship), and many others. By means of such terminations the designations of quite concrete and material objects can be applied to objects in the supra-sensible world of mind and spirit. This transfer is in its essence a metaphor.

There is another and no less interesting way of approach to the study of the growth of language by metaphor. Instead of taking language as it is and tracing back its words to their metaphorical origin, one takes groups of material objects and studies the metaphorical uses to which they have been put. One might take in turn the objects with which man has been surrounded from the beginning—his dwelling, his implements, his food, primitive occupations, his body itself, his domesticated animals, in short all the things with which he found himself in daily

---

[1] In the New Testament we have the interjectional imperative ἴδε, see ! behold ! (al. ἰδού) Ἴδε ὁ ἄνθρωπος, Ecce homo !
[2] *Figurative Language*, p. 202.

and hourly contact. One could then trace in any given language or group of languages the uses to which early man put the names which he gave these things. It is fascinating to watch, as it were, imagination play around these commonplace objects, to mark what curious and often fantastic analogies, what subtle likenesses it discovers or creates between them and some as yet unnamed object or idea, how what was at first perhaps a baby-name for some familiar thing is unconsciously adopted by grown-ups and then transferred to some new, and, it may be, elevated use. One thinks of the heights to which the infantine *ma* and *pa* have risen. Such rudimentary elements as primitive names for animals, domestic utensils, and parts of the body have, as a writer has expressed it, germinated in every direction and have enriched the dictionary with an entire world of ideas and of words. "La métaphore," the same writer continues, "cet agent puissant de l'évolution linguistique, après avoir fait pousser les germes, leur a communiqué la vitalité et le mouvement."

As examples of this line of investigation I may refer to two interesting, but I fear not very accessible, studies. One is by the writer just quoted, M. Lazare Sainéan.[1] Taking merely the domestic animals, the cat, the dog, the pig, and the rest, he traces through the Romance languages the metaphorical development undergone in course of ages by the names originally given to these animals, to their various limbs, cries, qualities, habits. Thus there are first the cat's names—beginning with the Low Latin cattus, catta, which appeared in the first century A.D. and has, with endless variations, been adopted into all the derived languages and dialects. Naturally

---

[1] " La création métaphorique en français et en roman," published in the *Zeitschrift für Romanische Philologie*, Verlag von Max Niemayer, Halle, 1905.

children gave it pet names corresponding to our pussy, tom, tabby, and the older grimalkin, such as the French *matou* and *minet*. Many of these were taken up into everyday speech and applied to new objects—take " pussyfoot " as a sample in English. Then there were a host of words descriptive of the cat's cries—mewing and purring and caterwauling and spitting. Then there were the cat's habits and characteristics, real and imaginary, which at once were seized upon to describe human beings. " Le chat est l'image même de la propreté, de la grâce, de la gentillesse." But it may also be the image of spitefulness and stealthiness. The words for its limbs and parts were used first to describe and then to designate objects resembling them, however faintly ; its claws, for instance, furnished a convenient name for anything hooked. In addition to all this there was what we may call the folklore of the cat as created by the popular imagination. One might recall, as something analogous in English, Puss in Boots, Dick Whittington and his cat, and the black cats, which were the familiars and accomplices of all genuine witches. One of the most interesting conclusions of the study is this, that, in default of a definite Latin or Germanic etymology for a word, one must seek in the *original* elements of the Romance languages, in their creative activity, the solution of most of the linguistic problems which have hitherto baffled research.

The other study referred to above, viz. *Essai sur la métaphore dans la langue grecque*, by Louis Morel,[1] carries the investigation further back. Like M. Sainéan he confines himself to names of animals used metaphorically. But he studies these metaphorical uses as they are actually found in the extant literature of Greece, and in particular in Homer, the Attic dramatists, and Plato. He shows how,

[1] Geneva, Imprimerie Charles Schuchart, 1879.

already in Greek, well-nigh every term concerning the animal in question had been turned to a variety of uses different, and often remote enough, from its primitive significance. " Among the causes," he writes, " which start a word on an adventurous career and concur to render its primitive meaning unrecognizable, we must reckon first of all the figurative transference of this word to notions or things which usage, time, or the literary language cause to be accepted or rejected. . . . It is in reality metaphor, in the broad sense of the word, that is the most active cause of these numberless variations in the meanings of words." The interest of M. Morel's study is enhanced by frequent references to similar usages in Latin and in modern languages.

Here, then, is another inviting field of investigation, as yet but imperfectly explored.

NOTE A

IMAGERY IN AKKADIAN AND HEBREW

A GOOD average example of the method followed and the results arrived at in Père Dhorme's L'Emploi Métaphorique des Noms de Parties du Corps en Hébreu et en Akkadien is afforded by his treatment of the metaphorical uses of the horn, Hebr. *qèrên*, Akkadian *qarnu*.[1] He shows that, besides its material uses in both languages for a receptacle for oil, wine, etc. (cf. Latin *cornucopia*), or for a trumpet (cf. English *horn*), it came to be used in two distinct metaphorical senses, corresponding on the one hand to the position of the horns as the highest part of the head and on the other to their use as weapons of attack. The existing Hebrew lexicons group all the metaphorical uses of *qèrên* under the meaning *robur* or *potentia*, strength or power. But just as the word for head both in

[1] pp. 34 sq.

Akkadian and in Hebrew may, when used with a verb meaning to raise up, express pride or exultation, so the horns, as being the highest part of an animal's head, may be used in just the same sense. The man who in exultation or pride holds his head high is likened to the animal that throws up its horns. This seems clearly to be the meaning in Ps. lxxiv, 5 : " I said to the arrogant, Deal not arrogantly and to the wicked, Set not up your horn on high. Lift not up your horn on high : Speak not insolently with a stiff neck." Similarly in 1 Kings ii, 1, where the exultation of the just is depicted : " My heart hath exulted in Jahwe, my horn has been high in Jahwe. My mouth has been opened wide against my enemies, for I have rejoiced in thy salvation." Again, Ps. lxxxviii, 18 : " For thou art the glory of their strength, and in thy favour our horn shall be exalted " (or, as Father Dhorme reads, " is exalted "). He thinks that the meaning exultant joy is indicated by the preceding verse : " In thy name do they exalt all the day and in thy justice are they lifted up." In the light of these passages Père Dhorme interprets Ps. cxxxi, 16, 18, where many commentators see mention of a *powerful* scion of David[1] : " Her priests also will I clothe with salvation : And her pious ones shall shout aloud for joy. There will I make the horn of David to shoot forth : I have prepared a lamp for my anointed."[2] The lamp, he notes, is a common symbol of joy. Another passage to the point is Ezechiel xxix, 21. This idea of exultation, of being uplifted in joy and victory came to be so associated with the word that " to take horns " came to mean to acquire glory, " to give horns," to confer glory.

---

[1] The expression "He hath raised up a horn of salvation to us in the house of David", in the canticle of Zachary (Luke i, 69), to which Père Dhorme does not refer, is thought to be derived from the passage in Ps. cxxxi.

[2] Cf. Ps. xci, 11.

Similarly to break the horn meant to humble the pride of some person or people, as in Ecclus xlvii, 8.

In a word the uses of horn, in the two languages, are parallel with those of head in the sense of highest part, top, of the body, in fact anything outstanding, jutting up (cf. the Golden Horn, the horns of the moon). Thus the rays of light issuing from the face of Moses were described as horns.

On the other hand there are certainly to be found passages in which horn has the other metaphorical sense of strength, force. There are in the first place many passages in which the word *qêrên* is used literally to mean the weapon of attack of rams, goats, bulls, or buffaloes.[1] But when to give horns to a person or a people came to mean endow with strength, the word was already used in a transferred sense. " Arise and tread, Daughter of Sion, for I will put on you a horn of iron and hoofs of brass : and thou shalt beat in pieces many peoples, etc." (Micheas iv, 13).[2] In Assyria and Babylonia horns, as symbols of power, were represented on the head-dresses of gods and of kings. And the latter in their inscriptions described themselves as striking down their adversaries with their horns. The expression *qarnâ bullû* " take away the horns," meant taking from a person all power to harm, just as in Zacharias ii, 1–4 : " These are the horns which have scattered Juda . . . and these (the smiths seen in vision) are come to fray them, to cast down the horns of the nations, that have lifted up the horn upon the land of Juda." And again in Jeremias xlviii, 25, there is the parallelism between the breaking of the " arm " of Moab and the cutting off of its " horn ".

A comparative study, therefore, of the metaphorical developments of the primitive image horn shows

[1] Dan. viii, 4 ; Ezek. xxxiv, 21 ; Deut. xxxiii, 17 ; Ps. xxi, 22.
[2] Cf. 3 Kings xxii, 11.

that the latter has given rise to the meanings joyous
exultation, pride, summit, corner, extremity, offensive
and defensive force. As a result light is thrown on
many passages of the Bible and the vagueness and
confusion of the dictionaries in this respect is remedied.

This brief summary gives a very inadequate idea
of the mass of erudition gathered into the seven pages
(out of 182) devoted to the study of the image horn.
But it may serve to show the value to the science
of language accruing from the study of imagery.

NOTE B

ANIMAL METAPHORS IN GREEK

As a sample of the interest and importance of M. Louis
Morel's *Essai sur la Métaphore dans la langue grecque*
we may take his treatment of the metaphors derived
from the horse. First in order are the metaphors
derived from the nature and form of the horse. In
classical times the horse was held in high honour, in a
sort of veneration. We see this in Virgil no less than
in Homer. The feeling about horses in the Homeric
age is evident from such a passage as that in the
seventeenth Book of the Iliad (lines 426 sqq.) where
the horses of Patroclus are represented as weeping
and as being comforted by Zeus himself. Similarly
Virgil (Aeneid xi, 89) makes the war-horse of Pallas
weep for him. Naturally then the main idea involved
in metaphors about horses is the nobility of the animal.
They usually imply praise and appreciation. The
very name of nobility in five languages beginning
with Greek comes from the horse :—

ἵππος ἱππεύς ἱππότης

    equus eques
    cheval chevalier
    caballo caballero
    cavallo cavaliere

METAPHOR AND LANGUAGE

Occasionally other and somewhat disparaging aspects of the horse appear in classical metaphors, for it was used not only for racing and for war but also as a beast of burden.

Indeed the uses of the horse as a domestic animal suggested a long series of metaphors. Quite early the winds were thought of as winged horses and ships as the coursers of the sea.

It lachrymans classique immittit habenas (Aeneid). A later Greek writer Diogenes Laertius speaks of practice in philosophy as καθιππάζεσθαι τῆς φιλοσοφίας.

The harness and caparisons of the horse have furnished metaphors innumerable. In particular the bit, the bridle, or reins, the spur, and the saddle have become fixed in language in certain metaphorical senses. The bit χαλινός, *frenum*, *frein*, is a symbol of absolute domination or else of restraint. Hence the English word refrain. To champ the bit δάκνειν τὸν χαλινόν indicated impatience under restraint.

The reins ἡνίαι, *habenae*, are a symbol of control. The image was early used as a metaphor for the administration of the State. As examples of its metaphorical uses such examples as the following may be quoted :—

'Ηνίας εἰς τὸ ὀπίσω ἑλκύσαι. Plato. Phaedr. 254 C.
ἐφεῖναι καὶ χαλάσαι τὰς ἡνίας τοῖς λόγοις. Protag. 338 A.
'Ενεδίδου τοῖς βουλήμασι τὰς ἡνίας. Dion Hal. 7, 35.

Finally ἡνιοχεύω came to be said of all intellectual and moral guidance. For comparison's sake we may take an example of the metaphorical use of reins from Latin poetry and one from Latin prose. Thus Lucretius :—

> Arboribusque datum est variis exinde per auras
> Crescundi magnum immissis certamen habenis.

And Cicero—Senatum servire populo cui populus ipse moderandi et regendi sui potestatem quasi

quàsdam habenas tradidisset (De Orat. i, 52, 226).
Compare the French :—

Tenir en bride un peuple sans raison. Corneille.

And Madame de Sévigné's Laisser courir sa plume
la bride sur le cou. To give free rein is a common
expression in English.

In the spur the Greek saw a symbol of energy,
of strength of will exerted by a higher power. It is a
favourite metaphor with the Greek tragedians.

Δηχθεῖσα κέντροις παιδὸς ἠράσθη σέθεν. Eurip. Hipp.
   1303.
'Εκπεπληγμένη κέντροις ἔρωτος. Ibid. 39.
Πρὸς κέντρα μη λάκτιζε, μὴ πταίσας μονῆς. Aesch.
   Agam. 1624.

Many other examples are quoted by the author :
it will suffice to mention *πρὸς κέντρον λακτίζειν,*
to kick against the goad (Pindar, Pyth. ii, 95).
The mordern word "recalcitrant" is this old metaphor
in fossilized form. In the following saying spur and
bridle are found together : *Δεῖ γὰρ αὐτοῖς ὡς κέντρου
πολλάκις, οὕτω δὴ καὶ χαλίνου.* Compare the Italian,
Tra la briglia e lo sprone consiste la ragione ; French,
Entre bride et éperon de toute chose gît la raison.
Fame is the spur that the clear spirit doth raise
(Milton).

There follow illustrations of the metaphorical
uses of saddle, stirrup, etc. All the horse's paces
and motions have been applied to the things of the
mind—gallop, trot, prance, rear, and so forth.

Further chapters deal with metaphorical expressions
derived from the nature, characteristics, and habits
of the cow, the bull, the ass, the mule, and the dog.
He had previously in a long introductory chapter
dealt with metaphors drawn from the names of
metals, colours, trades, and professions.

METAPHOR AND LANGUAGE

NOTE C

The Swedish writer T. Hilding Svartengren, in his very able thesis already referred to,[1] comes to some interesting conclusions. "What," he asks (p. 458), "are the interests of the English people as evidenced by their similes? We have noticed in the first place, that our hypothetic Englishman cares comparatively little for nature and its varied aspects, but he is immensely interested in *man* and *human life*. If we consider further his interests in things human, we notice that in spite of the similes with *sea*—they are largely literary—he is not much of a traveller. . . . He is an inland man, and he is no townsman. . . . There is extremely little to remind us of city life. And life in mines and factories and mills has left very few traces in these similes. Our Englishman's home is the quiet countryside. . . . He knows something about cattle and farming, mole-catching, deer-stalking, and some other branches of hunting. Otherwise he does not go in for sports very much, except perhaps bowling at the village green and a game of dice at the inn. He goes to church and knows his Bible well, but he fears the Devil more than God. He keeps away, on the whole, from politics, and what he has seen of State representatives with whom he has come in touch has not impressed him favourably. He is fond of his joke, in a mild way, and ready to poke fun at his neighbours and to criticize the craftsmen he has had dealings with. Although he does not seem to have gone very much beyond his three R's, he has some acquaintance with theatrical performances, and regards a play as a good thing. But even if he enjoys a piece of mummery, and a maypole dance on the green,

[1] *Intensifying Similes in English* (University of Lund), 1918.

he is far more interested in his own home. The word home does not occur in any simile, but the different parts of the house and the house itself . . . enter very largely into his stock of similes. Being a strong and healthy man ailments and diseases have very little hold on his imagination, but he cares a good deal for his body, its parts, and its normal functions. . . . He is profoundly interested in food and drink. Food, drink, seasonings, and their possible ingredients, have created a very large portion of our similes. The home of the English simile is the Farm."

He concludes :—" What characterizes the English simile as we have found it is its old-worldness and the strong predominance of elementary human interests " (p. 459).

CHAPTER II

Imagery in Rhetoric and Composition

I. GUIDING PRINCIPLES

In dealing with the functions of metaphor we have considered in a general way the manifold indebtedness of style to imagery. Metaphor is an integral element of style. It is inherent not merely in style but in language itself. It is impossible to write without using it and we use it constantly in speaking. The art of writing does not consist wholly in the use of imagery ; but the magic of style, its colour, brilliance, effectiveness, life, are very largely due to imagery.[1] It is therefore of no small importance to discover and lay down principles that may guide the writer or speaker in the use of imagery. And these principles might well form one of the most important chapters in any systematic treatise on the art of writing.[2] I shall make an attempt to formulate a certain number of leading principles.

1.   I have pointed out above (p. 109) that in order to fulfill its functions an image must first be in some degree *intelligible*. If wholly unintelligible it can neither aid thought nor stir emotion : it is useful neither for exposition nor for intensification. It is true that for the former function[3] a greater degree of clearness is required than for the latter, and the

---

[1] Albalat, *L'Art d'écrire*, p. 274.

[2] Composition and Rhetoric, which are coming to be used, especially in America, as synonyms, are the current terms used to designate such treatises.

[3] That is when the image is used as "illustrative or diagrammatical, providing a concrete instance of a relation which would otherwise have to be stated in abstract terms ". I. A. Richards, *Principles of Literary Criticism*, p. 239, London, 1925.

simile being more used for exposition than for intensification demands more clearness than the metaphor. An image of any kind may, as we have seen, be unintelligible or at all events obscure owing to various causes. The imported image which is brought in as an illustration may be so unfamiliar to hearer or reader as to be a mere word to him, calling up no image at all before his mind's eye. Or the " scope " of the comparison, implied in metaphor or expressed in simile, may be obscure to him : he misses the point. The image becomes an enigma rather than an illustration, thought is hampered rather than facilitated, the mind's eye is dazzled, not enlightened. Professor G. Lanson expresses this admirably :—" One cannot be too much on one's guard against metaphors whose sole effect is to set the reader wondering what is the literal notion hidden behind them. If the figure is merely a rebus, merely a word puzzle, it is bad and ought to be expunged. . . . The figure is a good one only if it calls up instantly the idea of the object without its being necessary for the mind to recall first the literal expression of that object, and if it present the idea accompanied, and so to speak enriched by all that the signified object and the figurative expression can suggest."

If as we have suggested, one of the uses of figurative language is to effect an economy in the reader's or hearer's attention by simplifying in some sort the apprehension of the idea presented to him, we have here an additional reason for clearness, for, as Spencer says, " if there be any obscurity in the meaning or application of the metaphor no economy of attention will be achieved." [1]

For the purpose of achieving clearness two practical rules may be suggested :—

[1] *The Philosophy of Style.*

GUIDING PRINCIPLES

(1) The "imported image" should be chosen from within the reader's or hearer's sphere of knowledge.

(2) The image ought to be intelligibly and otherwise suitably expressed, and, if need be, it should be gradually led up to so that the reader may be prepared for it.

2. In securing that a metaphor be familiar enough to be intelligible one is faced with the likelihood of its being so familiar as to be trite. Now a second principle in the use of imagery is to eschew the trite, the stale, the worn-out image. It is a good sound principle, but the application of it demands measure and reasonableness. For it is not possible to exclude from style every metaphorical expression that is not perfectly fresh. As we have seen, metaphor is of the very warp and woof of language, part of its permanent texture. All this imagery was once fresh and vivid : it called up a picture in the imagination. Then to its first users it seemed so aptly to express the idea which it had been used to illustrate that gradually it came to be retained as the habitual expression for that idea. Little by little it lost its vividness and freshness : it faded and finally reached the fossil stage, so as to be used without any consciousness of its being a metaphor. Clearly we are not called upon to eliminate from speech the whole of this deposit of dead and fossilized imagery. That is a first reservation.

A further reservation must, I think, be made in favour of metaphors that were originally so apt and have become so useful as to be all but indispensable. The present writer has not scrupled to use in the preceding paragraph metaphors which, without being fossilized, are certainly not fresh. Such are " warp ", " woof ", " texture " as applied to language, " fossil " as applied to metaphor, " trite," " stale," " worn-out " as applied to imagery in general. He does so without apology, though purists may be found to disapprove. And the justification seems to be this that these images continue to fulfil effectively one of the peculiar functions of imagery, viz. the making (by means of a familiar object) of a given idea easier for the mind to grasp. So long as an image continues to play its proper rôle with effect why should it be banished ?

It is when we turn to certain other functions of imagery that the value of the present principle becomes apparent. One of these functions, we have seen (pp. 81 seq.), is to bring ideas home to the mind through the imagination. To this end the image used by speaker or writer ought to stimulate the imagination of reader or hearer into the formation of a picture. Now this is what the entirely worn-out image fails to do. It has been used so often in place of a certain notion that the mind seizes at once upon the notion without troubling to form any picture at all. Take such stock phrases as, the flower of our manhood, stemming the tide, a load of sorrow, a spark of manhood, and the like, which we have all of us heard and read *ad nauseam*. Does anybody on hearing them picture to himself some beautiful flower, or the surge of the incoming tide, or a heavy burden that bows down the back, or a spark among half-extinguished embers ? Scarcely, I think. Nor do such images fulfil that other function of imagery, the arousing of emotion. They do not infuse any poetic quality into style. Neither do they surprise and delight.

It is well then to proscribe, as far as possible, what Emile Faguet calls " the residue of ancient images, metaphors, allegories, symbols, myths that have come to be no more than colourless signs of commonplace ideas, after having once been striking representations of natural or supernatural life ". The simple expression of a fact or an idea, on the other hand, never grows unpleasantly stale.

Instead of using the images instanced above it is better to say " the best or the pick of our manhood ", " the smallest remnant or trace of humanity ", " a heavy sorrow ", and so on. You may continue to say " it is raining " as often as the phenomena repeats itself. To keep saying " the skies are weeping " may become insufferable.

It would be easy to fill pages with a list of images which, by constant use, have lost their value as imagery It will be useful to give at least some samples in illustration. Thus we have grown familiar with the " poison of flattery ", the " torch of sedition ", the " strong arm of the Law ", and " the long arm of coincidence ", " the lap of luxury ", " parrot cries ", the " school of life ". We know such phrases as " written in letters of fire ", " beyond the pale ", " a place in the sun ", " hunger stalking through the land ", " a strangle-hold ", " poisoning the wells ", " backs to the wall ", " bubbling over " with something or other, to " bleed white ", " the crucible of . . .", " the tribunal of penance ", the " tip-toe of expectation ".

To the category of the stale belongs most of the imagery drawn from classical mythology—a disciple of Bacchus, Augean Stables, Herculean labours, a votary of Venus, rosy-fingered dawn, Phœbus and Diana and Mars and Neptune and Ceres and the rest of this faded paraphernalia. A writer of genius may, indeed, give new life to all this long-dead world and use its imagery with freshness. We have but to think of such poems as Tennyson's *Oenone* and *Ulysses*, Arnold's *Strayed Reveller*, Keats's *Hyperion*, or Swinburne's *Atalanta* in Calydon. But to do so the writer must call up and breathe again the atmosphere of the bygone times in which these things were realities, at least for the imagination. To the average writer such an effort of the constructive imagination would not be possible. He had better send forth his idea in its nakedness rather than array it in the frayed finery of a past literary period. Or, if he must needs clothe it, let it walk abroad in clumsy homespun rather than in garments stiff with the shabby brocade of a Euphues, or embroidered with the faded classic finery of the " Augustan Age ".[1]

The ideal image should spring spontaneously from inward feeling and personal imagination, created by an emotion and expressing an emotion. It is not necessary, nor even particularly desirable, that the object taken as an image be new. Fresh imagery can be made with the most familiar things—fields and flowers, the wind and the rain, nay the homeliest domestic objects. By means of such Christ our Lord Himself taught eternal truths in images that will last for all time.

3. In other words imagery ought to be *spontaneous*, and this is the third principle. Images ought to arise in the mind along with the thought which they clothe as though that thought could not be otherwise expressed. Goldsmith distinguishes between " those metaphors which rise glowing from the heart and those cold conceits which are engendered in the fancy ". But, as we have seen, we must make reservations in favour of those images which, while grasped and realized by our imagination, do not spontaneously present themselves but are chosen deliberately with a view to illustrate the thought. These cannot, I think, be ruled out as not spontaneous. But then their purpose is quite other than poetic,

---

[1] An excellent sample, too long to quote here, of a piece of modern prose full of stale metaphor will be found in Tract No. xi, *Metaphor*, p. 11, published by the Society for Pure English.

and it is to poetry and to the poetic element of prose style that this principle applies.

Moreover, it is quite possible for metaphors used many times before to become the genuine, and so far spontaneous, expression of a writer's thought. "Context," says Mr. Clutton-Brock, "may give life to a metaphor that has long seemed dead, as it gives life to the commonest words. If an image forces itself upon a writer because it and it alone will express his meaning, then it is his image, no matter how often it has been used before ; and in that case it will arrest the attention of the reader,"[1] and thus fulfil one of its proper functions.

It is, however, but too easy for writers to fall into the habitual use of faded and lifeless metaphors. Fearing that their thought may appear too commonplace if unadorned, they adorn it with familiar tags of well-worn imagery. Such imagery is not a spontaneous product of thought or a natural outcome of emotion. It is an effort to give interest and piquancy to what is felt to be commonplace, to give the impression of feeling where feeling is not. But the natural effect of such use of imagery is not to arouse but to dull attention. The imagination refuses to realize oft repeated tags and emotion to respond in any way to what has grown negligible through over-familiarity. It is dimly felt that the writer is using for plain statement of fact language which ought to be the product of emotion, the outcome of the poetic mood. As the same writer says, " If eloquence is reason fused with emotion, writing or speaking full of dead metaphors is unreason fused with sham emotion."

4. The fourth principle is concerned with *taste* in the choice of images and in the application of those chosen to the illustration of a given idea : in other

[1] *Metaphor*, pp. 11–15, Tract No. xi of the Society for Pure English.

195

words it insists on harmony between the first and second elements of metaphor and simile, viz. the " main idea " and the " imported image ". It requires that the latter be in all respects an apt illustration of the former. Now an image may possess for purposes of illustration certain good qualities: the underlying comparison may be accurate and striking: yet good taste may forbid its use. For, as we have seen, the tendency of imagery is not merely to explain or expound an object to our intellect but to raise or lower it in our esteem. There are, of course, purely expository images, but these are, for the most part, of the nature of formal and literal comparisons rather than figures of speech. All we demand of such is that they help to make the idea clearer. But account must be taken of the general tendency of figure to introduce into the expression of an idea an element of feeling. Now, if our feeling about a given object or idea is one of esteem and appreciation, it would be an error of taste to choose, in order to illustrate it, an image which, in the minds of readers or hearers, has mainly ignoble or vulgar associations. The illustration would lower and demean the subject, would be a kind of bathos. An opposite mistake is made by those who use noble and solemn imagery to illustrate commonplace and insignificant objects. This is bombast, rhodomontade, grandiloquence, fustian. In both cases " main idea " and " imported image " are out of harmony. A third offence against good taste in the use of imagery is affectation or preciosity. This last is an outcome of the use of imagery for its own sake and generally according to some false standard of taste prevailing at a given literary period. It results in sacrifice of substance to form, in far-fetched conceits, in tawdry decoration and embroidery.

As examples of illustration that demeans a subject

it will, I think, suffice to quote two passages, the first from Professor James Russell Lowell's essay on Shakespeare :—

" For such purposes of mere æsthetic nourishment Goethe always milked other minds—if minds those ruminators and digesters of antiquity into asses' milk may be called. There were plenty of Professors who were for ever assiduously browsing in vales of Enna and on Pentelican slopes among the vestiges of antiquity, slowly secreting lacteous facts, and not one of them would have raised his head from that exquisite pasturage, though Pan had made music through his pipe of reeds. Did Goethe wish to work up a Greek theme ? He drove out Herr Böttiger, for example, among that fodder delicious to him for its very dryness, that sapless Arcadia of Scholiasts, let him graze, ruminate, and go through all the other needful processes of the antiquarian organism, then got him quietly into a corner and milked him. The product, after standing long enough, mantled over with the rich Goethean cream, from which a butter could be churned, if not precisely classic, quite as good as the ancients could have made out of the same material."

Our second example is from De Quincey's *Essay on Language* :—" The Hebrew by introducing himself into the secret places of the human heart, and sitting there as an incubator over the awful germs of the spiritualities that connect man with the unseen worlds, has perpetuated himself as a power in the human system."

Many images even in Shakespeare are open to criticism on the score of propriety and good taste. Lord Kames, in the work referred to, has the hardihood to take the great poet to task on this score.

The writers of the Augustan Age in English literature, especially its minor writers, were possessed of a mania for the " noble " image and suffered from an inability to call a spade a spade. " Common " and " vulgar " objects, if mentioned at all, had to be draped in courteous circumlocution. A similar fashion prevailed among French writers of the late seventeenth and early eighteenth century such as Delille.

The fault of affectation and far-fetched preciosity could be abundantly illustrated first from the writings of the school of Euphues and then from the poetry of the " metaphysical " school, Abraham Cowley, and his fellows. Molière laughed at the fashion in his *Précieuses Ridicules*. "Mais, de grâce, monsieur, ne soyez pas inexorable à ce fauteuil qui vous tend les bras, il y a un quart d'heure ; contentez un peu l'envie qu'il a de vous embrasser."

A figure of speech ought not to be introduced for its own sake but for the sake of the thought or the emotion which it helps to express. To sacrifice the thought to the figure is to abuse the latter. As regards metaphor in particular it is a fault of taste to work it out in all its bearings, as is done in the example cited from James Russell Lowell. It ought not to be forgotten that the object of metaphor is to suggest to the mind a possible comparison, not to make a formal comparison. To quote Gustave Lanson once more, " Le charme s'évanouit si le développement de la métaphore emprisonne l'imagination : il ne faut pas tracer des sentiers, ni planter des jalons et des piquets dans le champs où l'on l'introduit. C'est une porte qu'on lui ouvre sur des espaces illimités dont elle visitera ce qu'elle voudra, selon son humeur paresseuse et vagabonde."[1]

5. Our next principle applies, not to a single isolated image, but to a succession of images. It might be formulated thus : Two wholly different

---

[1] *Principes de Composition et de Style*, p. 202.

objects must not be used to illustrate the same idea in such close juxtaposition that their images become superposed or confounded. The imagination can form only one clear picture at a time. It can pass quite rapidly from one picture to another provided one picture be shut off before the next appears. If on the contrary the pictures appear together or the second obtrudes itself while the mind is looking at the first, then much the same effect is produced on the mind's eye as that produced on the bodily sight by two slides being thrown together on the screen of a magic lantern. A feeling of confusion and bewilderment is produced, and the purpose of the use of imagery thereby defeated. " This is not the time to throw up the sponge when the enemy, already weakened and divided, are on the run to a new defensive position." Are we in the prize-ring or on the battlefield ? Apparently both together. " A real poet losing himself in the *meshes* of a foolish *obsession.*" Are we to see the hapless poet entangled in a net or to think of him as beset by an importunate thought as by a demon ?

Was the hope drunk
Wherein you dressed yourself ? Hath it slept since.

Hope seems to be spoken of as a person and a dress in the same breath. Even Homer sometimes nods and, if examples not a few might be quoted from Shakespeare, little wonder that they abound in lesser writers. Here is one from Corneille:—

Malgré des *feux* si beaux qui *rompent* ma colère.

And one from Père Monsabré:—

" Voilà, messieurs, *un bien gros et bien sombre nuage* sur le ciel de l'Eglise ; Mais rassurez-vous, elle n'en sera pas *écrasée* : on le croit plein de foudres, il n'est que plein de vent, et *il suffit des piqûres d'une sage et froide critique pour le dégonfler.*"

199

APPLICATIONS

We may next quote an example from Elizabeth
Barrett Browning :—

> Then the bitter sea
> Inexorably pushed between us both ;
> And sweeping up the ship with my despair,
> Threw us out as a pasture to the stars.

On this Bain comments thus :—" No Ossianic
juvenile ever perpetrated purer nonsense. What
possible resemblance can there be between a ship
and a pasture ? why and when do stars go out to grass ?
and wherefore, having so gone, they should feed on
ships and young ladies ?—these are questions of
insoluble mystery."

I have noticed the following in a MS by quite
a good writer given to me for revision :—" The
mainspring of his actions never soars above the body."

Sometimes a comic effect is produced by the
position in which an image is placed, as in these
sentences from Sir Leslie Stephen :—" Sir William
Temple, though he seems to have been vigorous and
in spite of gout a brisk walker, was approaching
his grave."   And again, " Even the high-churchmen
have thrown the Flood overboard."

We may add these few further examples :—

> Are we to let the *pendulum* swing back to the old *rut* ? "
> " Le *sabre* qui *gouvernait* (Napoléon 1er) ne *s'inquiétait* guère
> de Calderon et de Schiller."

> " He did not establish a throne surrounded by republican
> institutions, but a republic surrounded by the ghost of
> monarchical institutions."

How to surround a republic by a ghost is a problem
that would have puzzled Euclid.

In the following passage G. K. Chesterton pokes
fun at a mixed metaphor :—

" Mrs. Eddy summarizes the substance of her creed
in the characteristic sentence : ' But in order to enter
into the kingdom, the anchor of Hope must be cast

beyond the veil of matter into the Shekinah into which Jesus has passed before us.' Now, personally, I should prefer to sow the anchor of Hope in the furrows of primeval earth ; or to fill the anchor to the brim with the wine of human passion ; or to urge the anchor of Hope to a gallop with the spurs of moral energy ; or simply to pluck the anchor petal by petal, or spell it out letter by letter. But whatever slightly entangled metaphor we take to express our meaning, the essential difference between Mrs. Eddy's creed and mine is that she anchors in the air while I put the anchor where the groping race of men have generally put it, in the ground."

In the application of this, as of most literary principles, it is possible to be too meticulous, possible also to be too sweeping in condemnation of metaphors which at first sight seem incongruous or mixed. This verse of Malherbe has often been quoted as an instance of mixed metaphor.

> Donc un nouveau labeur à tes armes s'apprête ;
> Prends ta *foudre*, Louis, et va comme un *lion*
> Donner le dernier coup à la *dernière tête*
> De la rébellion.

As to this there is at least room for difference of opinion. M. Gustave Lanson would defend it[1] and thinks that only " chicane de grammairien " prevents us from enjoying it. While another French writer[2] on style holds it up as a typical example of a mixed metaphor. A similar divergency of view is noticeable regarding Shakespeare's phrase " to take arms against a sea of troubles ". It has been defended on the ground that both metaphors are so faded as no longer to evoke an image. The expression merely means " to contend against innumerable troubles ". Possibly. This, however, is a somewhat

---

[1] *Principes de Composition et de Style*, p. 196.
[2] Antoine Albalat, *L'Art d'écrire*, p. 276.

dangerous line of defence, for metaphors that appear not merely faded but dead have an unpleasant fashion of being on a sudden galvanized into momentary life on contact with other seemingly dead metaphors.

It is impossible to *crush* the Government's *aim* to restore the means of living and working freely.

" National military training is the *bedrock* on which alone we hope to *carry through* the great struggles, etc."

" The vogue of the motor car seems destined to help forward the provision of good road-communication, a feature which is sadly in arrear."

" The Geddes report is to be *emasculated* a little in the Cabinet and then *thrown* at the heads of the Electorate."

These expressions appear all the more incongruous because used in cold blood. When the emotions are aroused and the imagination working, as it were, at high pressure as in great poetry, image may follow image in rapid succession, nay one may be grafted on to another without any impression of incongruity or incoherence. To conclude, then, the principle may be expressed in the words of M. Gustave Lanson :

" The incoherence of metaphors jars upon us only when the words expressing them are closely subordinated to one another by relations of grammatical dependence, and it ceases to be objectionable when the metaphors are contained in parallel propositions ; then the mind sees defile before it images the most various, each of which flashes forth for a moment, disappears, and gives place to the next."

6. One more principle may be laid down. It aims at regulating quantity rather than quality. In the use of imagery, as in that of most things, excess is possible and excess is not only a fault against good taste in literary style but a hindrance to imagery in the attainment of its purpose. The business of the

writer is to arouse in the mind of his reader the fullest possible awareness of the idea or of the emotion that he is endeavouring to express. Imagery ought to help the reader not merely to *grasp* the idea that is being conveyed but to *realize* it imaginatively and emotionally. But this realization is very difficult if not impossible when image succeeds image, flash after flash, till the mind is merely dazzled. His mind has but half formed the image when it is gone and another has taken its place. Nay, a piece of writing may be so charged with imagery that its ideas are hidden and overlaid, its argument hard to disentangle.

Lastly there is a certain vulgarity in over-lavishness. The impression is as of a woman over-dressed. It suggests a want of sobriety of temperament, a lack of the sense of measure and propriety, a conscious straining after effect.

The principles I have been endeavouring to set forth apply in the first instance to metaphor, but they may be taken as applying with but little modification, to simile also. Nevertheless, it may be helpful to call attention, after a recent author,[1] to the principal dangers to be guarded against in the use of simile. We may group them under five heads :—

(1) *Artificiality*.—This is the fault of those who use a simile not because it arises naturally from the subject or with a view to illustrating or even adorning the subject, but who drag in similes because they make fine writing or in mere imitation of some imaginative writer. Simile may likewise be accounted artificial if it is obviously the outcome of too conscious art and too deliberate research.

(2) *Floridness*.—Over lavish use, like a dinner all of entrées or dessert, or music all of cloying melodies. Such style soon palls ; there is a sense of

[1] Grenville Kleiser, *Similes and Their Use*, New York, 1925.

surfeit. Professor Kleiser tells us that he has counted over sixty similes in the first six chapters of one of Conrad's earlier novels—the later are more sober. A writer must not forget that the realization of a simile uses up quite a considerable amount of imagining energy, and if his reader is forced through a series of such efforts he will have but little mental energy left for the story itself.

(3) *Falsity.*—A simile may be described as false when it does not genuinely represent the idea it purports to represent. The answer the writer gives to his own question, "What is my thought like?" is a falsehood, however unintentional. Truth is sacrificed to some attractive and brilliant image.

(4) *Obviousness.*—The opposite extreme to the last mentioned. Here the comparison is so true as to be a truism. The trite and obvious simile fails in that which is a principal aim of all figurative speech, which is precisely to turn aside from literal obviousness, so as to lend to speech a certain distinction, intensity, or beauty. Too obvious similes merely lend an air of the commonplace.

(5) *Over-elaborateness.*—That is, over-insistence on a particular simile, straining it to fit the idea at every point, working it out in endless detail. This is but artificiality under another form. Few similes will bear this elaboration without a note of falsity coming in. For *toute comparaison cloche.*

II. TOWARDS PRACTICE

THERE can be no doubt but that a vivid power of imagination is a great gift not only for literary work but for life. People who are ever garnering as they pass through the world a rich treasure of images are storing up priceless resources for expression and many a pleasing (alas! too, many a saddening) object

for brooding memory.[1]   In a former chapter[2] I have
set down some considerations on the general cultural
preparation for literary work. I do not propose
to revert to that subject here. I am at present
concerned with a more specific acquisition, the art
of using imagery. Can it be acquired ? There are
writers about the art of writing who maintain that
it can not, that it is a pure gift, that it is natural to
some minds to picture forth their ideas and emotions
by means of the facts and shows of the outer world,
while to others this power is denied.

Now in the first place one thinks, as we have seen,
by means of images : there can be no thought without
them. There would therefore seem to be in all
minds an inherent power of conceiving images of
some sort. It is not easy to see why this power could
not be used by anybody in the process of oral or
written expression of thought. True, different
individuals may possess the power of vividly conceiving images in very varying degrees. Equally
varying may be their inherent powers of expression.
But can any sufficient reason be put forward for
maintaining that these two faculties cannot be trained,
that the intensity and readiness of their action cannot,
to some extent at least, be increased by rightly directed
exercise ? I cannot but believe that skill in the
whole art of expression and in this department of
it in particular, viz. the use of imagery, may be
acquired, as all the arts are acquired, by education
and practice.[3]

In that belief some forms of exercise or practice
are suggested here. If they do not succeed in

[1] See " Imagery and its Recall ", being chap. iii of *Consider the Child*,
by Mary Eaton, London, 1925.
[2] Pt. I, Chap. V.
[3] " Note," says the author of *Consider the Child*, " that the store
(of images) is obviously acquired, and to a certain extent its richness
depends on the guidance given to children," in the course of their
education.

APPLICATIONS

increasing skill in figurative expression, they may at least increase one's power of appreciating that skill as seen in the great writers. This twofold object has suggested a twofold form of practice.[1]

A. The study and analysis from the point of view of imagery of any good piece of writing. This might be done in two stages :—

(*a*) One might take, say, one of the longer speeches in some play of Shakespeare and in it sift the figurative from the literal. Phrase after phrase should be examined with a view to determining whether it is the literal statement of some fact or idea or a pictorial expression of it, the words and epithets properly belonging to an object or idea of one class being used to make more intelligible or more vivid or more felt some object of a different class.

> O, pardon me thou bleeding piece of earth.

Is Cæsar's body quite literally a piece of earth ?

> Thou art the ruins of the noblest man
> That ever livéd in the tide of time.

"Ruins." Can a dead body be literally spoken of as the ruins of a living man ? And does not "tide" suggest the sea ; unless perhaps the word once had a wider meaning ? And then with "thy wounds . . . which, like dumb mouths, do ope their ruby lips" we have passed wholly into the realm of figure. The practice of such analysis ought to render one, in a sense scarcely intended by the poet,

> ". . . keen through wordy snares to track
> Suggestion to her inmost cell."

(*b*) A further process is to take the figures as we meet them in the books we read and to analyse or

---

[1] Some useful exercises in figures, somewhat on these lines, will be found in Professor Meiklejohn's excellent manual *The Art of Writing English*. See also Huntington, *Elements of English Composition*, Macmillan, 1904, p. 198, Ex. 56. Carpenter, *Exercises in Rhetoric*, Advanced Course, Macmillan, 1901, p. 200, Ex. xiii.

dissect them. Let us take an example already analysed : we speak of "uprooting an error"; to extirpate or eradicate is only the Latin form of the same metaphor (exterminate, i.e. banish from the territory, would be quite a different metaphor). Now here there is first an abstract idea "error" which the metaphor purports to render more concrete and easy to grasp. Secondly, there is a symbol which stands for error and helps to bring it home to us, viz. a weed. It is unexpressed but clearly indicated by the verb used. Now it is plain that error and a weed do not resemble each other in all respects. Error has no leaves, is not green, and so on. But when we speak of uprooting an error there is implied a comparison in some particular point. One might say, "as weeds in the midst of useful plants are out of place and harmful and ought to be got rid of, so when error insinuates itself (notice the snake-metaphor in this word) among wholesome truths it ought to be eliminated (i.e. put across the threshold). Finally, error and the weed are boldly identified and the former spoken of as if it were the latter. This particular metaphor is so commonplace that we are scarcely conscious of its being a figure of speech at all. But in every metaphor there are the four elements that we have mentioned.[1] Let us state them briefly as follows:—

1. An abstract or unfamiliar or otherwise difficult idea.

2. A concrete and usually familiar object.

3. A tacit or implied comparison, as regards some particular point or points, between the first and the second.

4. The identification of the first and second so that language applying properly and literally to the second is used of the first.

[1] Supra p. 48.

APPLICATIONS

In a simile the comparison (No. 3) is explicit and the fourth element is not present. Let this method of analysis be tried with such a figure as Shakespeare's.

> What custom rules in all things should we do't
> The dust on antique time would lie unswept
> And mountainous error be too high unheaped
> For truth to overpeer.

The exercise will not be found an easy one, but the result will repay the effort expended.

Again, taking the figures as one finds them in any piece of literary work, one might criticize them, judging them in the light of the qualities that, as we have seen, such figures should have if they are to fulfil their purpose. It is even useful, as suggested in Fowler's *English Exercises*, to collect the metaphors and similes in a given piece of writing and to classify them according to their sources.

B. The other form of exercise is to attempt original work in the use of figures. I do not expect all readers to agree with me, but I believe that such exercises have a solid value. I suggest the following :—

(*a*) Given the material symbol or image, use it to body forth some idea. This can be done in two stages. First take such common objects as a gate, a sword, a curtain, any metal or material, a ring, the fox, the rat, a hammer, a lamp, a key, mist, dawn, and so on. Try to recollect some common figurative use for these objects—it does not matter for the moment how hackneyed the use may be—an iron will, Kelly's Keys to the classics, the curtain of the future, a golden opportunity, etc., etc. A teacher might at this stage suggest how great writers have actually used these common objects : one needs not to be very well read to think of examples—

> Life's *leaden* metal into *gold* transmute . . .
> And shut the *gates* of mercy on mankind . . .

Two massy *keys* he bore of metals twain
The golden opes, the iron shuts amain . . .
Thy word is a *lamp* unto my feet . . . you are the *salt* of the
    earth . . .

Then endeavour to find new and original figurative
uses for these objects. My experience is that school-
boys do so readily enough. In attempting this one
must first ask oneself what are the characteristic
qualities of the object and then where else are such
qualities to be found ? Else one is working in the
vague.[1]

(*b*) Given the abstract idea find a symbol or image
to bring it nearer home. This is more difficult.
Take common notions such as death, life, peace, truth,
coming sorrow, fame, eloquence, the mind, the memory,
and so on. Begin with comparisons—" death is
like " . . . metaphors will suggest themselves later.
Here again let it be shown what images good writers
have chosen in order to make these too familiar
ideas once more fresh and vivid to their readers.

For Milton "*fame* is the spur that the clear spirit
doth raise ". While James Russell Lowell speaks of
reputation as " but a farthing candle of wavering
and uncertain flame and easily blown out, yet the
light by which the world looks for and finds merit ".
I shall have occasion presently to give many further
examples.

(*c*) I think that the learner in the art of expression
might with profit go somewhat further than this
and write brief essays on the figurative connotations,
implications, uses of such common things as water,
fire, aspects of the weather, and so on. The worlds
of matter and spirit are, as we have seen, marvellously
interlaced.

(*d*) Again one might take familiar metaphors

[1] For further examples see Huntington, *Elements of English Composition*, Macmillan, 1904.

such as life a stage, life a dream, life a pilgrimage or journey, the river of time, etc., and work them out in the form of an allegory somewhat on the lines of Addison's *Fame Machine* or the *Vision of Mirza*, or at least develop the metaphor in a fresh way as Shakespeare does in the case of the first mentioned.

In *Progressive Exercises in English Composition*, by C. E. L. Hammond,[1] the following forms of exercise are given:—

A. Express by means of metaphor the following:

1. He is always boasting.
2. He is getting into debt.
3. He has at last found a good post to suit him.
4. A divided command is dangerous ; one must direct.

And so forth. I am not sure that such sentences, tame in themselves and divorced from all emotional or imaginative connotations, are of the kind that lend themselves to metaphor.

B. Complete by adding a metaphor:—

A —— of hope. No cloud on the political ——.

A —— of doubt. A —— argument.

Without a —— of humour.

Love of money is the —— of all evil, etc.

Neither does this exercise appear to me of much value. Its result could only be to establish in the pupil's memory a number of *clichès* and trite figures that have lost all freshness and suggestiveness.

The most thorough and most systematic set of exercises on figures with which I am acquainted is that contained in Book II of *Model English*,[2] by Francis P. Donnelly, S.J. These exercises form

[1] Oxford : The Clarendon Press, 1924, pt. i, p. 31.
[2] Boston, etc. : Allyn and Bacon, 1919, chap. xi, Developing the Imagination.

portion of a course for the development of the imagination in view of literary expression. A first and very general stage of these exercises is the endeavour to *realize* what one reads in imaginative literature, i.e. to call up in the imagination the concrete pictures and to feel the emotions suggested. The next stage is the definite exercise of expressing abstract statements in concrete form. Here are some examples:—

> 1. The boast of heraldry, the pomp of power,
>   And all that beauty, all that wealth e'er gave,
>   Await alike th' inevitable hour ;
>   The paths of glory lead but to the grave.

Imagine concrete instances for all the abstract terms. Imagine the concrete pomp of a concrete power in Greek history, in Roman history, in your native place.

2. The New Testament parallel for asceticism is " Take up your cross daily ". What are the concrete parallels in the New Testament for perseverance, strength of character, good example, hypocrisy, unity of the Church, necessity of grace, Divine Providence, etc. ?

There follow four or five further skilfully devised exercises with the same end in view.

A third stage is to put the particular for the general, definite details to illustrate vague generalities. For example—

Exercise 1. Proverbs are general truths drawn from particular instances. What particular instances do you imagine for these proverbs ?

> More haste less speed.
> Procrastination is the thief of time.
> Evil communications corrupt good manners.

And so on. Eight or nine other varied exercises follow, models of the effective use of concrete details by Macaulay and other writers being given.

APPLICATIONS

The next step is an exercise in Synecdoche—"Put a significant part for the whole" thus, (1) "It is related that a lost traveller came in sight of a scaffold and cried, 'Now I know I have arrived at civilization.' Someone has said that the civilization of a country may be measured by the amount of soap it uses. A scaffold and soap are parts of civilization humorously suggestive of the whole. What would you imagine as suggestive of education, politeness, gratitude, humility, anger, democracy, autocracy, slavery, want, etc. ?" Model passages chiefly from Macaulay, Meagher, and Phillips, in which some idea is conveyed by means of significant features and characteristic traits are given, and the method is applied to the illustration of other ideas.

Then a series of excellent exercises in simile are provided.

1. Fill out these and other like phrases:—black as ——, red as ——, bitter as ——, still as ——, and so on. Imagine *new* comparisons, not old ones known to everybody.

2. Fill out these expressions with pictures from home, from the street, from business as well as from nature : easy as ——, busy as ——, sure as ——.

6. Imagine new pictures for the following trite comparisons.

7. Enumerate the concrete ideas associated with ——.

In every case excellent models from literature are provided.

Finally there are exercises in the expansion and development of comparisons which bring one to the threshold of allegory and parable.

Exercises of this kind methodically carried out ought to be of great assistance to the student of the art of writing.

But what of those whose literary education is

finished, who have frequent occasion to write and to speak in public but have no time to exercise themselves in the art of expression. To such I make a suggestion with a certain confidence in its soundness though aware that it would shock the literary dilettante. It is to make use, if necessary, of some systematic collection of illustrations, comparisons, similes, etc. Many such have been published. I have before me as I write a large tome containing a reprint of two old works of this kind, viz. *Things New and Old or a Storehouse of Similes, Allegories*, etc., etc., by John Spencer, 1658, and *A Treasury or Storehouse of Similes*, by Robert Cawdray, 1609. Another work not merely old but old-fashioned is *Flowers of Fancy, Exhibited in a Collection of Similes*, by Henry Schultes (London: Longman, Rees, Orme, Brown, and Green, 1829). There is an introduction, lengthy but of little value, the author's idea of a simile being a prosaic comparison of qualities which for the most part are not figuratively but literally like—" this paper is white as snow." His ideals of style are Tillotson and Robertson in prose, Akenside and Cowper in poetry ! His " similes " are arranged in alphabetical order according to the leading word of the phrase—Abhor it like the plague. Abhor his arms more than an aspic's twine or scorpion's clasp— and so on. All kinds of second, third, and fourth rate authors are drawn upon. Yet the book is not wholly without value.

Modern books of a similar type are numerous enough. We may mention here[1] Dr. Elon Foster's *New Cyclopædia of Prose Illustrations*, including metaphors and parables ; *The Cyclopædia of Illustrations for Public Speakers*, by Scott and Stiles (New York: Funk & Wagnalls, 1911) ; *A Dictionary of*

---

[1] Others will be noted in the Chapter on " Illustration in Homiletics ".

Similes, by Frank J. Wilstack (London: Harrap, 1917).

Finally, there is the very recent work already referred to *Similes and Their Use*, by Grenville Kleiser. This collection is in four parts, viz. :—1. Prose Similes, pp. 21–227, arranged alphabetically under the topic illustrated—Absence, Acquaintanceship, Admiration, etc. No references are given. 2. Miscellaneous similes arranged alphabetically according to the first word of the phrase. No references. 3. Poetic similes, arranged as in the first part but with reference to the authors. 4. Bible Similes, with chapter and verse.

CHAPTER III

ILLUSTRATION IN HOMILETICS

I HAVE dealt at some length in Chapter IV, Part I, with the functions of imagery in speech. Its rôle in rhetoric and composition has likewise been discussed. Consequently the application of the ideas already set forth to our present subject calls for but little elaboration.

It is plain that the preacher must in the first place aim at securing the attention of his hearers by arousing their interest. His task in this respect does not appreciably differ from that of other writers and speakers. It is in the nature of his subject-matter and in the object at which he aims that he differs from certain classes of writers and of speakers. His subject-matter, his theme or message, belongs to the supernatural world. His aim is to produce some definite effect not only upon the minds of his hearers but upon their wills. The former point is evident enough : there can be no true preaching that does not at least imply the supernatural. It is scarcely less evident that the preacher, as distinct from the lecturer, ever seeks to work upon the will. The dogmatic and even the controversial sermon aims at producing religious conviction, assent to revealed truths, faith. Now in faith, according to all schools of Christian thought, not the intellect only but the will is involved. As Saint Augustine said : " A man may enter the church unwillingly, he may draw near to the altar unwillingly, he may receive the sacraments unwillingly, he cannot believe unless willingly." [1] Still more obviously is the moral

[1] Tract 26 in Ioann., n. 2.

and hortatory sermon directed to producing some definite effect upon the will.

This being so, it is clear that the functions of metaphor which have been described in a former chapter find full play in Christian preaching. The intellectual function of imagery, viz. its rôle in rendering remote, unfamiliar, abstract truth concrete, real, vivid, graspable by the average mind, is peculiarly useful when as ever in preaching the theme is drawn from the sphere of the spiritual. Its emotional function is of much avail to add momentum to the impulse imparted to the will by intellectual conviction. Nay, the will may be wrought upon even in the absence of any very clear or definite grasp of truth. Even the æsthetic functions of metaphor have their use, though it be a use not unfraught with danger. Colour, vividness, freshness, are qualities that help to arouse interest in hearers no less than in readers. They create a favourable atmosphere for the acceptance of the message : they prepare the soil for the reception of the seed.[1] This is, of course, true not merely of metaphor and its kindred imagery, but of all forms of illustration—anecdote, parable, quotation, parallel. Such illustration is all the more necessary where the theme is an oft-told tale, in itself devoid of freshness and novelty.

We may reach the same conclusions regarding the importance of imagery to the preacher from historical study of the men who, in the sphere of religious oratory, have wrought positive and marked effects upon minds and lives. Those mighty preachers, the prophets of Israel, are richer in imagery than all the other writers of the Old

[1] " There is a natural delight which the mind has in this manner of teaching, appealing as it does not to the understanding only but to the feelings, to the imagination, in short to the whole man—calling the whole man with all his power and faculties into pleasurable activity." R. Chenevix Trench, D.D.

Testament, excepting, perhaps, the author of the Book of Job. A sixteenth century author[1] thus expresses the matter in a style that is quaint to us to-day :

" That the holy prophets were not only most exactly seen (skilled) in the peerless skill of divinity, but most exquisitely also furnished with the entire knowledge of all things natural, and not ignorant of any kind of learning or discipline may be sufficiently proved and manifestly gathered for that in their writings they use many similitudes, and make so many comparisons of things, fetched off, and from the very secrets and bowels of nature—as, namely, from wild and tame beasts, fowls, worms, creeping and swimming creatures, herbs, trees, the elements, rivers, brooks, wells, cisterns, seas, stars, pearls, stones, lightning, thunder, rain, dew, heat, drought, cold, winds, blasts, hail, snow, frost, ice, corn, seed, salt, leaven, nets, snares ; and likewise from the humours in a man's body—as blood ; women in travail, milk, dross, iron, gold, silver, and innumerable other things wherein they learnedly beautify their matter, and, as it were, bravely garnish and deck out their terms, words, and sentences with trophies (? tropes) and figurative phrases, metaphors, parables, comparisons, examples, shows, and other ornaments of speech, giving thereby unto their matter a certain kind of lively gesture, and so consequently attiring it with light, perspicuity, easiness, estimation, and dignity, stirring up thereby men's drowsy minds, and awaking slothful, negligent, careless, sluggish, and reckless people to the consideration and acknowledgment of the truth, and to the following and embracing of virtue and godliness."

In a later portion of this work I hope to show that

---

[1] Robert Cawdray, *A Treasury or Storehouse of Similes*, London, 1609. The passage occurs in the Epistle Dedicatory.

He who was and is the great Teacher of Mankind, the Preacher upon whom all Christian preachers must ever model themselves, delivered His message in great part through the medium of imagery. The sermon by the lakeside recorded by three evangelists is a series of parables. The Sermon on the Mount is figurative throughout—the disciples were the salt of the earth—but of what use is salt if it lose its taste. They were the light of the world—but men do not light a candle and put it under a barrel or under a bed. A village may be hidden in a valley, but a city built on a mountain top is conspicuous to all. It avails but little to hoard treasure that may perish by rust and the moth or may be stolen from its possessor. They must trust Him who feeds the birds of the air and clothes the lilies in the fields. They must not judge harshly, seeing the mote in a brother's eye but not the beam in their own. They must not throw pearls to the pigs. They may well pray with all confidence to a heavenly Father for He will not give them a stone instead of bread nor a serpent instead of fish. If they are to get into Heaven they must walk a narrow path and enter a narrow gate. They are to beware of teachers who masquerade as sheep but in truth are ravening wolves. Grapes cannot be gathered from thorn bushes nor figs from thistles. If they would build their house firmly, its foundations must be laid not upon the shifting sands but upon the solid rock. That is the manner of preaching of the Great Preacher.

It is very much to be noted that our divine Lord's illustrations were drawn from ordinary human life, and lay within the familiar experiences of His hearers. He spoke to peasants and so we find reference to sowing wheat and to the circumstances that favour or hinder its growth, to harvesting, winnowing, storing in barns, to the management of fig-trees and vineyards, and to bottling the wine. He spoke to house-holders and so we find reference to building houses, to the duties of servants, to leavening and baking bread, to sweeping and cleaning, to dogs lying under the table, to patching clothes, and lighting lamps. He spoke to fishermen, and so there is mention of boats and nets and fish. He spoke to common men and women of the common experience of life—marriage and childbirth, trade and the market place, rich men and beggars, debtors and creditors, children at play, prodigal sons. And with these simple images he brought the sublimest truths home to the hearts of men.

The points barely indicated above will be more fully dwelt upon when we come to deal with the subject of parable and allegory. Meantime I would refer the reader to a work by the Abbé Louis Picard[1] in which a fine study of Christ as preacher will be found. One remark may be quoted here :—" En général le peuple est un enfant. Il faut surtout lui parler en images. C'est pourquoi Jésus *image sa pensée.*" However that may be, it is certain that untrained minds are as little capable of sustained reasoning as children. Principles, general notions, abstractions, arguments often tell little with them. Persons and concrete objects seldom fail of their appeal. And so Christ said :—Consider the *lilies of the field* . . . *Solomon* in all his glory. . . .

From the few sermons of St. Paul that are sketched in outline in the Acts of the Apostles we cannot adequately judge his manner of preaching, but there can be little room for doubt that his discourses were at least as figurative as we know his letters to be.

The Great Christian preachers of the first centuries, Origen, Gregory Nazianzen, Basil, Chrysostom among the Greeks, Tertullian, Jerome, Ambrose,

[1] *La Transcendance de Jésus-Christ,* i, 383 seqq., Paris, 1905.

APPLICATIONS

Augustine, Cyprian, Gregory, among the Latins, all draw largely upon the world of imagery. Much of this imagery is derivative, drawn from Scripture, rather than original ; but a careful analysis of their style reveals a varying proportion of images that are freshly coined. We shall have occasion, when dealing with imagery in literature, to point to works in which the great preachers of the early Church are studied from the rhetorical point of view, and to indicate the findings of these studies.

I am not here attempting a history, even in the barest outline, of Christian preaching, but merely adducing instances of the value, as evidenced both by their precept and their practice, which Christian preachers of various periods have set upon the use of imagery.

A sample of popular mediaeval preaching is given us in a curious book, *The Metaphors of Brother Bozon*,[1] a translation into English of an old unpublished Norman French MS. preserved in the Library of the Honourable Society of Gray's Inns. It was written by a Franciscan Friar of the fourteenth century. The book consists of a series of short paragraphs in which some moral or religious truth is brought home to the people by means of allegories, parables, fables, quaint examples from Pliny's Natural History or from various mediaeval works such as *Le Bestiaire* of Guillaume le Clerc, Isidore's Etymology, the *Gesta Romanorum*, Bartholomew de Glanville's *De Proprietatibus Rerum*, the lesson being driven home by texts of Scripture. It is so full of good things that the choice of an example is difficult. Perhaps the following will serve as well as another :—

[1] London, 1913. An excellent edition of this work was brought out in 1889 by the " Société des Anciens Textes Français " under the title *Les contes moralisés de Nicole Bozon Frère Mineur*.

" Pliny, the philosopher, tells us in his book that the lion by nature bears hatred towards the ass, not deservedly, but through the desire which he has to eat the ass's flesh. So it is with rich men : they find cases against the poor, not at all because these have deserved ill, but because the rich want their goods. Wherefore says the Son of Sirach, ' As the wild ass is the lion's prey in the wilderness, so the rich eat up the poor' (Ecclus. xiii, 19). It is found in a fable that the lion made oath that he would not eat flesh all Lent if a beast did not give him too great cause to break his fast by committing an offence that deserved death ; soon he was hungry and had a mind to eat flesh. He turned to the right and saw a goat, and said to him, ' What do you think of my breath ?' ' It stinks vilely,' said the other. ' Forsooth,' said he, ' you have slandered me.' He assembled the court, and prayed judgment from the bailiff of the estate against him who had slandered him. To compensate him the goat was doomed to death. Another day he was hungry and met a foal. ' Sire,' said he, ' your breath is of sweeter scent than myrrh or cinnamon.' Said the other, ' Thou hast basely mocked me : all know that thou.hast lied. Therefore I shall feed on thy flesh by award of the court.' Next he met an ape in the way and put him the same question. The ape was silent and said nothing. ' What,' said he, ' do you disdain to talk to me ?' By judgment of the court he was sentenced to death. So it is with great lords ; they will never fail for lack of cause to fine the poor. Wherefore says the Bible, ' The rich man hath done wrong, and yet he threateneth withal ' (Ecclesiasticus xiii, 4)."

Elsewhere the Devil is a huntsman who hunts the hare (the soul) into his nets and snares by means of his four couple of hounds (various vices and evil passions)—Riches and Wilemyn, Havegyf and Bandewyn, Tristewel and Gloffyn, Beauviz and Trebelyn. " There is not," say the editors of the French version, " in all Anglo-Norman literature a second work which can give us such a complete idea of what popular preaching was in England and at the beginning of the fourteenth century." May we add that preachers of to-day might take from it many an excellent hint for their own sermons.

Coming to more modern times we may cite as

examples of a masterly use of imagery such great popular preachers as St. Francis de Sales, St. Leonard of Port Maurice, the Italian Jesuit Segneri, the French Oratorian Lejeune, and the Curé of Ars, St. John Baptist Vianney. Bossuet, in whose sermons the eloquence of the pulpit reaches its highest level, is also perhaps the greatest master of imagery at once elevated and restrained.

" Etudiez," says Gustave Lanson, " l'incomparable style de Bossuet. . . . Vous y verrez la métaphore brusque ou préparée, suivie on abandonnée. . . . lâchée dès qu'elle ne serait plus qu'une curiosité ou un obstacle, avec une souplesse et une fortune merveilleuses."

Among great pulpit orators of other Christian communions we may perhaps make special mention in this connexion of Liddon, Alexander MacLaren,[1] Henry Ward Beecher,[2] and Spurgeon,[3] as masters of the art of illustration.

Indeed, it may be said that at the present day the pulpit is the last refuge of eloquence. Political oratory, its rival in the past, is now exercised in such conditions that eloquence is at a discount, except in moments of great national crisis. Consequently, as Professor John Earle points out, " it is in the Sermon, perhaps more than in any other form of literature that we may find specimens of the figured

[1] There has been published a book entitled *Pictures and Emblems*, edited by James H. Martyn (London, 1885), which consists of a thousand illustrations (for the most part imagery) from Dr. MacLaren's sermons.

[2] " That greatest master of illustration with which [*sic*] God has yet blessed His Church." R. A. Bertram, *Parable or Divine Poesy*, London, F. Pitman, 1886. Preface. Mr. Beecher published a book entitled *Five Hundred and Ninety-five Pulpit Pungencies*, New York, 1866.

[3] One class of illustration much used by him is represented in his book *The Salt-cellars*, 1889, a collection of proverbs together with homely and often lively notes thereon. *Feathers for Arrows* or illustrations for preachers and teachers, New York, 1883, is a similar collection by the same writer.

diction which is requisite to form the highest order of prose. . . . Only in the pulpit (or in the study behind the pulpit) is there breathing time for the deliberate expansion of figurative illustration." [1]

The use of imagery, indeed of illustration in general, is a subject which, I venture to think, is not allotted its due importance in treatises on sacred oratory. It would be easy to name well-known and widely used manuals in which it is almost entirely ignored. Yet great preachers have insisted on it, not by their practice only but by their teaching. " Les similitudes," wrote St. Francis de Sales, " ont une efficace incroyable à bien esclairer l'entendement et à esclairer la volonté. On les tire des actions humaines, des histoires neturelles, des herbes, des animaux . . . et enfin de tout." " Not only," says Mgr. Dupanloup, " must we speak to them by ideas and sentiments, but we must employ images, stories, experiences, familiar comparisons drawn from things that they know, that they see, and that they do every day ; as our Lord Himself did. Otherwise they do not understand, they do not listen." [2] It would be easy to multiply such quotations but to do so would, I feel, be breaking in an open door.

I have in a previous chapter set down some considerations as to the manner in which a certain readiness and power in the use of imagery may be acquired. They apply no less to the preacher's than to the writer's preparation for their respective tasks. But in the present connexion it may be well to deal with this further point, whether, in default of such educative processes as have been indicated, any resource yet remains to the preacher. I consider that such a resource does exist and may well be drawn upon, though opinions may differ as to its value.

[1] *English Prose*, p. 236.
[2] *The Ministry of Preaching*, tr. Eales, p. 26.

APPLICATIONS

This resource consists of collections of illustrative matter. There are those who would debar the preacher from drawing on any such stores. Dr. John Watson humorously suggested that the Protestant Church should have an *Index Expurgatorius* wherein should be included in the first place *The Garland of Quotations, The Reservoir of Illustrations,* and the like. Dr. Henry Ward Beecher was of quite an opposite opinion. It is certain that, ignorantly used, such books would be a bane and not a benefit. But there are men of learning, of zeal, and of high moral value, but deficient in those qualities of imagination and of observation that are needed for the discovery and use of vivid and apt illustration. Why should not these supplement their natural poverty with the riches garnered by others ? " Books of illustrative material," says a recent writer on this subject, " similes, metaphors, allegories, parables, fables, stories, experiences, portrait galleries of saints and heroes . . . natural phenomena, natural history or science, literature, or art or history or trades or professions or the mechanical arts—why may he not, if they really help him to clarity of demonstration or to the stimulation of interest use them with a quiet conscience ? " Why, indeed ?

It may, therefore, be helpful to set down here the titles of a certain number of works of this kind :—

The New Handbook of Illustration (London : Eliot Stock), a classified treasury of themes, analogies, parables, similitudes, types, emblems, symbols, apologues, allegories, etc., arranged for ready reference.

A Dictionary of Similes, by Frank J. Wilstack (London : Harrap, 1917) ; a substantial volume of 490 pp. in which the similes, the majority of which are taken from published literature, are given in alphabetical order according to some leading word. There is an index of Authors. The book contains fifteen thousand similes. A much older book, now hard to obtain, is *Things New and Old, or a Storehouse of Similes,* by

ILLUSTRATION IN HOMILETICS

John Spencer. The first edition appeared in 1658, but there have been several since that date. It was reprinted in 1867 by Dickinson, London.

Parable, or Divine Poesy, by A. R. Bertram (London : 1866) ; illustrations in theology and morals selected from great divines and systematically arranged." The matter is arranged alphabetically (adversity, affliction, ambition, etc.), and there is an index of authors, subjects, and texts. The authors most drawn upon are Thomas Adams, Henry Ward Beecher, William Gurnall, John Downame, Jeremy Taylor, and Richard Sibbes.

Fifteen Hundred Facts and Similes for Sermons and Addresses, by J. F. B. Tinling (London : Hodder and Stoughton, 1897, 1908, etc.) ; *Eastern Proverbs and Emblems Illustrating Old Truths*, by Rev. J. Long (Boston : 1881) ; *The World of Parable and Proverb*, with illustrations from history, biography, etc., by Rev. J. Paxton Hood (1885).

Cyclopædia of Illustrations of Moral and Religious Truth, by John Bate (London : Jarrolds), includes, amid a vast mass of miscellaneous illustrations, many analogies, metaphors, similes, and emblems.

SOME FURTHER REFERENCES

The Power of Illustration, an Element of Success in Preaching and Teaching, by John Dowling (New York : 1858).

The Art of Illustration, by C. H. Spurgeon (New York : 1894).

The Art of Illustration, illustrated by John Edwards (London : Robert Culley, 1909).

Deals with the subject historically ; preachers of the early Church, mediaeval preachers, reformers, classic preachers of the English Church, Puritans, modern preachers ; modern Catholic preachers are omitted.

The Art of Sermon Illustration, by Harry Jeffs (London : Clarke, 1909).

Teaching by Illustration, by J. W. W. Moeram (1914).

Examples of San Bernardino of Silena, chosen by Ada Harrison (London : Gerald Howe), 1926.

CHAPTER IV

Metaphor and Logic

In treatises on Logic metaphor is wont to be severely handled. Logicians for the most part regard it as a foe and will have none of it. To them it is merely a popular method of false or at all events weak reasoning, a prolific source of fallacies. "The use of metaphorical language," says Welton, is a frequent source of false analogies."[1] "At present," writes Professor Alfred Sidgwick, "the words are few where metaphor is wholly absent and under metaphor wherever employed some danger lurks."[2] Similar expressions might be culled from almost any treatise on Logic. Writers on literary subjects are, when they think of Logic, almost equally mistrustful. Taine says of Shakespeare's images, that they dim with their brilliancy the pure light of logic. Another French writer, M. Gustave Lanson warns us that in expression emotion and imagination may easily outrun reason. "When this happens figures may hinder accuracy and clearness of thought. One may easily be duped by one's own metaphors, unaware that what one has been expressing are merely impressions ungraspable by the mind and untranslatable into the language of pure ideas, that, in a word, nothing reasonable, scientific, or practical has been said."[3] M. Darmesteter, another Frenchman, despite his Teutonic surname, sets down as one of the principal causes of the alleged obscurity of German philosophy the too metaphorical character of its language. He instances such picturesque terms as " Anschauung ",

[1] *Manual of Logic*, London, 1905, vol. ii, p. 268.
[2] *Fallacies*, London, 1883, p. 265.
[3] *Principes de Composition et de Style*, Paris, 1897, p. 214.

226

METAPHOR AND LOGIC

" Empfindung ", " Vorstellung ", " Begriff ", as contrasted with naked abstract terms such as intuition, perception, representation, idea.   The German words are metaphorical terms which produce various sensations in various readers : the French (and English) words accurately representing pure abstractions.   In the one case you have subjective and personal impressions, in the other, ideas.   For this precision French philosophical terminology is, he thinks, indebted to the Latin of the Schoolmen, the terms of which are almost all abstract " et ne donnent pas prise à ces trahisons qu'entraînment les expressions métaphoriques." [1]

Curiously enough M. Darmesteter has himself been betrayed by these treacherous metaphors.   On the first appearance of *La Vie des Mots* M. Michel Bréal pointed out that its very title is a metaphor and quite a treacherous one.   To say that words are born, live, and die—what is that but metaphor pure and simple ?   To speak of the life of language, to call languages living organisms is to use imagery which may indeed help us to understand things better, but which if taken literally would transport us into dreamland." [2]   Elsewhere he inveighs against the application to language of the term " organism ", a misleading, meaningless word much bandied about nowadays and used every time a writer shirks inquiry into the true causes. . . . To speak even in figure, of language as an organism is to obscure things, to sow a seed of error in the mind." [3]   I cull another example as cited by G. K. Chesterton.   " He (Rostand) suffers from a strange blunder which supposes that what is clear must be shallow.   It is chiefly founded on false figures of speech ; and is akin to the mysteriously

---

[1] *La Vie des Mots*, pp. 71–2.
[2] *Essai de Sémantique*, 5e éd., Paris, 1921, p. 280.
[3] Op. cit., p. 255.

meaningless saying that still waters run deep. It is repeated without the least reference to the evident fact that the stillest of all waters do not run at all. They lie about in puddles which are none the less shallow because they are covered with scum. Such were the North German philosophies fashionable at the end of the nineteenth century ; men believed in the puddle's profundity merely because of its opacity." Finally we have a recent English writer referring to metaphor as " a gravely illogical form of expression " on the ground that it is a product of emotion, warms the heart, and is incompatible with " the chill that settles on the mind along with the process of reasoning and logical statement ".[1]

We have already [2] shown at some length that of its nature metaphor has a tendency to obscure thought, though it by no means necessarily does so. This tendency to veil ideas rather than lay bare or explain them, to give rise to a vague impression rather than to a clear concept, is apparent even in ordinary speech and writing. We might expect it to be still more so when there is question of accurate scientific statement. But it should be remembered that, ordinarily speaking, metaphysics, logic, and science do not constitute the proper sphere of metaphor. It is rhetorical and poetical rather than philosophical. Yet we may with profit study it from the standpoint of Logic, for it is constantly being made to play a part in reasoning processes.

In order to ascertain the precise standing, as it were, of metaphor in the science of reasoning, we must return to the study of analogy. In a former chapter I endeavoured to show that metaphor is a form of analogy. It will now be necessary to point out more accurately the relations between the two.

[1] J. G. Jennings, *Metaphor in Poetry.*
[2] pp. 49 seq. supra.

METAPHOR AND LOGIC

What is analogy? Many writers are content to say that it is something midway between complete identity and complete diversity. You call a horse an animal and a dog an animal—the term animal is said to be used univocally as applied to each, i.e. its meaning is one and the same as applied to the one and the other. The same word " league " is used to describe on the one hand a measure of distance and on the other a bond or alliance, though there is no resemblance between these two objects. The term league is said to be applied equivocally to the two. Here we enter the region of puns and *double entendre*. Thirdly, you speak of a person's bodily constitution, of a certain climate, of certain food, and of somebody's complexion as " healthy ". The three last-named objects are certainly not healthy in precisely the same sense as the body is said to be healthy. Nor, on the other hand, does the word healthy when applied to these objects mean something entirely different in each case. It is neither univocal nor equivocal but analogous.[1] This, however, does not take us very far. We have yet to distinguish various forms of analogy before we can get an accurate idea of its nature.

The example given above may serve as a sample of the first form of analogy. It has been well termed analogy of extrinsic attribution. For health is not something intrinsic to colour, food, and climate. It is attributed to them merely because of their outward relations to the health of the body as its causes or results. This sort of analogy does not concern us at the moment. Indeed, in modern parlance it would be described rather as *transferred epithet* than as analogy.

The second form is the analogy of intrinsic attribu-

[1] *The Science of Logic.* By the Rev. P. Coffey, Ph.D., Maynooth. Longmans, 1918. Vol. i, p. 43.

tion. An example commonly given is the term " life "
as applied respectively to plants, animals, man,
and God Himself. Life is attributed to each of
these because of something that each is intrinsically,
but life in each case means something different from
what it means in the rest.[1] This distinction between
analogy of extrinsic and intrinsic attribution is no
doubt useful for philosophical and theological discussion, but I doubt if, in modern speech, it be correct
to say that a plant may be described as living only by
analogy with the life of human beings or with the
perfect life of God. Be this as it may, the basis of
this species of analogy is the resemblance of several
objects in some attribute or quality intrinsic to each
but possessed by them in varying measures or even
senses.

In the third form of analogy objects are said to be
analogous not because they possess the same quality
in differing measures, but because they each bear
to some other object a similar relation.   Thus God may
be said to bear the same relation to His personality
as man does to his, though the two objects described
as personality differ profoundly.   This may be
described as analogy of proportion. Analogy is
here used in the sense originally given to the word
ἀναλογία by Aristotle,[2] a sense which it still bears
in modern usage.   The term was first used of mathematical proportion, the equality of two quantitative
ratios expressible thus $2 : 6 :: 5 : 10$ or $\dfrac{A}{B} = \dfrac{C}{D}$.   It
was then extended to qualities, but did not wholly
lose its connotation of measure, for qualities are
capable of varying degrees of intensity.   The term
was further extended so as to include any " resemblance

[1] Bittremieux, *De Analogica nostra Cognitione et Prædicatione Dei*,
Louvain, 1913, p. 11.
[2] *Nicomachean Ethics*, Bk. v, 3 (8).

of relations " which is Whately's definition of analogy.
It may be expressed by the general formula $a: b :: x : y$,
the symbol $::$ standing for a resemblance which may
vary in degree from a mere likeness in a single point,
to practical identity.   The object a and the object x
are said to be analogous because they have relations
that are identical or similar to b and y respectively.
The similarity between a and x may end there: they
may be unlike in outward form and even in inner
nature—they are analogous if they stand in like
relations to certain other objects.   A stock example
is the analogy between the mind and the bodily sight
expressible thus:—

$$\nu o \upsilon \varsigma : \psi \upsilon \chi \acute{\eta} :: \ \breve{o} \psi \iota \varsigma : \sigma \tilde{\omega} \mu a.$$

Now it is plain that either of two cases may present
themselves.   The objects x, y may belong to the same
sphere of being as a, b, or they may belong to a different
sphere.   In the former case you have a real and literal
analogy of proportion between $a : b$ and $x : y$.   In the
latter case you have, as we have already seen [1] what
is in reality a proportion of proportions, an analogy
for which another name is metaphor.[2]   That not every
analogy of proportion is metaphorical will be evident
from examples given in discussing the nature of
metaphor.[3]   They are drawn from such exact sciences
as mathematics, physics, and biology, and might be
multiplied indefinitely.[4]

II

Such being the nature of analogy we next inquire
what is meant by analogical reasoning or reasoning

[1] Supra, p. 50.
[2] " Metaphors are simply analogies of this kind compressed into
a single word or phrase."   Coffey, ii, p. 161.
[3] Supra, p. 71.
[4] Debaisieux, *Analogie et Symbolisme*, Paris, 1921, p. 28.   Minto,
Logic Deductive and Inductive, p. 367.   I find it impossible to accept
Sidgwick's statement that " the difference between analogy and
metaphor is a gradual difference depending on the degree of explicitness merely."   *Fallacies*, p. 198, footnote.

by analogy. It would seem that the term is used by present day writers on Logic in two distinct senses. According to one use of the term analogy is understood in the sense just described, viz., as an equality or resemblance of relations. If we prove or assume that $a : b :: x : y$, then we may proceed to argue that a is c and that therefore x must be c. Or, more fully, a is related to b as x is to y. Now from the relation of a to b the consequence c follows. Therefore c will also follow from the relation of x to y. For example "it might be said that the relation of his patients to a doctor is the same as that of his customers to a tradesman, and that therefore as a customer is at liberty to deal at once with rival tradesmen, so a man may put himself at once in the hands of several doctors ".[1]

Before considering the validity of this form of reasoning mention may be made of the other sense in which the term analogy is used. Nowadays it is commonly taken to mean a resemblance of any sort and an argument from analogy is an inference based on such resemblance. Mill has stated it plainly thus. "Two things resemble each other in one or more respects ; a certain proposition is true of one. Therefore it is true of the other."[2] Two individual objects a and b resemble each other in a certain number of points 1, 2, 3, 4. We conclude that a and b resemble each other in point 5 known to belong to a but not known to belong to b. Or more simply, two things agree in many respects, therefore in this other.[3] For example, cholera has been proved to be due to a certain known bacillus. Here is some

---

[1] Joseph, op. cit., p. 493.　　[2] *Logic*, iii, chap. xx, § 2.
[3] Coffey, op. cit., ii, p. 153. Joseph, op. cit., p. 496. Veitch, *Institutes of Logic*, p. 465. Minto, *Logic Inductive and Deductive*, chap. x. Would limit the term to " a preponderating resemblance between two things such as to warrant us inferring that the resemblance extends further."

other disease which is seen to present many symptoms similar to those of cholera. Therefore this disease also probably has its origin in the action of some bacillus. We shall not further discuss this acceptation of analogical reasoning as it is merely an extension of the form previously described and does not, it would seem, differ from it essentially.[1]

To revert then to the first mentioned form of analogical reasoning we may ask what is its value. If it is to be valid, if it is to lead to a certain conclusion and amount to proof, we must ascertain two things : (1) Are the two relations $a : b$ and $x : y$ really identical, in other words does the symbol :: stand for a real equality? (2) Does what we infer from this identity depend entirely on it? Thus, in the example given, we ask, Are the relations between a doctor and his patients really the same as those between a tradesman and his customers? If so, it must be because of the fact that both are paid, and our inference will be in virtue of some such general principle as, Those who employ the services of others for pay are at liberty to employ as many in one service as they pay for? But is this principle universally true? However, even if it be granted that the relations $a : b$ and $x : y$ are not in all respects the same, what we infer from them might still be true if they were the same in the particular respects that affect our inference. But are they? And does the consequence (c) that we draw follow solely from the resemblance of these relations? " We may say that two relations are similar and yet doubt whether they are similar in the way that would justify the inference." [2] It is plain that this method of reasoning, though possibly fruitful up to a certain point, is treacherous if

[1] Coffey, loc. cit., p. 161. " Between this ' Aristotelean ' analogy and analogy in the modern sense there is no essential difference."
[2] Joseph, op. cit., p. 494.

relied upon without close scrutiny and if pushed too far.

If this be so in cases where the analogy is literal, involving a likeness of relations between two pairs of objects belonging to the same sphere of being, much more will it be so in cases where the analogy is metaphorical, involving relations between objects drawn from different spheres of being.[1] Thus if we establish the analogy, A mother-country is to colonies as parent to child, we must first recognise that mother-country (a nation or state) and parent (an individual human being) belong to different orders and that we are dealing with metaphor. May we infer that the reciprocal rights and duties of colony and mother-country are the same as those of parent and child ? Only if we can persuade ourselves that the two pairs of relations are in all respects the same. That they have a certain resemblance may be granted. But are they so much alike that everything true of the one must be true of the other ? Only a popular orator in the heat of the moment would maintain such a proposition, or a partisan journalist with his tongue in his cheek.

Logicians vie with one another in exposing the weakness of arguments from analogy. "We cannot," says Professor Minto, "conclude with any degree of probability from an analogy alone." Sidgwick describes analogical reasoning as "argument from indistinct resemblance". Elsewhere he writes, "The argument from analogy is not so much a mode of

---

[1] The Rev. Richard F. Clarke (*Logic*, Stonyhurst Series, p. 407), defining analogy as "a reasoning from one instance to another similar instance in a different order", says: "If Example is prone to mislead, much more is Analogy. It adds to the weakness of Example the further weakness of transference to another order of things which may be governed by altogether different laws " . . . When we argue from analogy it is not illustration but metaphor that we employ. This is true only if analogy be understood in the sense in which the author had defined it."

attempting proof as a mode of attempting to dispense with the serious labour of proving."[1] The careless thinker is attracted by certain superficial resemblances between two objects or two relations and immediately concludes that the resemblance extends to all particulars or at all events to those from which he wants to draw a conclusion. "Our conclusion from an inference by analogy," says Welton, "can only be more or less probable. Hence there is no proof by analogy, but only a suggestion as to the direction in which proof may be found."[2] The old adage is right : "Comparaison n'est pas raison," unless some perceived analogy be confirmed by experimental verification.

Indeed, as Professor Joseph points out, arguments from analogy can often be found pointing to opposite conclusions. To such arguments it is often a sufficient reply to change the analogy or even to change the metaphor. If it be argued that colonies must ever remain united to their "mother-country", as children to parents, with bonds of subordination and mutual service, one may answer with Alexis de Tocqueville by comparing the colonies to fruit which drops off from the "parent" tree when ripe. In further illustration we may borrow a page from George Eliot.

"It was Mr. Stirlling's favourite metaphor that the classics and geometry constituted that culture of the mind which prepared it for the reception of any subsequent crop. I say nothing against Mr. Stirlling's theory. I only know that it turned out as uncomfortably for Tom Tulliver as if he had been plied with cheese in order to remedy a gastric weakness which prevented him from digesting it."

"It is astonishing what a different result one gets by changing the metaphor. Once call the brain an intellectual stomach, and one's ingenious conception

[1] *Fallacies*, p. 232.
[2] *Manual of Logic*, vol. ii, p. 71. Cf. Lotze, *Logic*, § 214.

of the classics and geometry as ploughs and harrows seems to settle nothing. But then it is open to someone else to follow great authorities, and call the mind a sheet of white paper or a mirror, in which case one's knowledge of the digestive process becomes quite irrelevant. It was doubtless an ingenious idea to call the camel the ship of the desert, but it would hardly lead one far in training that useful beast. O Aristotle, if you had had the advantage of being ' the freshest modern ' instead of the greatest ancient, would you not have mingled your praise of metaphorical speech as a sign of high intelligence with a lamentation that intelligence so rarely shows itself in speech without metaphor—that we can so seldom declare what a thing is except by saying it is something else."

Elsewhere George Eliot speaks of " the sound thinker in those parts (the borough of Treby Magna) who observed that property was ballast and when once the aptness of that metaphor had been perceived, it followed that a man was not fit to navigate the sea of politics without a great deal of such ballast ".

Any reader of the newspaper press must be aware how many worthless arguments are set before the public in the alluring form of metaphor, how many wholly invalid deductions are drawn from popular images. Let us glance at a few familiar instances. It is common to speak of a country's capital city as its head or its heart. So far so good. The metaphor is not without its significance. But may we proceed to infer that, if the capital becomes very large, similar results will follow to those brought about by the abnormal growth of those two bodily organs ? Smollett in *Humphrey Clinker* says of London : " The capital is become an overgrown monster ; which like a dropsical head, will in time leave the body and extremities without nourishment and support. . . ." Again, what is more common than to attribute personality to a state or nation and then to work out in all its consequences the analogy between nation and person. A man, it is argued, must go through successive periods of growth, maturity and decline, and therefore a nation must do the same. As though the decay of nations were, as it is in man, the inevitable consequence of mere prolongation of life. Burke in his *Letters on a Regicide Peace*[1] thus deals with this false analogy :—

" I am not quite of the mind of those speculators who seem assured that necessarily, and by the constitution of things, all states have the same periods of infancy, manhood, and decrepitude, that are found in the individuals who compose them. Parallels of this sort rather furnish similitudes to illustrate or to adorn, than supply analogies from whence to reason. The objects which are attempted to be forced into an analogy are not found in the same classes of existence. Individuals are physical beings, subject to laws universal and invariable. The immediate cause acting on these laws may be obscure : the general results are subjects of general calculation. But commonwealths are not physical but moral essences. They are artificial combinations, and, in their proximate efficient cause, the arbitrary productions of the human mind. We are not yet acquainted with the laws which necessarily influence the stability of that kind of work made by that kind of agent." Yet in political discussions men will go on talking of the rights and duties of the nation, of its honour, liberty, greatness, its birth and death, as though all that held good of the individual man must also hold good in quite the same sense of the nation. The author of *A Course in Philosophy*[2] carries analogy to extremes. A syllogism for him, is an illustration of the same principle as

---

[1] London, Bell, 1925.
[2] Quoted by *Welton*.

sexual reproduction and "the biological organisms are to the earth as a nervous system is to a biological organism ".

Thus it is not difficult to see the perils of the misuse of metaphor and of the attempt to build arguments upon a metaphorical basis. The astute and the designing may make a skilful use of metaphor to mislead an easily led public. The mind naturally likes to note resemblances, delights in generalizations and simplifications. The unthinking, and these are the majority of men, are content with the crudest generalizations and will readily accept a picture for an argument. Counting on this the mob orator, the none too scrupulous journalist, the popular writer in general, will tacitly assume that such and such a resemblance or analogy is complete in all points and will begin to draw arguments therefrom. All opposing facts or differences are quietly ignored. Moreover the appeal is not really to reason, even unreasonable reason, but rather to passion. " In orations of praise and in invectives," wrote Hobbes, " the fancy is predominant, because the design is not truth, but to honour or dishonour, which is done by noble or vile comparisons," i.e. similes or metaphors. It is the task of the popular orator to enlist emotion on his side, as Antony did so skilfully in presence of Cæsar's corse, to turn reasoned judgments of approval or disapproval into love or hate, enthusiasm or anger. Metaphor, as we have already pointed out, as it is the outcome of emotion, is in its turn a powerful evoker of emotion.

In view of all this we have little difficulty in accepting the conclusion of a recent writer as to the rôle of metaphor in this connexion. " Metaphor is the first tool seized by the eulogist or the detractor. By the black art of metaphor damaging evidence is concealed, an outlook is confined, or the mind extravagantly prejudiced to praise or blame."[1] For a highly trained and cultivated mind the dangers of metaphor are comparatively slight and diminish with the growth of the critical and analytic faculty. " The power of recognizing metaphor as metaphor is one of the latest and highest acquisitions (so far as it is acquired) of mankind ; an outgrowth of the accurate spirit which marks off modern science from the ancient reign of florid imagination."[2]

Must we then banish metaphor remorselessly from the realm of logic ? No : it has a useful though modest and minor part to play there and may be tolerated though under close surveillance.[3] It has in the first place a rôle in logic akin to that which it fulfils in literature generally, viz. as an illustration, a device whereby abstract truths are brought home to the imagination and the heart of us and made to *live* in the mind. In the next place it may claim a modest share in the rôle conceded to analogy even by the logicians. " It is as pointing out the direction in which more rigorous investigations should be prosecuted that considerations of analogy have the highest scientific value. . . . There is no analogy, however faint, that may not be of the utmost value in suggesting experiments or observations which may lead to more positive conclusions."[4] A very different writer, Father Tilman Pesch, S.J.,[5] equally recognizes this rôle of imagery, " As in the method of investigation it is of importance to the inquirer to note the likenesses and differences of things, so, in teaching, the use of comparisons and images is greatly to be commended, for a matter that is somewhat obscure,

---

[1] Henry W. Wells, *Poetic Imagery*, New York, 1924.
[2] Sidgwick, *Fallacies*, p. 265.
[3] Cf. Eucken, *Bilder und Gleichnisse in der Philosophie*, Leipzig, 1880.
[4] *Logic*, iii, chap. xx, 3. Cf. Sidgwick, *Fallacies*, p. 261.
[5] *Institutiones Logicales*, Pars. i, n. 463. Dr. Coffey points out that analogy is by far the most fruitful source of scientific hypothesis (*The Science of Logic*, vol. ii, p. 151).

when likened to another that is known, becomes clearer and is more firmly grasped. Moreover, since in this universe of perceptible and non-perceptible things there is universal cohesion and all things are interconnected in a multitude of ways, from the use of apt comparisons this consequence will follow that the mind of the student will be aroused to exercise its proper activity and to think in many different directions. Thus images and similitudes prepare the way for the discovery of truth."

CHAPTER V

METAPHOR AND THEOLOGY

PERHAPS for theology the principal interest of the study of metaphor arises out of the important rôle which metaphor plays in the inspired records on which theology in its discussions and arguments so continually draws and upon which its conclusions are so largely based. With that aspect of the subject we hope to deal in a subsequent portion of this work, and it shall not be further pursued in the present chapter.

I

Allusion has already been made[1] to the practical necessity of imagery in the formation of concepts of things spiritual and religious and in the expression of such concepts. This necessity is recognized by Christian theology.[2] Not content with ample acknowledgment of it we find St. Thomas insisting upon the helpfulness and desirability of a use of imagery when dealing with the spiritual world. He discusses the question at some length both in the Summa[3] and in his commentary on the Book of Sentences.[4] *Convenientissimum est divina nobis similitudinibus corporalibus designari.* It is most fitting for us to designate things divine by material or physical similitudes—such is the thesis.

---

[1] Pt. I, Chap. II.
[2] St. Thomas says in a general way (Prologue to *Commentary on the First Book of Sentences*, q. 1, art. 5), Oportet modum istius scientiae (i.e. Theology) esse metaphoricum, sive symbolicum vel parabolicum.
[3] Prima Pars., q. 1, art. 9.
[4] In Lib. Sent. I dist. xxxiv, q. 3, a. 1.

APPLICATIONS

His first argument is based on the manner of apprehending truth which is natural to the human mind. We are unable, he argues, to grasp the truth of things divine in the way in which God comprehends them; accordingly we must needs grasp them in the way natural to ourselves. Now it is natural to us to arrive at objects proper to the intellect through objects proper to the senses (a sensibilibus in intelligibilia venire); and therefore objects of the intellect are set before us under the figure of sense-perceptible things, so that the mind may rise from known things to unknown. Such is the purpose of all symbolism, which plays in the world of tangible objects much the same rôle as imagery plays in the world of thought and language.[1] The whole object of the symbolism of worship—liturgy, sacraments, sacred music, sacred art, ought to be to raise the minds of the worshippers into the spiritual world. From physical actions and material objects the mind ascends, in a manner entirely in accord with our human make-up, to those things of the spirit which they remotely shadow forth. Long before St. Thomas this idea had often been dwelt upon by the great Christian writers. The constant presence of figurative language and Anthropomorphism[2] in the Scriptures is no discovery of modern times. It had been observed and commented upon from the earliest Christian times. Thus St. Thomas's arguments are mainly drawn from the early writer now known as Pseudo Dionysius, but long taken to be Denis the Areopagite. St. Cyril of Alexandria[3] writes :—

"If Scripture when speaking of God refers to

---

[1] See *Contra Gentiles*, l. iii, c. cxix.

[2] Anthropomorphism may be described as a species of metaphor whereby we transfer to God what properly belongs to man, attributing to Him, for instance, human limbs, faculties, ways of acting, an underlying comparison being, as in metaphor, always understood.

[3] *Adv. Anthrop.*, c. Ii, Migne, P. G., t. 76, col. 1078–9.

parts and members it speaks according to what our intellect is capable of understanding. For there is for us no other way of understanding things divine, Scripture must speak of God in terms of body because of the poverty of our understanding and speech. The things of God are altogether ineffable ; for it is impossible that we, bound up as we are in material and palpable bodies, could come to understand what it is necessary for us to understand unless by taking by way of example our bodily members and using them to attain some notion of God."

Similarly St. John Damascene[1] :—

" It is fitting for us to be aware how impossible it is for us, wrapped in gross flesh as we are, to understand and express in speech those lofty and immaterial actions of the Godhead unless by availing ourselves of figures and images and signs consonant with our nature."

A second argument of St. Thomas for the usefulness of imagery in theology is drawn from a consideration of God's providential dispositions. " As there are in us," he says, " two cognoscitive faculties, the intellectual and the sensible, divine wisdom has so ordered things that both of them in so far as that is possible should be led to things divine ; and consequently He has employed figures drawn from material objects which can be grasped by our senses, these latter being unable to attain directly intellectual ideas of the divine."

His third argument is that through metaphor and anthropomorphism we come to realize better God's transcendence. He contends that our notions of what God is not are more strictly accurate than our positive notions of what He is. For nothing that we affirm of God is to be understood in the sense in which it would be understood if affirmed of creatures.

[1] *De fide orthod.*, lib. i, c. ix, Migne, P. G., t. 94, col. 842.

Consequently to avoid all delusion that we are capable of describing God accurately in strictly proper terms we do well to use metaphors drawn from the humblest and most material things and thus speak of Him in terms which we are fully aware must not be understood literally. " It is quite fitting to signify divine things by material appearances so that, becoming accustomed to these latter, the human intellect may learn that none of the statements made about God can be made of Him otherwise than according to a certain analogy based on the creature being in a measure an imitation of the Godhead."

For writers of a rationalist or modernist tendency, however, that is by no means the whole of the matter. Not merely would they acknowledge the frequent need of speaking of God in metaphorical terms, they would hold that all our statements about the world of spirit are merely metaphorical or symbolical, anthropomorphism or figure of speech. In the view of Hegel and his school to attribute personality to God is a mere anthropomorphic metaphor, to conceive of God as a person is to think of Him in human form and constitution. Stuart Mill argues in a similar way about God's attribute of goodness. According to Herbert Spencer it is impious to speak of God's wisdom, liberty, personality, for to do so is to attribute to Him mere human characteristics and faculties. Sabatier writes,[1] " Quand l'élément métaphorique a disparu, la notion elle-même s'évanouit en tant que notion positive . . . Ainsi de nos idées générales sur l'objet même de la religion [Dieu]. Quand tout élément métaphorique en est éliminé, elles deviennent simplement négatives, contradictoires, et perdent tout contenu réel." MM. Loisy and Le Roy write in a similar strain. The former accuses theology of retaining an " extremely anthropomorphic " idea

[1] *Esquisse d'une philosophie de la religion*, pp. 394-6.

of God, " quite disconcerting for science and contemporary philosophy." The latter formulates the
dilemma :—" Si cette existence est analogue à la
nôtre, nous voici dans l'anthropomorphisme. Si elle
est transcendante, que signifie-t-elle pour nous?"
Again, speaking of the theological doctrine of divine
revelation, he writes, " Dieu a parlé, dit-on. Que
signifie ' parler' dans ce cas ? A coup sûr, c'est
une métaphore."

To enter fully here into the question of the mode
and extent of man's knowledge of the divine would
be to go beyond the scope of this work. But I shall
be keeping well within its scope in setting forth the
following points :—

(1) Many of our statements about God and the
spiritual world in general are undoubtedly metaphorical
or anthropomorphic.

(2) True concepts may be formed and consequently
true statements may be made about God and the
spiritual world which are neither metaphorical nor
anthropomorphic.

(3) Even metaphorical and anthropomorphic statements are not necessarily false but are capable of
conveying truth.

It would seem scarcely needful to insist in the first
place that the Bible abounds in metaphorical and
anthropomorphic descriptions of God's being and
attributes.[1] It will suffice to recall some examples.
" The Lord thy God is a consuming fire."[2] " God
is light and in Him there is no darkness."[3] The
Church, developing the metaphor, speaks of the
Word proceeding from the Father as *lumen de lumine*.
In the Psalms God is spoken of now as a rock or rock-
fortress, now as a shield, and again as a shepherd,

---

[1] Hujusmodi analogiâ Sacra Scriptura plena est de Deo metaphorice
notitiam tradens. Cardinal Cajetan, *De Nominum Analogia*, p. 16.
[2] Deut. iv, 14 ; Heb. xii, 29.
[3] 1 John i, 5.

a potter, a bridegroom.   The prophets describe Him
as a high tower, a lion, a Shepherd.   The promised
Messiah is described under a variety of figures.
Christ described His own nature and relations with
mankind under many images : He is a Shepherd
and the gate of the sheepfold, a vine, the way, the
light of the world.   His apostles are now light, now
the salt of the earth, now shepherds and anon a
little flock.

The Church, whether in prophecy or on the lips
of Christ or in the writings of the apostles, is presented
to us under a multitude of images.[1]   It is the New
Jerusalem, the vineyard, the Spouse, the Kingdom,
the mystical Body of Christ.   Scripture, too, abounds
in anthropomorphism, which is a species of metaphor.[2]
To the Godhead are attributed bodily organs : eyes,
ears, mouth, hands, feet, etc., and human actions,
walking, breathing, scenting, touching, sitting, and
many others.   God is represented as affected by
emotions such as sorrow, joy, regret, hatred, indigna-
tion.[3]   He deliberates and resolves, remembers and
forgets.

Metaphorical expressions, generally based on some
text of Scripture, are sometimes retained in the
expression of dogmatic truths as when, in the Creed,
Christ is said to " sit at the right hand of God ".

Such expressions have never presented a difficulty
to theology, and in reading or using them a well-
instructed Christian is aware of their figurative nature.
He is also aware that such expressions, not being taken

---

[1] See *L'Eglise : Figures et Métaphores*.   By the Abbé Gaston le Brun,
Brussels, 1921.   Also Kolbe : *The Four Mysteries of the Faith* (London,
1926), ch. xiii–xv.

[2] " Anthropomorphismus nihil aliud est nisi determinata quaedam
species sub genere metaphorae."   Bittremieux, op. cit., p. 238.

[3] An extended list of such anthropomorphisms is given by
Bittremieux, *De Analogica nostra Cognitione et Praedicatione Dei*,
p. 256.

literally, do not falsify any dogmatic truths about the nature of God which form part of his creed. As St. Thomas expresses it, " Radius divinae revelationis non destruitur propter figuras sensibiles quibus circumvelatur . . . sed remanet in sua veritate, ut mentes quibus fit revelatio non permittat in similitudinibus permanere, sed elevat eas ad cognitionem intelligibilium." [1] The average instructed Christian, then, is at least dimly aware that in speaking of God and the supernatural he uses ways of speech which are not literally true and yet express truth.

But writers who for the most part would accept the designation modernist commonly maintain not only that popular religious notions are metaphorical and anthropomorphic but that dogma itself thinks and speaks in metaphor under the impression that it is thinking and speaking literal truth. [2] For these writers all the attributes we make use of in describing the divine nature—goodness, personality, mercy, and the like, are necessarily metaphorical. For the Catholic theologian these attributes are not metaphorical but analogous. That is to say in applying to God an attribute such as wisdom, which is also applied to human beings, the theologian is fully aware that he does so with a difference, yet not with such a difference that the word wisdom when applied to God loses its proper meaning and can only be used in figure. [3] In fact in the real nature of things it is

---

[1] Prima Pars., q. 1, art. 9 ad 2[m]. The passage may be translated thus : " The light of divine revelation is not destroyed because of the sense-perceptible imagery wherein it is veiled . . . but abides in its truth, not allowing the minds to which the revelation is made to stop at the mere similitudes, but raising them to a knowledge of the intellectual ideas they body forth."

[2] This is very much the position taken up by Mr. Guy Kendall in an article entitled " Dogma as Metaphor " in the *Hibbert Journal*, July, 1924.

[3] Chr. Pesch, *Praelectiones Dogmaticae*, ii, n. 103, 104. He says : " When we use certain words in reference to God and to creatures such words are not used *univocally* (with precisely the same sense

only to God that the term wise can be applied in its fullest and highest sense. Men are wise only by analogy with that supernal wisdom. They possess a participated, one might almost say a reflected, wisdom, inasmuch as human nature is an image, an imperfect imitation, of the divine. The mind is capable of conceiving a wisdom, a goodness, a beauty wholly freed from the conditions which limit and trammel them in human nature, and it is such wisdom, goodness, and beauty that Christian theology attributes to God. But such a way of conceiving things has simply no meaning for those who repudiate, not merely the remoter conclusions, but the very foundations, of what we may call Christian philosophy.

Assuming, however, these foundations, the matter may, in untechnical terms, be set forth as follows : Certain notions may be entertained and certain terms used of the divinity which involve imperfection. If these be applied to God unpurged of their imperfection, they can be applied only in figure. Obviously such terms as express what is corporal and material come under this head. Many of them have been noted in a preceding paragraph. Under this head likewise fall expressions that imply in God senses of the body, emotions and passions of the soul. To say that God "repented of what He had done" is merely to speak *humano modo*. Next there come notions and terms the concept of which involves no imperfection. No lack of perfection, for instance, can be found in notions such as being, life, wisdom, goodness. Can we apply such notions to God? Yes, but only

of content) of both, because God, for instance, is wise with an essential wisdom, man with merely ' accidental ' wisdom. Therefore the meaning of the word is not quite the same in the two cases nor can it be defined in the same way as can the word animal, when applied to a horse and to a man. But these words are not used *equivocally*, for creatures are effects and images of God and therefore not wholly unlike Him. Consequently such words are used *analogously*, ' nam analoga sunt quorum essentiae habent similitudinem imperfectam.' "

by analogy.[1]   For, if they involve no imperfection in their concept, the manner in which they exist in human beings is very far from perfect.   In applying them to God we at least implicitly withdraw all limits and imperfections.   Wisdom in God is not an attribute laboriously acquired from intercourse, experience, and books.   Nor is it limited by capacity of brain nor cramped by " this muddy vesture of decay ".   In scholastic terms such perfections are asserted or predicated of God *quoad rem ipsam et ipsam rationem significatam* but not according to the manner in which they exist in us.[2]

Not content with seeing metaphor everywhere in all that may be stated regarding the divine nature, many modern writers imply that all our attempts to express our ideas about the divine are false, misleading, or have at best a pragmatic value as statements determining one's attitude of mind and practical directions for conduct.[3]   In a preceding chapter [4] I have endeavoured to show that truth may be conveyed through the medium of metaphor with all the varying degrees of accuracy that literal statement may convey. In all metaphor there is implied an equation of ratios, and the question simply is : Is this equation justified by the truth of the matter.   To say " God is a consuming fire " is doubtless false if taken literally, but if analysed it is seen to convey an expression of the terrible nature of the divine wrath and of divine chastisement.   The term " lion " when applied to God, says St. Thomas,

---

[1] Pesch, *Praelectiones Dogmaticae*, ii, n. 103.   The *kind of* analogy in this case is termed *analogia attributionis intrinsecae* or *internae* as distinguished from *analogia proportionalitatis* which is the term applied to metaphor.   Thus Suarez, *Metaphysicae Disp.*, xxviii, § 3, n. 11 sq. According to Hontheim, *Theodicaea* (n. 511, 515), analogia proportion- alitatis being practically metaphor, analogia attributionis is practically metonymy.

[2] St. Thomas, *Summa*, 1ª pars., q. xiii, a. 3.   Brittremieux, op. cit., pp. 252–3.

[2] Le Roy, *Dogme et Critique*, p. 133 and passim.

[4] Supra, pp. 70 seq.

means merely that God " similiter se habet ut fortiter operetur in suis operibus sicut leo in suis ". In other words the proportion

God : his works :: lion : his actions

the point of the comparison, permitting of this equation, being the common attribute of energy and power. Similarly St. Augustine, commenting in one of his letters[1] on those verses in the Psalms, " Shew forth thy wonderful mercies ; thou who savest them that trust in thee from them that resist thy right hand. Keep me as the apple of thy eye : protect me under the shadow of thy wings," says " Just as when we read about ' wings ' we understand protection, so when we read of ' hands ' we understand work being done, when we read of ' eyes ' we understand the intellectual vision whereby God knows ; and anything else of this kind recorded in Scripture is to be spiritually understood ". The principle thus expressed by St. John Damascene " per illa quae nobis congruunt ea quae supra nos sunt edocemur ",[2] is surely a simple and obvious one. And in describing things " above us " by things which " nobis congruunt " we frequently use expressions that are metaphorical. Is it because we have no ideas about that which we describe ? Surely not. " Have not," says Mr. Kendall himself, " the profoundest truths been expressed in metaphor ? " " Toute métaphore," says Père de Tonquedec,[3] " implique une idée et le rapport de ressemblance qu'elle énonce est même quelque chose de fort abstraite." Moreover, " l'idée analogique est réellement definissante à sa manière." Thus a person quite unable to define in philosophical terms the personality of God may

[1] Epist. cxlviii, cap. vi, 13.
[2] *De fide orthodoxa*, lib. 1, c. xi.
[3] Etudes, *La notion de Verité dans la philosophie nouvelle*, 1907, tome 112, p. 348.

describe it quite correctly in terms which are analogical or even metaphorical—" a person is a somebody to whom one can speak and who listens, whom one can love, who responds in some way."   That is, there is in God something which corresponds to that which in man makes him somebody to whom one can speak, etc.   It is just that analogy of proportion which, as I have endeavoured to show, underlies all metaphor. To accept Mr. Kendall's illustration, then, the poetic epitaph in Macbeth

After life's fitful fever he sleeps well.

" does not convey less truth, less objective truth, than might be embodied in a bulletin published in a Court Circular to the effect that " His Majesty's temperature is now normal and he passed a restful night with six hours continual sleep ".   " Duncan," continues Mr. Kendall, " had no fever and he was not asleep.   It was ' mere metaphor '."

But it would surely be impossible to maintain the very sweeping thesis of the same writer viz. that " Christian dogma commonly, if not universally, expresses truths in a metaphorical, that is to say poetical, form because in no other form can the profoundest truths about reality and the relation of God to the world and to man be adequately expressed ".   One would be led to suppose that in the opinion of the writer the literal or non-literal character of a given passage of scripture was to be determined on aesthetic (or possibly pragmatic) principles.   " There are those who apparently think," he writes, " that the words of Jesus at the Last Supper were more significant and valuable and true if He was making a statement about the properties of the food before Him than if they bore some purely spiritual meaning metaphorically expressed."   And again, " Let us assume that He was using a metaphor and see if anything is lost by so doing.   No, we have left the most profound and significant suggestion that was ever made in metaphorical language. The doctrine of Transubstantiation is a reduction to mere prose of the poetry of the Eucharist." But the question is one of fact, to be decided upon rational principles of interpretation which we shall later endeavour to set forth. Antecedently to the examination of a text upon these principles it may or may not be true in literal fact that, as Mr. Kendall says, " the voice of the Lord God was literally heard in a real garden by a historical Adam and Eve " or that " an actual song was heard by actual shepherds ". If these and many similar statements in the Bible are to be accepted as poetical and figurative doubtless they would not thereby lose all significance. That is not the question. The question, I repeat, is one of fact. What did the writer actually mean to state ? Once this has been ascertained the question of fact is, for Catholics and indeed for all who believe in the Bible as the word of God, decided.

I think it is permissible to conclude that, viewed in a general way, the use of metaphor in theology presents no real difficulty : all the difficulty lies in the application of general principles to particular cases. That application must in the long run be left to the trained theologian.

II

The problem of the relations between idea and image plays a noteworthy part in the history of Christian dogmatic teaching. The constant use of analogies and figures gives to early theological controversies a peculiar character. And one of the most frequent causes of departure from orthodoxy has at all times been the taking of some metaphorical expression for literal statement of fact or at least the working out of a legitimate metaphor into details which formed no part of the underlying analogy which gave rise to it.

St. John, in order to convey an idea of the nature and the generation of the eternal Son, used a term which was current in Greek philosophy,[1] ὁ λόγος, the Word.[2] It was, of course, a metaphor, but helped the minds of the evangelist's contemporaries to grasp an aspect of the truth. The more, however, that analogy was developed the greater was the risk of deviating from the truth. In expounding and developing the doctrine the theologians had recourse to terms used of Philo's very different Logos, and spoke of λόγος προφορικος and λόγος ἐνδιαθετος. These terms can be applied to the eternal Word, but with restrictions and adaptations. They were partial analogies at best and easily lent themselves to abuse. Heresy used them for its own purposes. The Sabellians seized upon the term ἐνδιαθετος so as to confound together the first and second persons of the Trinity: the Arians used the term προφορικος to diminish the Second Person. In the end it was found necessary to proscribe altogether the use of this particular image.

Again, before the Council of Nicaea, the theologians, in order to bring out the obedience of the Son, used the metaphor whereby the Son is said to be the minister, servant, or executor of the Father's behests. This metaphor expresses a truth and must ever continue to express a truth. It was helpful in combating the Gnostic and Sabellian heresies. But to forget that it is a metaphor and proceed to treat it as literal statement, is to fall into the early heresy known as Subordinationism. The Fathers felt this and were careful to insist that the metaphor must not be pressed.

[1] Not only in Philo, but as early as Heraclitus and in the Stoic and Platonist schools.
[2] In these paragraphs I follow closely Père de la Barre, S.J., in his work *La Vie du Dogme*, Paris, Lethielleux, 1898, p. 195 sqq.

" Itaque," says St. Basil, " quod dicitur mandatum ne sermonem imperiosum per vocalia organa prolatum intelligamus, Filio veluti subdito praescribentem, etc." [1]

Once more, to explain to their contemporaries the stupendous truth of the Incarnation, the early Christian writers called to their aid all the resources of language as men spoke it then. They had recourse to metaphors and similitudes in order to convey some notion of the mystery to minds to which these ideas were new. Their imagery usually took one of two forms. On the one hand they spoke of Christ *assuming* human nature, taking it and making His dwelling in it. His human nature is spoken of as theophoros, God-bearing and the Word is described as sarkophoros, flesh-bearing. On the other hand they speak of the intimate compenetration of the two natures, of their being confused together in a human-divine compound or mixture. Both images are imperfect as indeed all imagery must be which seeks to convey an immaterial idea. Over insistence on one of these images would lead and did lead to Nestorianism, over insistence on the other to the heresy of Eutyches.

But the fact that imagery may be misused by those who allow the image to dominate the idea is no sufficient reason for avoiding altogether the use of imagery. We have seen the useful services it may render in theology as in other spheres of thought. Those powerful and subtle thinkers, Gregory Nazianzen, Irenaeus, Athanasius, Augustine, and the other Doctors of Christianity, clothed their ideas in an imagery suited to their times and the exigencies of the moment. But they seldom allowed their minds to be dominated by the image to the detriment of the great ideas they were striving to express.

[1] *De Spir. Sancto*, n. 20.

METAPHOR AND THEOLOGY

III

In a beautiful and suggestive book,[1] which appeared while the present work was passing through the press, the author, Mgr. Frederick Kolbe, of Capetown, has very amply developed this thought of the usefulness and even need of metaphor in lifting the mind to spiritual truths and mysteries of faith. " Since," he writes, " we have no direct vision of things divine, revelation must be to us of an indirect character : it must come to us by analogy, by simile, by type, by parable, by something or other which shall translate the truth into terms within our capacity." And again, " the mind of man must gradually be led from symbol to reality, from metaphor to mystery." This last phrase expresses the theme of the entire work.

To speak through sign and symbol rather than by explicit utterances has been from the beginning an essential feature of the divine economy of revelation. The average human mind needs much preparation for the reception of any deep truth, and this preparation must be suited to the stage of its development. The binomial theorem or the theory of relativity could not be explained to a mind unprepared for the acceptance of such ideas. Now if intellectual truths require intellectual preparation, far more do divine truths require divine preparation. Things beyond our experience can be explained to us only by analogies, and by their very definition the mysteries of faith are truths outside of human experience.

Dr. Kolbe shows in detail how the ultimate revelation of each of the four cardinal mysteries of Christianity—the Trinity, the Incarnation, the Church, and the Eucharist, was preceded by many an adumbration, was gradually led up to by symbols and analogies,

---

[1] *The Four Mysteries of the Faith,* London, 1926.

255

was embodied in metaphor and parable. Metaphor to mystery—that is the normal process whereby God has chosen to reveal to mankind truths that lay beyond its ken.

In this book, therefore, is set forth far more adequately than has been possible to the present writer in the brief sketch here concluded, the true relation of metaphor to theology.

CHAPTER VI

METAPHOR IN COMMON SPEECH

IT is interesting to take an ordinary piece of very simple prose, a passage say in some school " Reader ", and to examine it word after word with this question in mind : " Is this word capable of use, either itself in a metaphorical sense or as an element in a figurative expression ? " There can, of course, be no question of prepositions, conjunctions, pronouns, articles, but apart from these it is surprising how seldom the answer will be : No. Let us take an example at random. I find the following in a book of simplified *Æsop's Fables* that forms one of W. T. Stead's " Books for the Bairns ".

> As a cock was scratching up the straw in a farm-yard, in search of food for the hens, he hit upon a jewel that by some chance had found its way there. "Oh," said he, "you are a very fine thing, no doubt, to those who prize you; but give me a barley-corn before all the pearls in the world."

In the first place the entire fable has a significance in a sphere wholly different from that to which the tale belongs. Its meaning can be expressed in general, abstract terms, " We value only what we can use." Then, taking the nouns, verbs, and even the adjectives—

The word cock is used in a transferred sense for one who domineers over people somewhat insolently. We say of somebody that he is " cock of the walk ", and " to cock over " is a local slang term for to bully. We say of a reformer whose reforms are not very thorough or of a writer who is superficial, that they have merely " scratched the surface ". " Straw " is given a significance above itself in such an adage as

APPLICATIONS

" A straw shows which way the wind blows ", which being translated into literalness means " From trifles we may learn the trend of events ". Then we have " To make bricks without straw " for an impossible task ; " a man of straw " for a man of no account ; and so forth. For " farm " and " yard " I do not recall very familiar uses, unless " Europe's back yard ", said, at one time, of certain nations. But the metaphorical possibilities of these two words are evident enough. " Search " is used for spiritual seekings as well as physical. " Food " recalls that saying of Christ, " My food is to do the will of Him that sent me." The notion of mental pabulum or spiritual nourishment is a quite familiar metaphor. " Hen " recalls [1] another saying of Christ : " How often would I have gathered these as the hen gathered her chickens under her wings." The metaphorical uses of words like jewel and gem are many. We call to mind the setting given to the former by Shakespeare :

> Sweet are the uses of adversity
> Which, like the toad, ugly and venomous,
> Bears yet a precious jewel in his head.

" Way " is more familiar in its numerous metaphorical uses than in such literal physical senses as " the permanent way ", " kindly tell me the way ". Christ our Lord exalted it into a description of His own significance for mankind : " I am the way, the truth, and the life." A committee of ways and means is not concerned with roads and paths. We " prize " not only things with calculable money values, but objects with intellectual and spiritual values. " Barleycorn " is not only, as in this fable, the literal name of an ear of barley, but a symbol of insignificance, as when a nominal rent is paid in the shape of a barley-corn. " Pearl " reminds us at once of the

---

[1] A " hen-pecked " husband is an expression hardly to be taken literally.

" pearl of great price " in the Gospel parable and it has many other transferred uses, as, for instance, when we speak of the Pearl of the Antilles. Finally, " world " means for us now not merely this planet of ours and its inhabitants. It has a deep and mysterious significance, the spirit of aloofness from God, nay, of opposition and hostility.

I think it will be found that an average passage of simple prose with plenty of concrete words will reveal equally rich possibilities of metaphor. " It is certain," says Sidgwick, " that there are comparatively few words in daily use which are not frequently extended to metaphorical uses. It is not easy to find many words which have quite escaped this fate." [1] Consequently the very stuff out of which is wrought our common speech is also metaphor-stuff and may belong to the world of imagery.

That is one aspect of the matter. Another and more interesting aspect is the prevalence of actual metaphor in daily talk and such writing as is but the reproduction of daily talk. Here I recall a distinction observed by most writers on the subject, viz. between " radical " metaphor, the result of a process which is part of the original making of language, and " poetical " metaphor, the result of the working of imagination and emotion on thought. Radical metaphor, as we have seen (supra, p. 38), may be described as having reached the *fossil* stage as contrasted with poetical metaphor which is still *living*. In using the former we are no longer aware that we are not speaking literally, in using the latter two significances of the word, its original proper sense and its transferred sense, are present to the mind.

As to radical metaphor the matter is clear enough. The main object of Mr. Grindon's fine work,[2] to

[1] *The Application of Logic*, 1910, p. 116.
[2] *Figurative Language*.

which we have referred above, is " to show that the bulk of all language is figurative essentially ". Speaking of this process, originally poetical, which has given to language so many words from which poetic significance subsequently faced, Carlyle says [1] : " Thinkest thou there were no poets till Dan Chaucer ? No heart burning with a thought, which it could not hold, and had no word for—what thou callest a metaphor, trope, or the like ? For every word we have, there was such a man and poet. The coldest word was once a glowing new metaphor, and bold questionable originality. ' Thy very attention, does it not mean an *attentio*, a stretching-to ? ' Fancy that act of the mind, which all were conscious of, which none had yet named, when this new ' poet ' first felt bound and driven to name it ! His questionable originality, and new glowing metaphor, was found adoptable, intelligible ; and remains our name for it to this day."

I may now attempt to show a little more at large how full is ordinary speech of metaphor, simile, and the like. A great proportion of our current metaphors are heirlooms,[2] they belong to a common stock that has been handed down to us, growing as it went. As regards their poetic value they are, many of them, much faded, but have not yet reached what we have called the fossil stage. In using them we are at the very least vaguely aware that what we say is not to be taken strictly *au pied de la lettre*.

---

[1] *Past and Present*, Bk. ii, chap. xvii. " That idioms are a kind of crystallized poetry," says a writer in the Literary Supplement of *The Times*, " appears from the strong flavour of metaphor in many or most of them." And again, " These idioms are the crystallization in a sort of racial memory of those flashes of comparison which belong to the genius of language at its source and form in their original and salient applications the very substance of poetry."
[2] L. Pearsall Smith, *Words and Idioms*, p. 235 sq., gives lists of idioms (most of them metaphorical) found not only in English but in French and many of them in other European languages as well.

METAPHOR IN COMMON SPEECH

It is curious to note that every category of objects, even the most unlikely, has been pressed into the service of expression, not merely literary, poetical expression but the expression of the notions of daily life. From every sort of human activity we have borrowed words and phrases that help us to express the infinite variety and complexity of human life. Each kind of human activity has its own vocabulary, its terms to describe its materials, its methods, its difficulties, and its aims ; and from these activities words and phrases are taken up into standard speech. " Sailors at sea, hunters with their dogs, labourers in the fields, cooks in their kitchens, needing in some crisis a vigorous word of command or warning or reprobation, have often hit upon some expressive collocation of words, some vivid and homely metaphor from the objects before them ; and these phrases and metaphors, striking the fancy of their companions, have been adopted into the vocabulary of their special sport or occupation. Soon a number of these phrases are found to be capable of a wider use ; often for convenience, often with a touch of humour, they come to be applied to analogous situations ; a sailor applies his sea phrases to the predicaments in which he finds himself on land ; the fisherman . . . talks of life in terms of fishing ; the housewife helps herself out with metaphors from her kitchen or her farmyard ; the sportsman expresses himself in the idioms of his sport ; and little by little the most vivid and the most useful of these phrases make their way . . . from popular speech into the standard language, and come to be universally understood."

We can but glean examples here and there.[1] The sea and all that concerns it has ever been a fruitful

[1] Not a few are taken from *The Romance of Language*, by Alethea Chaplin. Many further examples may be found in *Words and Idioms*, by Logan Pearsall Smith, London, 1925, 2nd ed., pp. 188 sq.

source. A person in a fit of anger reminds us somehow of the sea in a high wind. We speak of his "tempests", of his being shaken by "gusts" of passion, we refer to him as "storming" and "raging" and then "calming" down again. Coming obstacles and troubles are "breakers ahead". Somebody in pecuniary straits is "on the rocks". We wonder whether a person in serious trouble will succeed in "weathering the storm", or whether he will "go under". We speak of one man's happiness being "wrecked", of another man drowning his cares. We are surprised that such another manages "to keep his head above water". A man who has succeeded fairly well so far is admonished not to "rest on his oars". As though we had once been in the smuggling business we sometimes look about to see if "the coast is clear", and so on almost indefinitely.[1]

The language of sport gives us much help in eking out our ideas. We still talk of "drawing the long bow", as though quite familiar with archery, and the title of one of Mr. G. K. Chesterton's latest books is *Tales of the Long Bow*. From the same sport come such expressions as "hitting the mark", "feather in one's cap", "two strings to her bow", "point blank" (the blanc or white being the bull's eye), "beside the mark". Similarly from bear-baiting comes "to stave off", from court-tennis "from pillor to post", from bowls "there's the rub", from marbles "to knuckle under", "to knuckle down", from billiards to "put on side". Many

[1] She "sailed" majestically into the room, his last illusions "went by the board", much "leeway" to make up, "sailing under false colours", "taking in tow", "full steam ahead", "flotsam and jetsam", "getting into deep water", "quite at sea", "to sail close to the wind", to be "left stranded", to "look out for squalls", to "cut the painter"—we remember the significance of this last phrase in discussions on the Constitutional relations between England and Ireland!

current metaphors are derived from card-games : a trump card, to play one's cards badly, to show one's cards, or to lay one's cards on the table, a winning hand, to follow suit, to force the hand of, etc. Nowadays we borrow metaphors from cricket, football, and golf : " It isn't cricket ", " bunkered ", " stumped ", " clean bowled ", " to have the ball at one's feet ", and so on.

St. Paul borrowed metaphors from the arena, the stadium, and the palaestra ; and their modern equivalents furnish us with many a vigorous figure. From boxing we have " under the belt ", " throwing up the sponge ", a " knock-out blow ", " counted out ", " to bring to the scratch ". It will be remembered how Mr. Micawber occasionally descended to the use of such colloquial expressions.

" The friendliness of the gentlemen " (meaning Mr. Dick), said Mr. Micawber to my Aunt, " if you will allow me, ma'am, to cull a figure of speech from the vocabulary of our coarser national sports—floors me."

Thousands of people who never saw a race or a cross-country run interlard their talk with metaphors of the hunting-field and the turf : " drawing a blank," " in full cry," " at bay," " to carry weight," " a fair field," " a false start," " in the running," " on the wrong scent," " drawing a herring across the track," " in the long run," to " run to earth ", to win at a canter or hands down, " neck and neck ", " a dark horse," " also ran."

The tendency is for the speech of ordinary folk to absorb more and more of that of specialists in these various pursuits : the seafaring man, the " horsey man ", the more or less professional sportsman, the talk of a Captain Cuttle or an Educated Evans, or others of that ilk.

War was once so common a feature of life that ordinary speech borrowed from it many an image.

APPLICATIONS

War has totally changed in all but its essential feature : the effort of two bodies of men to slaughter one another. But we still go on using expressions borrowed from wars and weapons of the past : to " throw down the gauntlet " and to " run the gauntlet ",[1] " a foeman worthy of one's steel ", " not worth his salt " (i.e. salary or salt-money), the " honours of war ", " enter the lists ", " charge full tilt ", " with flying colours ", " to pass muster ", " to change front ", " a flash in the pan " (the old flint-lock), " up to the hilt ".

Somewhat more modern are " sticking to one's guns ", " marking time ", " taking by storm ", " masking one's batteries ", " between two fires ".

The Great War gave us a new batch of words, an entire vocabulary, in fact, of which a few obvious specimens are " camouflage ", " funk-hole ", " shirker ", " over the top ", " no man's land ", " a smoke screen ", all of which daily talk has appropriated for uses quite other than those of war.

Mr. Pearsall Smith is able to fill fourteen pages in double columns merely with *somatic* idioms, that is, phrases in which we use words properly referring to the body and its parts to express mental and moral and social states and facts.[2] Many of them are delightfully racy. Take the head alone. We say to keep one's head and to lose one's head, swelled head, to put one's head in a noose, to have one's head screwed on the right way, to be off one's head, over head and ears, to cudgel one's brains, to split hairs, to cut off one's nose to spite one's face, to see no further than one's nose, to pay through the nose, to have one's

---

[1] A different word from the preceding gauntlet (from *gant* = glove), being a corruption of *gantlope* from the Swedish word *gatlopp*, formed from *gata* " lane " and *lopp* " course ". L. P. Smith, *Words and Idioms*, p. 195.

[2] In this collection about fifty parts of the human body, the head and its features, the arms and hands and fingers, the legs and feet and toes, the heart, the bones, the blood, and breath within the body, are all put to vivid figurative uses.

nose kept to the grindstone, his nose is out of joint, etc., etc.

Common speech has likewise borrowed metaphors from the blacksmith's forge and the carpenter's shop, from tools and handicrafts, from the theatre and the tavern.

But there is perhaps no sphere from which such homely and such racy metaphors have come into common speech as those drawn from the household. The commonest household furniture and utensils have lent themselves to the concise and picturesque expression of ideas. Here are a few that are familiar to everybody : To fall between two *stools*, to be on the *shelf*, a skeleton in the *cupboard*, a *peg* to hang something on, to *bolster* up, to put back the hands of the *clock*, as stiff as a *poker*, to burn the *candle* at both ends, a new *broom*, that won't wash, to wash one's dirty *linen* in public, a storm in a *tea-cup*. The kitchen has furnished a goodly contingent : to boil down, to keep the pot boiling, to cook someone's goose for him, to make hash of, to put the lid on, to make mincemeat of, to have a finger in the pie, to go to pot, to stew in one's own juice, a half-baked convert, in apple-pie order, the fat's in the fire, in hot water, the pot calling the kettle black, to take pot-luck.

A widely prevalent tendency in common speech is to use with nouns denoting immaterial things adjectives and verbs applying properly to quite concrete and material things. We talk of our hopes being " kindled ", or " quenched " or " shattered ", our ardour being " damped ", of a man being " spurred on " by ambition, or " goaded " into retaliation. An orator's arguments are " threadbare " or else they " will not hold water ". We implore people not to " rake up " the past, not to use " stinging words ". People's hearts are " cold " or " warm ", " heavy " or " light ", " soft " or " hard ". They can be " broken ". Even one's spirit may be broken or crushed.

Moreover the English language in particular possesses an entire class of verbs, usually known as " phrasal verbs ", which, originally denoting physical motion, have come to be used in a vast number of idiomatic expressions, mostly metaphorical, by means of which human relations, actions, feelings, and thoughts of all kinds are given expression. The metaphorical transfer is effected by the simple device of an added preposition or adverb. Such verbs are " go ", " come ", " run ", " fall ", " turn ", " stand ", " get ", " take ", " look", " put", " set", " lay". All these denoted originally a simple bodily action of a very general kind. But in combination with adverbs and prepositions of abstract direction they are made to describe a wonderful variety of mental and moral attitudes and activities. " We can take *to* people, take them *up*, take them *down*, take them *off*, or take them *in* : keep *in* with them, keep them *down* or *off* or *on* or *under* ; get *at* them, or *round* them, or get *on with* them ; we may fall *in* with them or fall *out* with them ; do *for* them, do *with* them or *without* them, and do them *in* ; make *up* to them, make *up with* them, make *off with* them, make *up for* them ; set them *up* or *down* or hit them *off*—indeed, there is hardly any action or attitude of one human being to another which cannot be expressed by means of these phrasal verbs.[1]

It is to be noted, however, that these expressions belong to a species of imagery different from that with which we have for the most part been dealing. They are not so much visual images like " on the rocks ", " under a cloud ", but rather images derived from the sensations of the muscular efforts which

[1] The Oxford Dictionary records fifty-two meanings of " take up " and sixty-seven of " set up ".

accompany the attitudes and motions of the body. Psychologists have given to these the name " kinæsthetic " (i.e. perception-of-motion-al) images and the metaphors formed in this way are termed " kinæsthetic " metaphors.

All kinds of current sayings, wise saws, and adages take metaphorical form, a natural fact being taken as a sort of picture of a moral truth, and thus given a significance quite other than the meaning which, taken literally, it would convey. Such are the sayings which recall familiar fables—sour grapes, borrowed plumes, dog in the manger, to cry wolf, to blow hot and cold ; or stories from classical literature : sword of Damocles, to tantalize, herculean task, a Gordian knot, in stentorian tones, Augean stables, Scylla and Charybdis. Such, too, are sayings about the " thin end of the wedge ", " taking the bull by the horns ", " having several irons in the fire ", or " two strings to one's bow", " striking the iron while it is hot", " making hay while the sun shines " (two expressions for taking advantage of present opportunities), " throwing dust in people's eyes ", " laughing up one's sleeve " (a difficult feat with modern sleeves). Many popular proverbs, too, are cast in this form : " a rolling stone gathers no moss " (few people, I think, are clear as to whether this does or does not constitute a dereliction of duty on the part of the stone), " a bird in the hand ", " killing too birds with one stone " (often applied in a way that in reality is scarcely complimentary), " the last straw " (alluding to the camel's back), " a cat's paw " (alluding to the historic manner in which the monkey picked chestnuts out of the cinders), " letting sleeping dogs lie ", where there is no question of dogs of flesh and blood, " drawing in one's horns ", " coming out of one's shell ", " breaking the ice ", though how this particular expression has come to mean overcoming mutual constraint and setting up friendly relations, it is not easy to say.

Then there is the language of slang. " All slang," says Chesterton, " is metaphor," and we may assent, with but few reserves. Slang seldom invents entirely new words ! It seizes upon old ones and in a flash of imagination transfers them to new senses. The French equivalent of " cheek ", *le toupet*, literally meant merely a top-knot ; *le panache*, a word immortalized by Rostand in the sense of dare-devil courage, meant a plume—" a feather in one's cap ", by the way, is metaphor for something to pride oneself upon. One need not go far to find examples. A youngster is a " kid " ; the French *piocher* (lit. to use a pick) means to study hard ; in American slang *shucks* (an old word for husks or pods) is used to mean nonsense, rubbish, *fluff* is expressive slang for foolish.

Slang as the product of imagination and emotion is a sort of rough poetry. " I do not imagine," Chesterton writes, " that it is necessary to demonstrate that poetic allusiveness is the characteristic of true slang. Such an expression as " Keep your hair on " is positively Meridithian in its perverse and mysterious manner of expressing an idea. The Americans have a well-known expression about " swelled head " as a description of self-approval, and the other day I heard a remarkable fantasia upon this air. An American said that after the Chinese War the Japanese wanted " to put on their hats with a shoe-horn ". . . . The world of slang is a kind of topsy-turvey-dom of poetry, full of blue moons and white elephants, of men losing their heads and men whose tongues run away with them—a whole chaos of fairy tales."

We may add this confirmation from a recent scientific work on language : " La métaphore est un des procès favoris de l'argot. . . . La métaphore et la métonymie sont employées en argot avec une fréquence particulière ; comme il s'agit d'accuser et de maintenir la différence qui distingue l'argot de la langue commune les métaphores s'usent assez vite et ont besoin d'être renouvelées."[1]   Hence the perpetual changefulness of slang.

It is a prevailing fashion among modern popular speakers and writers, journalists in particular, to couch ideas of all kinds in terms of familiar concrete objects.   Such a device catches the popular imagination and does duty for argument.   We are all familiar with the statement that " blood is thicker than water " and commonly accept it as a conclusive argument that certain (imaginary) Anglo-Saxons in the United States are bound to (almost equally imaginary) Anglo-Saxons on this side of the Atlantic by ties, instinctive and unacknowledged, perhaps, but none the less real, of affection and regard.   The enunciation of the phrase " hands across the sea " is counted upon to confirm a similar conviction.   We remember how during the South African War the British public was comforted by being told how its army was engaged in " wiping something off a slate ", though how that somewhat primitive process illustrated the situation is not at all easy to see.   The doings of modern statesmen are described in terms of " exploring avenues ", or " building bridges " or " bridging chasms ", or " delivering the goods ".   Their doings and pronouncements are disrespectfully referred to by their opponents as "eyewash" or "window-dressing " or " backstairs intrigues ", while the endeavour of these opponents is to " cut the ground from under them ", " to take the wind out of their sails ", or "to steal a march on them ".   Their policy may be a mere " bread and butter " policy or it may

---

[1] Joseph Vendryes, *Le Langage*, Paris, 1921, p. 259.

a policy of "bread and circuses" (Panem et circenses).

This tendency in popular speeches and newspaper articles of the day may be illustrated by a page from an Irish comic paper. It purports to be a series of drawings from the Blatherskite Bequest, recently added to the British Museum. They are labelled as follows : Scales removed from the eyes of the people in December, 1921 (the drawing is of a pair of weighing scales) ; actual wires pulled by Mr. H. ; fig which Mr. O'H. didn't give for the Opposition ; dogs to which the country is going according to Mr. D. ; pin pricks inflicted on the Government by the Farmers' Party ; herring drawn across the trail by various Election speakers ; actual inch which Sir J. C. didn't budge ; axe which has been applied to Old Age Pensions ; and so forth.

Skilfully used this device renders the most abstract disquisitions pleasant and even entertaining. Here is a passage from Chesterton that might be matched by scores of others from the same writer :—

> An intelligent persecutor, an intelligent heresy hunter, right or wrong, is not like a man with a blunderbuss. He is like a man with a rifle who is so good a shot that he can pick out some man without touching the man beside him. But the blunderbuss is broad-mouthed as its owner is broad-minded. The blunderbuss is a large, a liberal, a universal instrument . . . a gun that scorns to have anything so narrow as an aim. The blunderbuss merely explodes ; that is, it merely expands ; it is the natural weapon of those who pride themselves on ideals of expansion and evolution, etc., etc.

A writer of the last century, now undeservedly forgotten, writes a delightful essay on immaturity under the title "Concerning Veal."[1]

> "By Veal I understand the immature productions of the human mind ; immature compositions, immature opinions, feelings,

[1] *Leisure Hours in Town*, by the Author of *The Recreations of a Country Parson*, A. K. H. Boyd, London, 1871.

and tastes . . . the work, the views, the fancies, the emotions which are yielded by the human soul in its immature stages."

Speaking of Miss Edith Sitwell's poetry, Mr. Robert Graves writes in a recent book :

" She will even quite sincerely avow herself a traditionalist, but that is no more than lightly bearing home the family pitcher after it had gone to the well once too often."

One more example, this time from the Literary Supplement of *The Times*. "The essayist, in Mr. M.'s new perception or impersonation of him, is a chewer of the cud. He begins as a starer with wide absorptive eyes that drink the world ; but at last his nature brims, he broods upon his treasure in a ' long meditativeness ', and distils from it a pleasant flowing stream of warm reflection . . . and the thoughts upon which one mind has fed become food for the multitude."

This tendency, though excellent in many ways, has nevertheless its dangers. The proper rôle of metaphor is the illustration of thought and the embellishment of speech. Not infrequently metaphor usurps to itself a further rôle. All unknown to the speaker or writer it proceeds to frame his thought for him, to guide it along certain lines. If you begin by thinking of learning as the food of the mind and think out in full the parallelism between learning and food, your views on learning will not follow the same lines as if you had started with the notion that the mind is soil upon which learning falls, like seed, and takes root, springing up as weeds or corn, according to circumstance. The following passage which has already been quoted from *The Mill on the Floss* will illustrate this point.

" It was his (Rev. Mr. Stirlling's) favourite metaphor that the classics and geometry constituted that culture of the mind which prepared it for the reception of any subsequent crop. I say nothing against Mr. Stirlling's theory. I only know that it turned out as uncomfortably for Tom Tulliver as if he had been plied with cheese in order to remedy a gastric weakness which prevented him from digesting it.

"It is astonishing what a different result one gets by changing the metaphor. Once call the brain an intellectual stomach, and one's ingenious conception of the classics and geometry as ploughs and harrows seems to settle nothing. But then it is open to someone else to follow great Authorities, and call the mind a sheet of white paper or a mirror, in which case one's knowledge of the digestive process becomes quite irrelevant. It was doubtless an ingenious idea to call the camel the ship of the desert, but it would hardly lead one far in training that useful beast. O Aristotle, if you had had the advantage of being 'the freshest modern' instead of the greatest ancient, would you not have mingled your praise of metaphorical speech as a sign of high intelligence with a lamentation that intelligence so rarely shows itself in speech without metaphor—that we can so seldom declare what a thing is, except by saying it is something else." ·

For a variety of reasons founded in human nature or in social convention common speech is wont to shirk the bald statement of unpleasant realities by the device of language known as euphemism.[1] Now for euphemistic purposes metaphor is invaluable. "Les tropes," says Du Marsais, "sont d'un grand usage pour déguiser les idées dures, désagréables, tristes, ou contraires à la modestie." All languages have an astonishing variety of metaphors to describe the state of intoxication without using the brutal word "drunk". The disagreeable fact of death is

---

[1] "L'Euphémisme n'est qu'une forme polie et cultivée de ce qu'on appelle l'interdiction du vocabulaire"; i.e. the process by which certain words gradually become taboo. J. Vendryes, Le Langage, Paris, 1921.

clothed in softening imagery.[1] " I will waive the point," says Chesterton somewhere, " whether death is a mist or a fog or a front door or a fire escape or any physical metaphor ; being satisfied with the fact that it is there, and not to be removed by metaphor." Yet we love to " call it soft names "—a sleep, a frontier line, a *quai de départ*, a " short dark passage to eternal life ".[2]

And euphemism, as life is constituted, has its uses. But there are moments that call for plain speaking and when euphemism becomes an impertinence, if not a danger. A figure of speech may exercise a sort of hypnotic influence if we forget that it is but a figure of speech and fail to penetrate to the reality behind. Harm has been done to weak natures by the easy use of phrases such as " to tide over ", " to bide one's time ", " to lie fallow ", " to sow one's wild oats ", " to try one's luck ", " in for a penny in for a pound ", and by a multitude of proverbs that are only half-truths. Such phrases cannot salve conscience or determine a line of action. " Let us beg you," says a thoughtful writer now little read, " to draw a line where any high moral principle is involved . . . for there the mischief of euphemism (and of all figure) lies. When something vital is touched we must put our proverbs away, we must no longer speak in parables. In life or death matters hard, straight-flying words are best. Metaphor is not good in essentials." [3]

---

[1] Au lieu de mourir nous disons en français périr, passer, trépasser, décéder, s'endormir, rendre son âme à Dieu, simplement même partir ou s'en aller. Ibid., p. 258.

[2] Folk-speech and local dialects have numberless curious euphemisms for death. Some of these are recorded in *Rustic Speech and Folklore*, by Elizabeth Mary Wright (Oxford, 1913). Here are samples : " He has put his spoon in the wall," " he has gone to the mole country," " he's singing whillalooya to the day-nettles." " Gone west " is a modern equivalent.

[3] W. Carew Hazlitt, *Offspring of Thought in Solitude*.

APPLICATIONS

Nor are metaphors—at all events stock metaphors—always good where simple explanation and lucid exposition are called for. They are often a cheap means of securing colour at the expense of clearness. Often enough the writer or speaker is not clear in his own mind as to what is the literal meaning he intends to convey by his figures. He merely takes them as he finds them in current speech. For example, there is Bacon's metaphor about the books to be tasted and the books to be chewed and digested. Few who use it begin by examining the correctness and relevancy of the image. In what sense, for instance, is the mind said to " chew " and in what to " digest " received information ? But a vigorous thinker will seize upon this well-worn metaphor, refashion it to his own purpose, and give it a new life. " We talk," says Ruskin, " of food for the mind as of food for the body ; now, a good book contains such food inexhaustibly ; it is a provision for life, and for the best part of us, yet how long most people would look at the best book before they would give the price of a large turbot for it ! " This analogy has been freshly and ingeniously worked out in a chapter entitled " Books as Mental Food " of *De Libris : Being Six Chapters on Books*, by F. J. Grierson.[1] If books be mental food, he argues, then it behoves our reading, like our bodily food, to be wholesome, regular, varied. Then there are considerations on the " digestion " of information and on " exercise " as being as necessary for the growth and development of the mind as for that of the body.

One of the resources of modern humour, notably of the humour of Mr. G. K. Chesterton, is to take these worn-out metaphors and current sayings and to galvanize them into unexpected vitality. Examples abound in his writings. The following examples must

[1] Dublin, 1909.

suffice :—" It is by rather an unlucky metaphor that we talk of a madman as cracked ; for in a sense, he is not cracked enough. He is cramped rather than cracked ; there are not enough holes in his head to ventilate it. There is no way of letting in daylight on his delusions." Again :—" If the Christians had accepted (this fusion of religions) they and the whole world would certainly, in a grotesque but exact metaphor, have gone to pot. They would all have been boiled down to one lukewarm liquid in that great pot of cosmopolitan corruption in which all the other myths and mysteries were already melting."

Common speech, then, is shot through with metaphor. It would not, I think, be difficult to show it likewise shot through with other forms of imagery akin to metaphor.[1] What, for instance, are such adjectives as cowardly, ruffianly, saintly, homely, ghostly, childlike, birdlike, homelike, but a sort of abridged simile ? So with metonymy: even in most familiar talk we say *irons* for fetters, *glasses* for spectacles or for drinking vessels, *the knife* for surgery. *Canvas* for sails or for tents, and so on. And synecdoche—sixty *head* of cattle, a rumshop, a gin palace, a cut-throat (for any sort of murderer), a hangman (for any sort of executioner), etc., etc.

So common a feature of our daily speech are figures that we are all of us in the position of the person in Hudibras of whom it was said—

> For Rhetorick, he could not ope
> His mouth but out there flew a trope.

NOTE A

Metaphor in American Slang

The following extract will be of interest in this connexion. It is from *The English Language in*

[1] This has to some extent been done in *Words and Their Ways in English Speech*, by James Bradstreet. Greenough and George Lyman Kittredge, London and New York, 1902.

APPLICATIONS

America, by George Philip Krapp, New York, The Century Co., 1925, vol. i, pp. 319–23.

Examples of striking picturesque metaphor in American slang are legion. It is in this direction that the artist in slang exerts himself. No metaphor is too remote for him, no allusion too subtle. Novelty is the very breath of life to the artist in slang. This quest for freshness naturally causes the slang of the moment to become archaic with the passing of the moment. Illustrations must almost necessarily belong to the history of slang, but antiquated examples are just as useful for illustrating the psychological processes as the last word. Thus *warm* or *hot society*, meaning gay society, is vigorously self-explanatory ; *bunch*, a number of persons or a number of anything not usually tied in bunches suggests its metaphorical origin. A *lemon* can be an unpleasant person, experience, remark, anything not sweet or agreeable. A hat may be a *scream* by the same process as that which the poet employs when a smile becomes a summer's day. Or a hat becomes a *lid*. One can *freeze on to* a thing when one holds it fast, as water freezes to cold metal. The science of bacteriology has brought certain new ideas within the limits of popular apprehension, especially the notion of germs. The germ, however, becomes a *bug*, and so a person with a particular fad or notion is said to have that *bug*, or to be *bug house* in a certain direction. Some slang has local associations, like *tenderfoot*, *cinch*, *corral*, and an infinite number of words from the West. Sometimes slang is complicated in its suggestiveness, like *cackleberry*, meaning *egg*. . . . The metaphor sometimes depends on a phrase, as in *nobody home*, meaning you do not get me, you have not caught on, you are off the trolley, etc., or *Good night* as a general expression of finality. Or it may be a generalization derived from an individual or personal quality, as in *Jonah*, meaning anything or any person that brings bad luck, or the reverse *mascot*, something which brings good luck, usually a living animal, from *La Mascotte*, the luck-bringing heroine of a French comic opera popular in America in the last quarter of the nineteenth century.

    ·   ·   ·   ·

The picturesque metaphor of slang as it has been used in popular American expression has certain manifest virtues, but also obvious limitations. It is usually concrete, direct, and vigorous, but it makes the mistake of saying everything and leaving nothing to the imagination. It is too adequate, too pat. A hat is a lid by a very appropriate metaphor. A hat fits a head as a lid fits a pot—nothing could be more apt or more final. But when one gets the point, there is nothing more to get. The metaphor leaves nothing unrealized, nothing to be imagined. It is like a remorselessly precise epithet, so completely satisfactory that it removes the situation from further human interest. The literary value of such a style is obviously low. One can admire or smile at the ingenuity employed in securing so striking a metaphor or epithet, but the mechanical perfection of the complete adaptation of the image to its purpose can have only a momentary or mechanical interest. This character of finality is found not infrequently in popular speech. Persons of limited but absolutely certain experience sometimes express themselves with a picturesque precision and conclusiveness of effect which seems as unsought and unescapable as a happening in the world of nature. Their figures are on the same level imaginatively as the platitude in the intellectual world. The striking metaphors of slang are imaginative platitudes, fatal to genuine poetry. As slang always arises in concrete and familiar situations, in it a highly effective machinery of expression is applied to a relatively low order of thought. The Society for Pure English has recently issued as its Tract No. xxiv (Oxford : Clarendon Press) a *Glossary of American Slang*.

NOTE B

The extent to which metaphor and kindred imagery form an element of common speech differs greatly in the various languages. The study of these differences would prove a fascinating bypath of comparative semantics, and would throw many an interesting sidelight on national psychology.

Spanish, for example, is a language peculiarly rich in those popular and proverbial sayings that are so commonly metaphorical. Spanish proverbs have been reckoned to number some 24,000. The Dictionary of the Spanish Academy is well known for its wealth of metaphorical expressions. The Gaelic language also abounds in proverbs which, however, seem comparatively seldom to take metaphorical form.

It is when we consider from this point of view a language which has no affinities with our Western tongues that we find ourselves as it were in an entirely new region of the world of imagery. The Chinese language is of particular interest in this connexion. Let me give a number of samples which I owe to a missionary of many years standing.

For spies the Chinese say " eyes and ears ", for a thief " three hands ", for shameless " face-skin-thick ". The moon is " heaven's lamp " or (in complimentary language) " golden mirror ". A worthless person is a " rice sack " and the body is the " skin sack ". The death of a wife is spoken of as " breaking the strings of a guitar ". Moss or lichen is " the rock's clothes ", brothers are " hands and feet ". To study is " to gnaw letters and lick characters ". A minister of state is " middle of the hall " and so forth. A writer in *Our Missions*,[1] organ of the Society of the Divine Word, Techny, Illinois, wonders whether this profusion of metaphor in daily talk is due to love of pretentiousness or to a mistaken sense of humour. There seems to be no sufficient reason for thinking that it is due to either one or the other. It is sufficiently accounted for by two causes— the poverty of the Chinese language and the ceremonious politeness habitual to Orientals.

As regards the former cause it should be noted that Chinese is almost devoid of abstract terms. Its sole means of expressing abstractions is to join two concrete nouns. Thus length is, strangely to our way of thinking, expressed by " long-short " ; a thing or object in general by " West-East " : a composition is " pencil and ink " : climate is " water and earth " : inconstant, irresolute is " three hearts two thoughts " meaning = " character's eyes ": con- duct = " coming and going ": rheumatism = " wind and damp ": beginning and end = " head and tail."

Then there are the expressions of courtesy. In China politeness demands that references to the person addressed be accompanied by a magnifying epithet, references to the speaker by a depreciatory one. Thus one says, " A thousand pieces of gold " for your daughter, " the honourable thing of your house " for your mother, " flowery pencil " for your letter, and so on.

[1] June, 1925.

279

SUPPLEMENTARY BIBLIOGRAPHY TO PART II

General

H. Arminius, *Die Tropen und Figuren.* Innsbruck, 1890.
J. Bauer, *Das Bild in der Sprache.* Anspach, 1878, 1889.
A. Biese, *Das Metaphorische in der dicterischen Phantasie.* Berlin, 1889.
—— *Die Philosophie der Metaphorischen.* Hamburg, 1893.
A. Braun, *Versüch über die Tropen.* Munnerstadt, 1847.
W. Caspers, *Ueber die Tropen und Figuren.* Recklingshausen, 1873.
Gustav Gerber, *Die Sprache als Kunst,* 2 vols. Bromberg, 1871.
K. Tumlirz, *Tropen und Figuren.* Prague, 1883.
Friedrich Brinkmann, *Die Metaphern. Studien über den Geist der modernen Sprachen.* Bonn, 1878.
Gertrude Buck, *Figures of Rhetoric : A Psychological Study.* Contributions to Rhetorical Theory (University of Michigan).

Works on the Science of Language

E. Bourciez, *Elements de linguistique romane.* Paris, 1910.
J. van Ginneken, *Principes de linguistique psychologique.* Paris, Amsterdam, Leipzig, 1907.
A. Hovelacque, *La Linguistique.* Paris, 1888.
F. de Saussure, *Cours de linguistique générale,* 1916.
A. H. Sayce, *Introduction to the Science of Language,* 2 vols. London, 1890.
Ch. A. Sechehaye, *Progrès et méthodes de la linguistique théorique.*
B. Leroy, *Le Langage.* Paris, 1905.

Works on Rhetoric and Style.

J. Bascom, *The Philosophy of Rhetoric.*
G. Campbell, *The Philosophy of Rhetoric.* 1823.
G. R. Carpenter, *Exercises in Rhetoric* (Advanced Course).
Jas. de Mille, *Elements of Rhetoric.*
John Earle, *English Prose.*
A. S. Hill, *Foundations of Rhetoric.*
—— *Principles of Rhetoric.*

SUPPLEMENTARY BIBLIOGRAPHY

D. J. Hill, *The Science of Rhetoric.*

E. E. Hale, *Constructive Rhetoric.* New York, 1896.

Gayley and Scott, *Methods and Materials of Literary Criticism.*

Marmontel, *Elements de Littérature.*

E. Elster, *Prinzipen der Literaturwissenschaft.* Halle, 1897.

W. Wackernagel, *Poetik Rhetorik und Stilistik.* 2 Aufl., Halle, 1888.

W. C. Robinson, *Forensic Oratory.*

Scott and Denney, *Composition and Rhetoric.* Boston, 1897.

Sherman, *Analytics of Literature.*

J. Stirling, *System of Rhetoric containing all tropes and figures necessary to illustrate the Classics.* London, 1764.

A. Thomkins, *The Science of Discourse.*

Capmany y Montpalau, *Filosofia de la Elocuencia.* 1826.

George Lansing Raymond, *Poetry as a Representative Art*, 1886. Seventh edition. New York, Putnams, 1899.

Ch. Bailly, *Traité de stylistique française*, 2 vol. Paris, 1909.

—— *Précis de stylistique.* Genève, 1905.

—— *Le Langage et la Vie*, Genève, 1913.

PART III

ILLUSTRATION

THIS third part of the work consists of a classified selection of metaphors and similes which I have met with and noted down in the course of a few years' reading. None of them, so far as I can recollect at the moment, have been taken at second hand from previous collections or from works on composition and rhetoric. To that extent at least they are fresh. The collection might have been much richer but for the fact that the bulk of my reading during those years was of a professional character, largely in Latin and French, and of a type in which the imagination, the creator of imagery, had but little scope.

The collection is included in the present volume with a view to illustrating, more fully than it was possible to do in the body of the work, certain aspects of the subject. One may for instance infer from it how great a value for literary expression even the simplest and homeliest object may have when used as an image. Clearly the humblest things may be made images of the highest, as a lamb was made an image of the Incarnate Word, or the trefoil was used as a symbol of the Trinity. It is mainly with a view to showing this that I have arranged the selection according to the objects used as images. Incidentally it will appear how, seized upon and transfigured by imaginations of different tone and quality, the same object may serve as an image of ideas that differ altogether from one another.

Again, one may gather from this collection, small though it be, what an astonishing wealth of resources

283

language may draw upon. Compared with the entire world of imagery these are but as a few shells picked up by children on some seashore, a few meadow and hedgerow flowers gathered in a day's ramble.

And these samples of imagery have with gathered flowers this other resemblance, that set apart from the spot in which they first sprang up, they lose much of their life and freshness. Its original setting is almost as necessary to the vividness, aptness, beauty of the image as its native mossy bank is to the comeliness of the primrose. I have therefore sought to choose such figures as would lose least by being torn away from their first setting. As a consequence most of the examples given belong to that type of figure which calls attention to itself. And this is commonly not the best. For the true rôle of imagery is not to be a mere ornament stuck on to save prose from being too prosaic or to make poetry out of prose in metrical form. It ought to be an integral element of the expression of thought. Here it has not, of course, been possible to give each image its true setting in the general unfolding of some idea, but it will, I think, be found that the majority of the images set down express an idea which is at least intelligible by means of the image alone.

The collection may serve for another use. It is not intended as a store from which the writer reduced to penury of literary expression may pilfer and purloin. Yet it may help the learner, and we are all learners until we lay down the pen for ever, to realize the various values of imagery in the style of good writers. It will afford, not a headline to copy, but a source of suggestion and inspiration.

I have given *poetic* examples somewhat sparingly and chiefly for purposes of comparison. For images are the very life and breath of poetry and may be found in profusion in the works of any poet. Nearly every line of Thompson's *Hound of Heaven* might have found a place in this selection. My object has been rather to illustrate what imagery can do to lift prose out of the rut of convention and commonplace, to put into it spirit and life, colour and suggestiveness, to lend it humour or sublimity.

I. THE BODY : ITS PARTS, STATES, AND MOVEMENTS

OF this class of metaphors it may be said that all or well nigh all the words we use to describe the spiritual element of our nature, its states, activities, qualities were originally borrowed from the qualities, activities, and states of the body. In speaking of the mind we suppose it to have something of the nature of a body. We speak of it as impressed, struck, touched, stung. Or we talk of the material brain as though it were the equivalent of intelligence. Hence such expressions as scatter-brained, to cudgel one's brains, a brainy person, full of brains, he has no brains (a rather alarming statement if taken literally). The language of sense-perception is similarly borrowed to express soul states—wounded feelings, a sour temper, cut to the quick, bitter grief, hard-, soft-, tender-hearted, a ruffled temper, a sweet disposition. The mind is enlightened, dazzled, blinded.

If you meditate a subject, you should first long roll the subject under the tongue to make sure you like the flavour before you brew a volume that shall taste of it from end to end.—R. L. Stevenson, *The Morality of the Profession of Letters.*

It is also inquired whether the imagined stampede of students flying in panic from the Irish language is not a disagreeable dream arising from indigestion of facts.—Professor Eoin MacNeill.

ILLUSTRATION

As a theory his Æsthetic seems lean, not to say starved ; but to see it applied, or at any rate applied by Croce himself, is to realize that lack of flesh need not necessarily imply absence of muscle.—G. L. Bickersteth in *Quarterly Review*, April, 1921.

> I think that I shall never see
> A poem lovely as a tree,
> A tree whose hungry mouth is prest
> Against the earth's sweet-flowing breast ;
> A tree that looks at God all day,
> And lifts her leafy arms to pray.
> A tree that may in Summer wear,
> A nest of robins in her hair ;
> Upon whose bosom snow has lain ;
> Who intimately lives with rain.
>
> Joyce Kilmer.

We are concerned with what the mind does when it takes the leap of metaphor : whether it skips in a delicate conceit, or places us for the moment on an imaginative elevation.—H. W. Wells, *Poetic Imagery*, 1924.

> To drop head foremost in the jaws
> Of vacant darkness and to cease.
>
> *In Memoriam.*

For the last three centuries, above all for the last three-quarters of a century, that same Pericardial Nervous Tissue (as we named it) of Religion, where lies. the life-essence of Society, has been smote at and perforated, needfully and needlessly ; till now it is quite rent into shreds ; and Society, long pining, diabetic, consumptive, can be regarded as defunct ; for these spasmodic, galvanic, sprawlings are not life. —Carlyle, *Sartor Resartus*.

But efforts to heal deep wounds by superficial plasters are likely to breed disappointment.—*Times Literary Supplement*, July, 1925.

THE BODY AND DRESS

He needed not to mask familiar thoughts in the weeds of unfamiliar phraseology.—Lowell, *English Poets*.

In this [Collins's *Ode on the Passions*], despite its beauty, there is still a soupçon of formalism, a lingering trace of powder from the eighteenth century periwig, dimming the bright locks of poetry.—Francis Thompson, *Essay on Shelley*.

For the present, it is contemplated that when man's whole Spiritual Interests are once *divested*, these innumerable stript-off garments shall mostly be burnt ; but the sounder Rags among them be quilted together into one huge Irish waistcoat for the defence of the Body only.—Carlyle, *Sartor Resartus*.

Art thou not by this time made aware that all Symbols are properly Clothes ; that all forms whereby Spirit manifests itself to sense, whether outwardly or in the imagination, are Clothes ; and thus not only the parchment Magna Charta, which a Tailor was nigh cutting into measures, but the Pomp and Authority of Law, the sacredness of Majesty, and all inferior Worships are properly a Vesture and a Raiment ; and the Thirty-nine Articles themselves are articles of wearing apparel (for the Religious idea) ?—Carlyle, *Sartor Resartus*.

The most gorgeous, tarnished, threadbare, patchwork set of phrases, the left-off finery of poetic extravagance.—Hazlitt, *Table Talk*.

> In words like weeds I'll wrap me o'er
> Like coarsest clothes against the cold.
> Tennyson, *In Memoriam*.

His [Rupert Brooke's] passion for loading his lines, like the fingers of some South American beauty, with gem after gem.—*The Times Literary Supplement*.

ILLUSTRATION

II. FAMILIAR OBJECTS

PHOTOGRAPHIC PLATE.—Above all, must the mind be disencumbered, clean, and plastic when, like a sensitive plate, it is set to receive the impression of a work of art.—Geo. Wyndham, *Studies in Romantic Literature*.

DYE-HOUSES.—Wherever Shakespeare dipped, it [English] came up clear and sparkling, undefiled as yet by the drainage of literary factories, or of those dye-houses where the machine-woven fabrics of sham culture are coloured up to the last desperate style of sham sentiment.—Lowell, *English Poets*.

MOTOR-CAR.—Think as well as read. Don't fly through the shires of literature on a motor-car with motion as your sole object.—Arnold Bennett.

GRAMOPHONE.—He knows exactly when to put the patriotic, religious, comic, or seamy side disc on the gramophone of his mind.—A Writer in *Everyman*, 1919.

NET.—The greatness of prose heightened and coloured by poetry, lies in the fact that the poetry remains *latent* in it. Even when struggling to escape she is unconscious of herself. The net holding her loveliness grows alive with light : her personality thrills along the webbing and saturates it with glory. But once the silken filaments are broken and their prisoner is free, nothing remains except a coarse coil of hemp—Poetry is not only released but annihilated, for a man has ravished her secret and revealed it to the world.—Theodore Maynard, *Carven from the Laurel Tree*.

CUDGEL.—The author belabours modern " progressive " political theory with vigorous, if occasionally puzzling, strokes of an Aristotelian cudgel. —*Times Literary Supplement*, Jan., 1926.

TRAPPINGS OF DEATH.—I was angry that he [Walter

Pater] should treat English as a dead language, bored by that sedulous ritual wherewith he laid out every sentence as in a shroud—hanging, like a widower, long over its marmoreal beauty or ever he could lay it at length in his book, its sepulchre.—Max Beerbohm, *Diminuendo* in *Works*.

MUSICAL INSTRUMENTS.—

Unfaith in aught is want of faith in all.
It is the little rift within the lute
That by and by will make the music mute
And ever widening slowly silence all.
Tennyson, *Merlin and Vivien*.

And now my tongue's use is to me no more
Than an unstringed viol or a harp,
Or like a cunning instrument cased up,
Or, being open, put into his hands
That knows no touch to tune the harmony.
Richard II, Act i, 3.

I have sounded the very base-string of humility.
I *Henry IV*, ii, 4.

The imagination infuses a certain volatility and intoxication. It has a flute which sets the atoms of our frame on a dance, like planets.—Emerson, *Books*.

AEROPLANE.—The supreme felicities of Keats or Shelley seem to come when the engine of the brain is shut off and the mind glides serene but unconscious. —*The Times Literary Supplement*.

LOOPHOLE.—It is this illogical but living sense of things which looks out at us through the idiomatic loopholes in rational language.—L. P. Smith, *Words and Idioms*.

CISTERN.—They have forsaken me, the fountain of living waters, and have digged to themselves cisterns, broken cisterns, that can hold no water.—Jeremias ii, 13.

WELL.—Suspended in the dropping well of his imagination the commonest object becomes crusted with imagery.—Francis Thompson, *Essay on Shelley*.

ILLUSTRATION

FOUNTAIN.—

> And now my heart is as a broken fount,
> Wherein tear-drippings stagnate, spilt down ever
> From the dank thoughts that shiver
> Upon the sighful branches of my mind.
> > Francis Thompson, *The Hound of Heaven.*

SHEARS.—It is true he shared the fate of nearly all the great poets contemporary with him in being unappreciated. Like them he suffered from critics who were for ever shearing the wild tresses of poetry between rusty rules, who could never see a literary bough project beyond the trim level of its day, but they must lop it with a crooked criticism.—Thompson, *Essay on Shelley.*

TAPESTRY.—Enriched with warm thoughts and frolic fantasies, shreds of purple and gold from tapestries of the imagination.—Article in the *Tablet.*

SCREEN, QUILT.—The stupid book is tiresome enough because it ends by making one feel that there is a real human being that one cannot get at behind all the tedious paragraphs, like someone stirring and coughing behind a screen—or even more like the outline of a human figure covered up with a quilt, so that one can just infer which is the head and which the feet, but with the outlines all overlaid with a woolly padded texture of meaningless words.—A. C. Benson, *The Silent Isle.*

NINEPINS.—

> And set him up as ninepin in their talk
> To bowl him down with jestings.
> > E. B. Browning, *Aurora Leigh.*

BOLT.—Wordsworth really led the way into a new century of poetry, and shot back a bolt in the human breast which almost the whole of the present century has busied itself in securing against any recoil.—R. H. Hutton, *Brief Literary Criticisms.*

FAMILIAR OBJECTS

LAMP.—In the school of her (Ireland's) history are treasured records which are by some accounted as equal to a promise for the future. But the world moves on ; there is no return of evil or good days ; what comes, comes new from the fount of destiny ; and what of past pride and joy we keep are but lamps hung in the pavilions of memory, that may hearten and make cheer for us indeed, but can throw only a dim radiance on the hidden hours of to-morrow.— Filson Young, *Ireland at the Cross Roads*.

> For e'er the six years that he hath to spend
> Can change their moons and bring their times about,
> My oil-dried lamp and time-bewasted light
> Shall be extinct with age and endless night.
> *Richard II, i, 3.*

CANDLE.—

> How far that little candle throws his beams
> So shines a good deed in a naughty world.
> *Merchant of Venice.*

These people were by this time quite accustomed to the idea that the old Christian candle-light would fade into the light of common day. To many of them it did quite honestly appear like that pale yellow flame of a candle when it is left burning in daylight. It was all the more unexpected . . . that the seven-branched candlestick suddenly towered to heaven like a miraculous tree and flamed until the sun turned pale.— G. K. Chesterton, *The Everlasting Man*.

.   .   .   .

There are the multitudes to whom civilization has given little but its reaction, its rebound, its chips, its refuse, its shavings, sawdust, and waste, its failures.— Alice Meynell, *Solitude*.

Nay in any case would Criticism erect not only finger-posts and turnpikes but spiked gates and impassable barriers for the mind of man.—Carlyle, *Sartor Resartus*.

ILLUSTRATION

TAPER.—A touch of Steele's tenderness is worth all his (Congreve's) finery; a flash of Swift's lightning, a beam of Addison's pure sunshine, and his tawdry playhouse taper is invisible.—Thackeray, *English Humourists*.

CHIMNEY.—In civilized society law is the chimney through which all that smoke discharges itself that used to circulate through the whole house and put everybody's eyes out. No wonder therefore that the vent itself should sometimes get a little sooty.—Scott.

STAINED GLASS.—

The One remains, the many change and pass.
Heaven's light for ever shines : earth's shadows fly.
Life like a dome of many-coloured glass
Stains the bright radiance of eternity,
Until Death shatters it to fragments. . . .

Shelley, *Adonais*.

The Church is like a stained glass window—all darkness and confusion without, all order, beauty, and light within.—Newman.

" As common windows are intended only to admit the light, but painted windows also to dye it, and to be an object of attention in themselves as well as a cause of visibility in other things, so, while the purest prose is a mere vehicle of thought, verse, like stained glass, arrests attention in its own intricacies, confuses it in its own glories, and is even at times allowed to darken and puzzle in the hope of casting over us a supernatural spell."—George Santayana, *Poetry and Religion*.

BRIDGE.—Those accustomed never to plunge for a moment into that torrent of sensation and imagery over which the bridge of prosaic associations habitually carries us safe and dry to some conventional act. How slight that bridge commonly is, how much an affair of trestles, and wire, we can hardly conceive until. . . .—Ibid.

FIRE.—Yet when he [Newman] is in possession of

his subject his imagination often catches fire and gives out a pale, steady light as different from the smoky torch of Carlyle as from the conflagration of Burke.

LIGHTS.—Considering our present advanced state of culture, and how the Torch of Science has now been brandished and borne about . . . for five thousand years and upwards ; how . . . not only the Torch still burns, and perhaps more fiercely than ever, but innumerable Rushlights, and Sulphur-matches, kindled thereat, are also glancing in every direction, so that not the smallest cranny in Nature or Art can remain unilluminated.—Carlyle, *Sartor Resartus*.

ELECTRIC LIGHT.—As a man might sit in a darkened room, having at his hand the electric light and refusing to use it. So Jesus all his mortal life had at his command the glory of the Godhead but put it away from Him.— J. Rickaby, S.J., *Waters that go Softly*.

BOTTLE.—Man at the best is a narrow mouthed bottle. Through the conduit of speech he can utter— as you, my hearers, can receive—only one word at a time.—Sir A. Quiller-Couch, *The Art of Writing*.

MONEY.—Words are the only currency in which we can exchange thought even with ourselves.—Ibid.

SIEVE.—General definitions and theories, through the sieve of which the particular achievement of genius is so apt to slip.—Ibid.

MILL WHEEL.—These professors lived by a mere Reputation, constructed in past times . . . by quite another class of persons. Which Reputation, like a strong, brisk-going undershot wheel, sunk into the general current, bade fair, with only a little annual repainting on their part, to hold long together, and of its own accord assiduously grind for them. Happy that it was so, for the Millers.—Carlyle, *Sartor Resartus*.

MILL.—" Shall your Science proceed in the small

chink-lighted, or even oil-lighted, underground work-shop of Logic alone ; and man's mind become an Arithmetical Mill, whereof Memory is the Hopper, and mere Tables of Sines and Tangents, Codification, and Treatises of what you call Political Economy, are the Meal ? "—Carlyle, *Sartor Resartus*.

BOOMERANG.—The charge of obscurity against a poet is a boomerang that may return not to the critic's feet but at his head.—*Times Literary Supplement*, 1919.

RAILWAY.—The beginnings of Mr. Wells's books are apt to be better than the endings. Nobody can start out so well—he is already doing his sixty miles an hour before he is clear of the suburban entanglements of the first chapter. But towards the summit level of the middle pages the locomotive begins to labour, the pace gets slower and slower, and finally we come to a full stop at Sociological Junction ; the guard discusses modern thought with the engine-driver, the station master intervenes with a dissertation on the superior advantages of State railways, and finally Mr. Wells the Reformer pokes his head out of the window, and Mr. Wells the romancer, having taken his ticket to the terminus, quietly curls himself up in a corner and goes to sleep. It is a discouraging situation, not provided for in the ordinary time tables of fiction. Eventually, of course, the train starts again, but the swing and the rush and the glory of the first rapid motion have vanished ; and as we crawl through the last wayside stations, we notice that the weary attendants are already putting out the lamps with a series of explosive dots. . . .—*The Edinburgh Review*, Jan., 1923.

DUMB-BELLS.—In a passage too long for quotation, De Quincey (*Essay on Style*) compares the two separate clusters of Greek literature (viz., the age of Pericles and the age of Alexander) to the globes at each end of a dumbbell and Isocrates to the cylinder that connects them.

LUMBER-ROOM.—" The art of history, like other arts, consists in selection, in the choice of a few samples from the unassorted bundles which litter the lumber-rooms of the past."—Arnold Lunn, *Roman Converts*.

TIGHT-ROPE.—Keble and Pusey continued for the rest of their lives to dance upon the tight-rope of High Anglicanism, in such an exemplary manner, indeed, that the tight-rope has its dancers still.—Lytton Strachey, *Eminent Victorians*.

FROTH.—

> My words are only words and moved
> Upon the topmost froth of thought.
>
> Tennyson, *In Memoriam*.

BUBBLE.—Military glory is a bubble blown from blood.—Douglas Jerrold.

> Seeking the bubble reputation
> Even at the cannon's mouth.
>
> Shakespeare.

In *Antony and Cleopatra* the surface of imagery is often far more buoyant than the emotions which are intimated to lie beneath. Bubbles play about the brim. —H. W. Wells, *Poetic Imagery*.

SICKLE.—

> Les astres émaillaient le ciel profond et sombre ;
> Le croissant fin et clair parmi ces fleurs de l'ombre
> Brillait à l'occident, et Ruth se demandait,
> Immobile, ouvrant l'œil à moitié sous ses voiles,
> Quel dieu, quel moissonneur de l'éternel été
> Avait en s'en allant négligeamment jeté
> Cette faucille d'or dans le champ des étoiles.
>
> Victor Hugo, *Booz endormi*.

WINDOW BLINDS.—If your life is dark, is this not perhaps owing to the fact that all the blinds are drawn ? Many a man is made so impervious by egotism that no light from above, no warm ray from without, can penetrate into his soul.—Bishop von Keppler, *More Joy*.

KEY.—The Hegelian master-key has proved much too simple to fit the words of so intricate a lock [viz. the problem of the rise of the Christian Church].—*Times Literary Supplement*, 21st May, 1925.

FURNITURE.—"Whose minds still display faded suites of the intellectual furniture of the Macaulay and Froude periods.—J. S. Phillimore in Preface to Bishop Fisher's *Penitential Psalms*.

CARPET AND PAVEMENT.—Eastern paganism is really much more all of a piece, just as ancient paganism was much more all of a piece, than the modern critics admit. It is a many-coloured Persian carpet as the other was a varied and tessellated Roman pavement ; but the one real crack right across that pavement came from the earthquake of the Crucifixion.—G. K. Chesterton, *The Everlasting Man*.

POT.—There is a vast sediment of potential voting power in Ireland that has never been stirred up, even when the political pot was boiling its hottest, and nobody knows how the whole political brew might be flavoured if that sediment was stirred up and mixed into the normal voting population.—A. E. in *The Irish Statesman*.

"George A. Birmingham" called one of his novels of Irish political life *The Seething Pot*.

COBWEB.—Was it merely the restless spirit of German speculation ever eager for a new cobweb.—Professor Blackie, *Horae Hellenicae*.

BELL.—As for the poets, there is but one among so many of their bells that seems to toll with a spiritual music so loud as to be unforgotten when the mind goes up a little higher than the earth, to listen in thought to earth's untethered sounds.—Alice Meynell, *The Spirit of Place*.

VEIL.—The florid style is the reverse of the familiar.

The last is employed as an unvarnished medium to convey ideas ; the first is resorted to as a spangled veil to conceal the want of them.—Hazlitt, *Table Talk*.

STILTS.—Anyone may mouth out a passage with a theatrical cadence, or get upon stilts to tell his thoughts.—Ibid.

BRAKE.—Natural conservatism and the instinct of thriftiness, virtues in themselves, often become brakes on the wheel.—*Times Literary Supplement*, December, 1925.

WHEELS.—The rusty wheels of our disused nature must be moved, and as they move the unction of God's grace must flow over them. At first the motion is heavy, grinding, clumsy, and agonizing, but as the sacred oil of Divine grace flows over them the movement becomes freer.—B. W. Maturin, *Self-knowledge and Self-discipline*.

CRUST.—Such has been the fate of most of the civilizations of the past. Their cake of custom has so hardened as to become brittle, incapable of partial modification and growth, so that, like a crystal, it must either resist completely every modifying influence or be shattered irretrievably.—W. Bagehot, *Physics and Politics*.

BUILDINGS.—Did the personality of such an one stand like an open watch-tower in the midst of the territory it is erected to gaze on ? and were the storms and calms, the stars and meteors its watchman was wont to report of, the habitual variegations of his everyday life, as they glanced across its open roof or lay reflected on its four-square parapet ? Or did some sunken and darkened chamber of imagery witness, in the artificial illumination of every storied compartment we are permitted to contemplate, how rare and precious were the outlooks through here and there an embrasure upon a world beyond, and how blankly would have pressed on the artificer the boundary of his daily life, except for the amorous diligence with which he has rendered permanent by Art whatever came to diversify the gloom.—R. Browning, *Essay on Shelley*.

What is there in them that should stir vague hopes and long-forgotten regrets and set all the vaults of our memory echoing.—Stephen Gwynn, *Tennyson*.

Did he ever, in rapture and tears, clasp a friend's bosom to his; looks he also wistfully into the long burial aisle of the Past, where only winds and their low, harsh moan give inarticulate answer ?—Carlyle, *Sartor Resartus*.

But the rooms of literature lead to stairways up and down. No one knows in what chamber, reception-hall, or garret or cellar, the explorer shall find his own kingly treasury. But the mansion is full of windows and glorious.—Sir A. Quiller-Couch.

Though it is easy at any given moment to eject from our minds the notion that style is ornament, and to bolt the door against it, the notion is persistent. It may come back through the keyhole.—J. Middleton Murry, *The Problem of Style*.

III. Food and Common Substances

Wine.—Jeremy Taylor compels his clipped fancy to the conventional discipline of prose and waters his poetic wine with doctrinal eloquence.—Lowell, *English Poets*.

The Reformation had passed the period of its vinous fermentation, and its clarified results remained as a element of intellectual impulse and exhilaration ; there were small signs yet of the acetous and putre-factive stages which were to follow.—Ibid.

Ice.—The usual deputation of Nonconformists followed and the audience watched with keen interest the very dexterous way in which the dissenting spokes-man and the Bishop successfully skated over thin ice.

FOOD AND SUBSTANCES

Cotton Wool.—Everybody who in the name of duty, decency, self-control, and such like catchwords, has stuffed his ears against the pipes of Pan with the cotton-wool of aggressive respectability.—W. L. George, *A Novelist on Novels*.

Metals.—

Life's leaden metal into gold transmute.—Omar Khayyam.

Leaden eyed Despairs.—Keats.

Time crawled across her life with leaden feet.
John Masefield, *The Daffodil Fields*.

The coming of death is a fearful blow.
To hearts unencompassed with nerves of steel.—Shelley.

All lovers of poetry have always felt in their bones, if they have not expressed it in set terms, that the poetry which has one or two atoms of the true gold in it is infinitely more valuable than all the silver verse in the world. Men have sought the true gold high and low, putting up with a great amount of copper and other alloys and even baser admixtures, but fully satisfied if they could find some trace of the authentic treasure.—J. St. Loe Strachey, *Edinburgh Review*.

Ashes.—

The worldly hope men set their hearts upon.
Turns ashes. . . .—Omar Khayyam.

Clay.—

The purest treasure mortal times afford
Is spotless reputation ; that away
Men are but gilded loam, or painted clay.
Richard II, I, i, 177.

How hast thou merited ?
Of all men's clotted clay the dingiest clot.
Francis Thompson.

Cake.—

In —— [a new novel] the icing with which Mr. X is wont to cover his confections seems a little sweeter and the cake within a little less substantial, than in days gone by. There are the characteristic ingredients. —*Times Literary Supplement*.

ILLUSTRATION

In the wedding-cake Hope is the sweetest of the plums.—Douglas Jerrold.

He turns and twists his subject in a score of different ways ; he hashes it ; and he serves it up cold ; and he garnishes it, etc.—Thackeray, *English Humourists*.

PITCH.—People who know no more cunning way of exhibiting the brightness of Christianity, than by smearing the face of heathenism indiscriminately over with pitch.—Professor Blackie, *Horae Hellenicae*.

JAM.—It is, indeed, the writing of a child ; or, perhaps, of an exceptional boy who . . . has broken into the store-closet of literary conserves, and cloyed himself in delicious contempt of law and ignorance of satiety, tasting all capricious dainties as they come. —Francis Thompson, *Sidney's Prose*.

MUD, ASHES.—

> Rassasié de pain, de silence et d'extase
> Le limon de mon cœur descend au fond du vase.
>
> *   *   *
>
> Triste serait l'accent et cette longue histoire
> Remuerait trop de cendre au fond de ma mémoire.
> > Lamartine, *Nouvelles Méditations*.

BREAD.—I gathered here an ear or two, there something more, elsewhere a whole handful. And now I bring these scattered stalks together into a sheaf from which somebody may thresh out the ears of fact, to be turned by him into the flour out of which he will make the bread of history.—W. F. Butler, *Gleanings from Irish History*.

IV. THE ELEMENTS

FIRE.—Failure counts for nothing, defeat, disappointment—these matter nothing at all, so long as hope sits patiently, stirring the embers, watching and tending the fire, coaxing the flame, never despairing and never leaving the wind to work its will.—Bede Jarrett, O.P.—*Meditations for Layfolk*.

Yet when he [Newman] is in possession of his subject his imagination often catches fire and gives out a pale steady light as different from the smoky torch of Carlyle as from the conflagration of Burke.

These speeches have parts which glow, but rarely burst into flames, or if they flare with the brightness of sheet-lightning, they fail to condense into the quivering lines that have the flash of death in their leap.—F. P. Donnelly, *The Art of Interesting*.

And every world will burn like a red spark from hell.
John Masefield, *The Daffodil Fields*.

But there is another fire that may burn within us, before whose lurid flames the Divine light grows pale and dim and at last dies out. The fire that at first as the faintest spark burns in the flesh and grows with a fearful rapidity, demanding ever more and more fuel, till all that is noblest in the soul is sacrificed to feed its all-consuming flames, and the heavenly flame dies exhausted and untended.—B. W. Maturin, *Self-knowledge and Self-discipline*.

"Pamphlets from which, like dry ashes, the heat of the fire that warmed them once has fled."—A. C. Benson, *From a College Window*.

LIGHT AND DARKNESS.—"Many a word offers in itself a flickering light, often dim to be sure, but enabling one to peer into the blackness of the past."—G. H. McKnight, *English Words and their Background*, 1923

His [Macaulay's] pages are illuminated not only by little sparks of antithesis but by broad flashes.—Minto, *A Manual of English Prose Literature*.

Considering our present advanced state of culture, and how the Torch of Science has now been brandished and borne about with more or less effect for five thousand years and upwards ; how in these times especially, not only the Torch still burns, and perhaps more fiercely than ever, but innumerable Rushlights and Sulphur-matches kindled thereat, are also glancing in every direction, so that not the smallest cranny or doghole in Nature or Art can remain unilluminated. . . . etc.—Carlyle, *Sartor Resartus*.

Light that makes things seen makes some things invisible. Were it not for darkness and the shadow of the earth, the noblest part of creation had remained unseen, and the stars in heaven invisible. The greatest mystery of religion is expressed by adumbration. . . . The sun itself is but the dark simulacrum, and light is but the shadow, of God.—Sir Thomas Browne.

AIR, WIND.—That all your lover's vows were empty air.—John Masefield, *The Daffodil Fields*.

Mr. Robertson enters the room of approved reputations and theories like a vigorous breeze, parting the curtains that have preserved a reverential half-light and blowing away the dust. But if his writing is, like a March wind, clean and invigorating, it is apt to be petulant too.—*The Times Literary Supplement*, 18th October, 1923.

Language is, as it were, the atmosphere of philosophical investigation, which must be made transparent before anything can be seen through it in the true figure and position.—J. Stewart Mill, *Three Essays on Religion*.

V. ASPECTS OF NATURE

WEATHER AND ITS PHENOMENA.—The thickest clouds, black and violent with menace of approaching storm, may yet gain a strange splendour from the wintry sunset, or catch a reflexion of wild and rugged beauty from the breaking of the boisterous morn. Thus even the shadow of sorrow to come, even the threatenings of impending grief, may be touched by the sad brightness of a smile of sympathy or softened

ASPECTS OF NATURE

by the simple charms of a happy home.—Father Robert Kane, *Good Friday to Easter Sunday*.

Oh that the words that make the thoughts obscure
  From which they spring, as clouds of glimmering dew
From a white lake blot heaven's blue portraiture
  Were stripped of their thin masks and various hue.
    Shelley, *Ode to Liberty*.

He does not deal with prehistoric times, but "stands near the outer margin of the fog to observe and delineate the people as they emerge from darkness and twilight."—Standish O'Grady.

For when the blood ran lustier in him again,
  Full often the bright image of one face,
  Making a treacherous quiet in his heart,
Dispersed his resolution like a cloud.
    Tennyson, *Launcelot and Elaine*.

To add sunshine to daylight by making the happy happier.

Parnassus has two peaks ; the one where improvising poets cluster ; the other where the singer of deep secrets sits alone—a peak veiled sometimes from the whole morning of a generation by earth-born mists and smoke of kitchen fires, only to glow the more consciously at sunset, and after nightfall to crown itself with imperishable stars.—Lowell, *English Poets*.

He took the hands of his mother
  And answered in gentle wise,
Though his face was a cloud of anger
  And a quenchless flame his eyes.
    Ethna Carbery.

It takes a great deal of adversity to make night in some souls. Their sky keeps obstinately blue; their sun keeps shining on. But there are souls whose day is like the day of tropical latitudes, intensely lightsome while it lasts. But at evening there is no twilight, no softly creeping shades of dusk; night descends swiftly, suddenly, and in an instant there is blackness over all.

*   *   *

ILLUSTRATION

There is an obscurity of mist rising from the undrained shallows of the mind, and there is the darkness of the thunder-cloud gathering its electric masses with passionate intensity from the clear element of the imagination, not at random or wilfully, but by the natural processes of the creative faculty, to brood those flashes of expression that transcend rhetoric, and are only to be apprehended by the poetic instinct.—Lowell, *English Poets*.

If he [Shakespeare] had sorrows, he has made them the woof of everlasting consolation to his kind; and if, as poets are wont to whine, the outward world was cold to him, its biting air did but trace itself in loveliest frostwork of fancy on the many windows of that self-centred and cheerful soul.—Ibid.

An intenser play of passion condensing that misty mixture of feeling and reflexion, which makes the ordinary atmosphere of existence, into flashes of thought and phrase, whose brief but terrible illumination prints the outworn landscape of every day upon our brains, with its little motives and mean results, in lines of tell-tale fire.—Ibid.

Tiny breezelets of surprise, each one destroying the ripplets which the former had made—yet all keeping the surface of the mind in a bright dimple-smile.—S. T. Coleridge, *Anima Poetae*.

These Pensées [those of Maine de Biran] would be pitiful reading were they not relieved here and there by gleams of inspiration—great lightning-flashes of thought athwart the low thunder-clouds of despondency.—Canon Sheehan, *Under the Cedars and the Stars*.

Our pursuits are like the coloured ends of rainbows, seen through even while we pursue them and always receding before us as we advance.—F. W. Faber, *Bethlehem*.

There are some breezes from the candid novelist,

some harsh and poisonous blasts on which any window might be slammed. But what is curious to observe is the effect of coddling on the literary system, and the sickliness which becomes the habit of the mind unaccustomed to honest rigour and fresh air.—Francis Hackett in *Chicago Evening Post*.

We have unquestionably a great cloud bank of ancestral blindness weighing down upon us, only transiently riven here and there by fitful revelations of the truth.—W. James, *Talks to Teachers on Psychology*, etc.

" There is a great deal of unmapped country within us which has to be taken account of in any explanation of our gusts and storms."—George Eliot, quoted by F. C. Kolbe, *The Art of Life*.

You slip to and fro on the frozen levels of his [John Gower's] verse which gives no foothold to the mind.—James Russell Lowell.

" When storms blow high in the political atmosphere, the events of the day fill the sails, and the writer [journalist] may draw in his oars, and let his brain rest; but when calm weather returns, then comes, too, ' the tug of toil,' hard work and little speed."—S. T. Coleridge, *On the Principles of Sound Criticism*.

But if the place were grand, the time, the burden of the time, was far more so. The air overhead in its upper chambers was hurtling with the obscure sound ; was dark with sullen fermenting of storms that had been gathering for a hundred and thirty years.—De Quincey, *Joan of Arc*.

The cloud of mind is discharging its collected lightning and the equilibrium between institutions and opinions is now being restored. Shelley, Preface to *Prometheus Unbound*.

His [Emerson's] understanding played about a thought like lightning about a vane.—Francis Thompson, *Prose Writings*, Emerson.

ILLUSTRATION

Everyone has known, at one time or another in life, that strange unexpected calm that always falls like sudden snow on a storm-tossed country after some great crisis or upheaval.—Hugh Walpole, *The Cathedral*.

Like a torrent of sunshine falls her [Katharine Tynan's] lyric speech, large and sweet and spontaneous; lifting up things great and humble with equal diligence. About her pages there is the hush and innocent luxuriance of summer fields and blowing wild flowers. —Katherine Brégy, *Poets and Pilgrims*.

THE SEA AND SHIPS.—In due time these childish volumes, of which I still retain so kindly a recollection, were cast aside. How many a thing once precious do we cast aside, to be carried off by the ebb of the receding years.—*Lectures of a Certain Professor*.

It [Newman's Prose] flows round you ; it presses gently on every side of you, and yet like a steady current, carries you in one direction, too. On every facet of your mind and heart you feel the light touch of his purpose and yet you cannot escape the general drift of his movement any more than a ship can escape the drift of the tide.—R. H. Hutton.

Scarce one but thought he could gauge like an ale firkin that intuition whose edging shallows may have been sounded, but whose abysses, stretching down amid the sunless roots of Being and Consciousness, mock the plummet.—Lowell, *English Poets*.

So dark a forethought rolled about his brain,
As on a dull day in an ocean cave
The blind wave feeling round his long sea-hall
In silence.

Tennyson, *Idylls of the King*.

The fatal rocks towards which his logic desperately drifted.—Thackeray, *English Humourists*.

306

ASPECTS OF NATURE

And thus your pains
May only make that footprint upon sand
Which old recurring waves of prejudice
Resmooth to nothing.
                    Tennyson, *The Princess.*

They parted—ne'er to meet again ! . . .
They stood aloof the scars remaining,
Like cliffs that had been rent asunder ;
A dreary sea now flows between,
But neither heat, nor frost, nor thunder,
Shall wholly do away I ween,
The marks of that which once hath been.
                    Coleridge, *Christabel.*

A voyage of discovery into the regions of the memory will disclose here and there some bit of land, whether a tiny island of precarious volcanic origin or a more solid and greater continent not yet submerged by the waters of forgetfulness.—Francis P. Donnelly, *The Art of Interesting.*

The book is indeed a very Sea of Thought, neither calm nor clear, if you will ; yet, wherein the toughest pearl-diver may dive to his utmost depth, and return not only with sea-wrack but with true orients.—Carlyle, *Sartor Resartus.*

Let readers after intense consideration, and not till then, pronounce, whether on the utmost verge of our actual horizon there is not a looming as of Land ; a promise of new Fortunate Islands, perhaps whole undiscovered Americas, for such as have canvas to sail thither ?—Ibid.

Teufelsdröckh is now a man without Profession. Quitting the common Fleet of herring-busses and whalers, where indeed his leeward, laggard condition was painful enough, he desperately steers off, on a course of his own, by sextant and compass of his own. Unhappy Teufelsdröckh ! Though neither Fleet, nor Traffic, nor Commodores pleased thee, still was it not *a Fleet*, sailing in prescribed track, for fixed

objects ; above all, in combination, wherein, by
mutual guidance, by all manner of loans and borrowings,
each could manifoldly aid the other ? How wilt
thou sail in unknown seas ; and for thyself find
that shorter North-West Passage to thy fair Spice-
country of a Nowhere ?—A solitary rover, on such a
voyage, with such nautical tactics, will meet with
adventures. Nay, as we forthwith discover, a certain
Calypso-Island detains him at the very outset ;
and as it were falsifies and oversets his whole reckoning.
—Ibid.

The Oxford Movement may be a spent wave, but,
before it broke on the shore, it reared, as its successor
is now rearing, a brave and beautiful crest of liturgical
and devotional life, the force of which certainly
shifted the Anglican sands, though it failed to uncover
any rock-bottom underlying them. It is enough if
now and then a lone swimmer be borne by the tide,
now at its full, to be dashed, more or less ungently,
upon the Rock of Peter, to cling there in safety while
the impotent wave recedes and is lost in the restless
sea. M. A. Chapman, Art., " The Cresting Wave,"
in *Blackfriars*, April, 1921.

Things are always better done under one's own
steam than in somebody else's tow.—*Catholic Herald
of India*, March, 1924.

" A man, in whatsoever craft he sails, cannot
stretch away out of sight when he is linked to the
windings of the shore by the towing-ropes of History."
—De Quincey, *Joan of Arc*.

Two mighty vortices, Pericles and Alexander the
Great, drew into strong eddies about themselves all
the glory and the pomp of Greek literature, Greek
eloquence, Greek wisdom, Greek art. De Quincey,
On Style. Note.—At the beginning of the same paragraph he had expressed the same idea through a
different image. " Round these two foci . . . gathered

the total starry heavens of Greek intellect. . . . All that Greece produced . . . revolved like two neighbouring planetary systems about these two solar orbs."

The views advocated in this volume run counter to the trade wind of public opinion, so that, if noticed at all, I fear my venturesome craft will be severely buffeted by the waves of adverse criticism, if not sucked down mercilessly by the maelstrom of general indifference."—Max Müller, *Preface to the Science of Thought*.

No philosopher could think anything except that, in that central sea, the wave of the world had risen to its highest, seeming to touch the stars. But the wave was already stooping ; for it was only the wave of the world.—G. K. Chesterton, *The Everlasting Man*.

> Her heart still knew one star, one hope, it did not range
> Like to the watery hearts of tidal men,
> Swayed by all moons of beauty.
>> John Masefield, *The Daffodil Fields*.

Society had lost its moorings and gone adrift in the storm.—Thackeray, *English Humourists*.

" While Tennyson seeks for quiet waters and for harbours of refuge for the soul upon the voyage of life, Browning ' is glad to know the brine salt on his lips and the large air again '."—W. M. Dixon, *A Tennyson Primer*.

It is indeed difficult to account for the fact that a book so waterlogged with mediocrity should yet remain buoyant and seaworthy.—*Times Literary Supplement*.

The history of her [Arabia's] frontiers is a history of migrations ; heavy tides of men which in time burst even the strongest bulwarks opposed to them, and rush, or soak and trickle, into full possession of the civilizations beyond.—George Adam Smith, *Early Poetry of Israel*.

ILLUSTRATION

Hamlet *drifts* through the whole tragedy. He never keeps on one tack long enough to get steerage-way, even if, in a nature like his, with those electric streamers of whim and fancy ever wavering across the vault of his brain, the needle of judgment would point in one direction long enough to strike a course by.—Lowell, *English Poets*.

Much that is mere lumber and ballast floats upon the raft which is the name of Wordsworth; "Sumer is icomen in" breasts the billows proudly unsupported, bearing the surf that breaks upon the shore of eternity. —Nevile Watts, Introduction to *Love Songs of Sion*.

CLOUDS.—These [tall of feudalism, Schism of the West, etc.] were the loftiest peaks of the cloudland in the skies that to the scientific gazer first caught the colours of the *new* morning in advance. But the whole vast range of sweeping glooms overhead dwelt upon all meditative minds.—De Quincey, *Joan of Arc*.

Some of the stories undoubtedly saw it [the unity of the universe] as the clouds of mythology cleared and thinned away.—G. K. Chesterton, *The Everlasting Man*.

DESERT.—

> Full desertness
> In souls, as countries, lieth silent, bare,
> Under the blenching, vertical, eye-glare
> Of the absolute Heavens.
>
> E. B. Browning.

His [Wordsworth's] longer poems are Egyptian sand-wastes, with here and there an oasis of exquisite greenery, a grand image, Sphinx-like, half-buried in drifting commonplaces, or the Solitary, Pompey's Pillar of some towering thought.—Lowell, *English Poets*.

CAVE AND DESERT.—Thus has the bewildered Wanderer to stand, as so many have done, shouting question after question into the Sibyl-cave of Destiny, and receive no Answer but an Echo. It is all a grim Desert, this once-fair world of his ; wherein is heard only the howling of wild beasts . . . ; and no Pillar of Cloud by day, and no Pillar of Fire by night, any longer guides the Pilgrim.—Carlyle, *Sartor Resartus*.

SEASONS.—And what if joy pass quick away ? Long is the track of Hope before—long too, the track of recollection after, as in the Polar spring the sun is seen in the heavens sixteen days before it really rises, and in the Polar autumn ten days after it has set ; so Nature, with Hope and Recollection pieces out our short summer.—Coleridge.

> Now is the winter of our discontent
> Made glorious summer by the sun of York.
> Shakespeare.

ROADS AND PATHS.—The path to truth is overgrown with prejudices and strewn with fallen theories and rotting systems which hide it from our view. —Seeley, *Ecce Homo*.

> In shadowy thoro'fares of thought.
> Tennyson, *In Memoriam*.

" There is no longer any need to grope at random through a trackless forest. Fair roads have been opened. But the adventurous come to conceive a mislike of these very roads as too well frequented and trite. Is there no shorter cut to a desired goal ? Glory should assuredly accrue to such a discovery. And you may lighten baggage."—*Times Literary Supplement*, 1924, p. 838, in a review of a work on the genesis of religion.

INLAND WATERS.—His [M. Arnold's] verse is no great strain of the waters of life, bursting from the rock at the magic touch of the prophet's rod, for staunching the thirst of millions wandering athirst in the torrid wilderness. But it is a rivulet of crystal

311

ILLUSTRATION

purity that never runs dry, at which the solitary wayfarer may drink, to the refreshment of his soul.—W. T.
Stead.

Cut us off from narrative, how would the stream of
conversation, even among the wisest, languish into
detached handfuls and among the foolish utterly
evaporate.—Carlyle, *Sartor Resartus*.

The remorseless cataract of daily literature which
thunders over the remnants of the Past.—Frederick
Harrison, *The Choice of Books*.

> Never came reformation in a flood,
> With such a heady current scouring faults.
>
> *Henry V*, i, 1.

The stream of narrative flowing swiftly, as it
does, over the jagged rocks of human destiny must
often be turbulent and tossed ; it is, therefore, all
the more the duty of every good citizen to keep it as
undefiled as possible, and to do what in him lies to
prevent peripatetic philosophers on the banks from
throwing their theories into it, either dead ones to
decay, or living ones to drown.—A. Birrell, *The Muse
of History*.

> I would play you the music of laughter
> And set the smiles lighting your apple-bloom face
> In little, glad ripples that gather apace,
> As if the lone hush of lake waters were stirred
> In a wind from the swift sweeping wing of a bird
> Which trails the breeze after.
>
> Ethna Carbery.

The rivers of mythology and philosophy run parallel
and do not mingle till they meet in the sea of Christen-
dom.—G. K. Chesterton, *The Everlasting Man*.

When this movement pierced the dyke between
the east and west and brought more mystical ideas
into Europe, it brought with it a whole flood of other
mystical ideas besides its own. . . . They very
nearly flooded and overwhelmed the purely Christian

element. . . . All this dark tide out of the metaphysical sea in the midst of Asia poured through the
dykes simultaneously with the creed of Christ ; but
it is the whole point of the story that the two were
not the same ; that they flowed like oil and water.
That creed remained in the shape of a miracle ; a river
still flowing through the sea. And the proof of the
miracle was practical once more ; it was merely that
while all that sea was salt and bitter with the savour
of death, of this one stream in the midst of it a man
could drink."—Ibid.

To have read the literature of the seventeenth
and eighteenth centuries is to know that nearly everybody had come to take it for granted that religion
was a thing that would continually broaden like a
river, till it reached an infinite sea. Some of them
expected it to go down in a cataract of catastrophe,
most of them expected it to widen into an estuary of
equality and moderation ; but all of them thought its
returning on itself a prodigy as incredible as witch-
craft.—Ibid.

> You are water roughed by every wind that stirs,
> One little gust will alter your intent.
> John Masefield, *The Daffodil Fields*.

That wild source of inspiration has been stopped ;
it has been built over, lapped and locked, imprisoned,
led underground.—Alice Meynell, *Essays*.

> Fate . . .
> Bade through the deep recesses of our breast
> The unregarded river of our life
> Pursue with indiscernible flow its way ;
> And that we should not see
> The buried stream, and seem to be
> Eddying at large in blind uncertainty,
> Though driving on with it eternally.
> Matthew Arnold, *The Buried Life*.

N.B.—The same image runs right through the
poem.

ILLUSTRATION

As a beam o'er the face of the waters may glow,
While the tide runs in darkness and coldness below,
So the cheek may be tinged with a warm sunny smile
Though the cold heart to ruin runs darkly the while.

T. Moore.

Milton ! thou shouldst be living at this hour :
    England hath need of thee ; she is a fen
Of stagnant waters.

Wordsworth.

It is not to be thought of that the flood
    Of British freedom, which, to the open sea
    Of the world's praise, from dark antiquity
Hath flowed " with pomp of waters, unwithstood "—
Roused though it be full often to a mood
    Which spurns the cheek of salutary bands,
    That this most famous stream in bogs and sands
Should perish and to evil and to good
Be lost for ever.

Wordsworth.

The Gaelic waters reached everywhere either in occasional streams or in concealed floodings.—Daniel Corkery, *The Hidden Ireland*.

Both figures (Touchstone and Jaques) are set like boulders in the pellucid stream of the drama, contributing nothing to its movement, but making its hidden tendencies, its currents and cross-currents visible and explicit.—C. H. Herford, *The Works of Shakespeare*.

Remote as the mountain snows, yet near as the wind upon our face, is her [Alice Meynell's] song.—Katherine Brégy, *The Poets' Chantry*.

New circumstance, new care shall cause to wane
His very image, till your eyes no more
Behold him in the deep
Dark mere of memory.

Roden Noel.

The river of his History, which we have traced from its tiniest fountains, and hoped to see flow onward, with increasing current, into the ocean, here dashed

314

itself over that terrific Lover's Leap ; and as a mad-foaming cataract, flies wholly into tumultuous clouds of spray. Low down it indeed collects again into pools and plashes ; yet only at a great distance, and with difficulty, if at all, into a general stream. To cast a glance into certain of these pools and plashes, and trace whither they run, must, for a chapter or two, form the limit of our endeavour.—Carlyle, *Sartor Resartus*.

> Sweet are familiar songs, though Music dips
> Her hollow shell in Thought's forlornest wells.
> > Lord Lytton, *A Night in Italy*.

> O strong man, man of my love
> With eyes of dreams
> Pools of the dusk where move
> No starry gleams.
> > Ethna Carbery.

> She is Mary of the Curls—the swan-white, modest maid,
> Grey pools of quiet are her eyes, like waters in the shade.
> > Ibid.

HEAVENLY BODIES.—This Jacobin's club which at first shone resplendent, and was thought to be a new celestial sun for enlightening the nations, had, as things all have, to work through its appointed phases ; it burned, unfortunately, more and more lurid, more sulphurous, distracted ; and swam at last, through the astonished Heaven, like a Tartarean Portent and lurid Prison of Spirits in Pain.—Carlyle, *French Revolution*.

The coldest moon of an idea rises haloed through his vaporous imagination. The dimmest-sparked chip of a conception blazes and scintillates in the subtile oxygen of his brain.—Francis Thompson, *Essay on Shelley*.

He [Dante] was the Lucifer of that starry flock which in the thirteenth century shone forth from Republican Italy, as from a heaven, into the darkness of the benighted world. His very worlds are instinct with spirit ; each is as a spark, a burning atom of inextinguishable thought ; and many yet lie covered in the ashes of their birth, and pregnant with lightning that has yet found no conductor.—Shelley, *Defence of Poetry*.

His lines flow as simply as water in a brook. They ripple irregularly over the stones, but the chief impression they leave with us is not of irregularity but of onward sliding motion.—*Times Literary Supplement*.

MOUNTAINS.—The mind is confined by numberless concentric mountain barriers ; once stumble on a pass in the nearest, and the mind's eye ranges freely for ever to a vaster horizon with mountains of its own—peaks of Darien—in the distance.—Ibid., October, 1920.

VARIOUS.—Not unfrequently the Germans have been blamed for an unprofitable diligence ; as if they struck into devious courses where nothing was to be had but the toil of a rough journey ; as if, forsaking the gold-mines of finance and that political slaughter of fat oxen whereby a man himself grows fat, they were apt to run goose-hunting into regions of bilberries and crowberries and be swallowed up at last in remote peat-bogs.—Carlyle, *Sartor Resartus*.

As there are some days even in England when merely to go out and breathe the common air is joy. . . . So, to take up almost any one of Dr. Newman's books, and they are happily numerous, is to be led away from " evil tongues " and " the sneers of selfish men ", from the mud and the mire, the shoving and the pushing that gather round the pig-troughs of life, into a diviner ether, a purer air. . . .—A. Birrell, *Res Judicatae*.

The powers that history commemorates are but the coarse effect of influences delicate and vague as the beginning of twilight.—W. B. Yeates, *A Book of Irish Verse* (Introd.).

The constant flutter of culture, the flash of modernistic technique across the page, do not obscure the solid horizons of a great, sure tradition.—G. N. Shuster in the *Month*.

We are often surprised by the discovery of vast, unknown tracts of the spiritual life. They seem like great plains stretching out in mystery and wrapt in mists that sometimes for a moment lift, or sweep off and leave one looking for one brief instant upon great reaches of one's own life, unknown, unmeasured, unexplored.—B. W. Maturin, *Self-knowledge and Self-discipline*.

Nature is always clarifying her water and her wine. No filtration can be so perfect. She does the same thing by books as by her gases and plants. There is always a selection in writers and then a selection from the selection.—Emerson, *Books*.

VI. THE PLANT WORLD

PLANTS AND FLOWERS.—

He was
The ivy that had hid my princely trunk
And sucked the verdure out on't.
The Tempest.

Like other plants virtue will not grow unless its root be hidden, buried from the eye of the sun. Let the sun shine on it, nay do but look at it privily thyself, the root withers, and no flower will glad thee. —Carlyle, *Sartos Resartos*.

The temper of a party is sometimes greatly influenced by the courage which the Government show in framing their measure. Majorities, like nettles, need to be grasped.—*The Spectator*.

Every hidden root of thought, every subtlest fibre of feeling, was mated, by new shoots and leafage of expression, fed from those unseen sources in the common earth of human nature.—Lowell, *English Poets*.

Hence the vanity of translation ; it were as wise to cast a violet into a crucible that you might discover the formal principle of its colour and odour, as seek to transfuse from one language into another the creations of a poet. The plant must spring again from its seed or it will bear no flower.—Shelley, *Defence of Poetry*.

> The heart that has truly loved never forgets,
> But as truly loves on to the close
> As the sunflower that turns on her god when he sets
> The same look which she turned when he rose.
>
> Moore, *Irish Melodies*.

A fresh crop of mushroom periodicals.

These little poems [those of P. H. Pearse] are the first blossoms of a Spring that has scarcely begun —shy crocuses breaking through the earth where the barren foot of Winter still lingers.—Cathaoir O'Braonain in *Studies*.

> Yet freedom is itself a flower, which tops
> All growths except the weedy licence bred
> Within its rich vicinity.
>
> F. W. Faber, *Poems*.

A rambling rose-branch full of lovely flowers a little overblown, twined inextricably into that green laurel-garland, the classic art of France—such, at first sight, appears Madame de Sévigné.—*Times Literary Supplement*, 4th February, 1926.

Yet, when all is said, one hesitates to bring the " personal equation " too close to a poet's individuality or to criticize the passion flower because it is neither a rose nor an asphodel.—Katherine Brégy, *The Poet's Chantry*.

The whole Elizabethan flower burst from the old literary stalk that Catholic scribes and poets had built blindly and coralwise through the centuries.— Shane Leslie, Preface to *An Anthology of Catholic Poets*.

All the Arthurian legend is a wild flower growing out of the gargoyles of the Sanctuary.—Ibid.

GARDEN.—

> Like a child
> In some strange garden left awhile alone,
> I pace about the pathways of the world,
> Plucking light hopes and joys from every stem,
> With qualms of vague misgiving in my heart
> That payment at the last may be required,—
> Payment I cannot make,—or guilt incurred,
> And shame to be endured.
>
> A. H. Clough.

The excitement of conflict had proved a forcing bed for immature talent, which had burst prematurely into bloom at a season when, under healthier conditions, it should still have been thrusting its tap roots deeper into the nourishing and sustaining soil of normal experience.—Wilfrid Wilson Gibson in a lecture, 1921.

Speaking of English Conservatism the American Ambassador at London, Walter H. Page, writes to President Wilson : " This moss that has grown all over their lives (some of it very soft and most of it very comfortable—it's soft and warm) is of no great consequence—except that they think they'd die if it were removed."

In a similar context Carlyle, inveighing against the preservation of institutions that are unjust or decadent, writes :—

The bough that is dead shall be cut away, for the sake of the tree itself. Old ? Yes, it is too old. Many a weary winter has it swung and creaked there, and gnawed and fretted, with its dead wood, the organic substance and still living fibre of this good tree ; many a long summer has its ugly naked brown defaced the fair green umbrage ; every day it has done mischief, and that only : off with it, for the tree's sake, if for nothing more ; let the Conservatism that would preserve cut *it* away. Did no wood-forester apprise you that a dead bough with its dead root left sticking there is extraneous, poisonous ; is as a dead iron spike, some horrid rusty ploughshare driven into the living substance ;—nay, far worse ; for in every windstorm (commercial crises, or the like) it frets and creaks, jolts itself to and fro, and cannot lie quiet as your dead iron spike would.—*Past and Present*.

Here the metaphor is so developed as to become an allegory.

TREE.—Wondrous, indeed, is the virtue of a true book ! Not like a dead city of stones, yearly crumbling, yearly needing repair ; more like a tilled field, but then a spiritual field ; like a spiritual tree, let me rather say, it stands from year to year, and from age to age . . . and yearly comes its new produce of leaves (Commentaries, Deductions, Philosophical, Political Systems ; or were it only Sermons, Pamphlets, Journalistic Essays), every one of which is talismanic and thaumaturgic, for it can persuade men.—Carlyle, *Sartor Resartus*.

The edelweiss of spiritual joy cannot possibly take permanent root among the thorns and thistles and stinging nettles of a life where work is feared and duty neglected, nor in the swampy morass of lewdness and intemperance, nor in the hard, stony soil of laziness, nor in the desert wastes of a soulless, godless brutish existence, nor in the quicksand and mire of frivolity. In such soils will flourish only short-lived plants of evil odour with poisonous berries.— Bishop von Keppler, *More Joy*.

SEEDS, HARVEST.—Until the mind can love, and admire, and trust, and hope, and endure, reasoned principles of moral conduct are seeds cast upon the highway of life, which the unconscious passenger tramples into dust, although they would bear the harvest of his happiness.—Shelley, Preface to *Prometheus Unbound*.

The ancient philosophy was a treadmill, not a path. It was a contrivance for having much exertion and no progress. Every trace of intellectual cultivation was there, except a harvest. There had been plenty of ploughing, harrowing, reaping, thrashing. But the garners contained only smut and stubble.— Macaulay, *Essay on Lord Bacon*.

They quietly assumed that the Norman and Saxon elements would disappear under the Gaelic genius like the tracks of cavalry under a fresh crop.—Davis, *Essay on the Ballad Poetry of Ireland*.

The art-producing fields get weary, as it were, of a crop too often sown ; their harvests dwindle ; until in the fulness of time a new vegetation, drawing upon fresh sources of nourishment, springs suddenly into vigorous and aggressive life.—A. J. Balfour, *Criticism and Beauty*.

The world is found to be subsisting wholly on the shadow of a reality, on sentiments diluted from passions, on the tradition of a fact, the convention of a moral, the straw of last year's harvest.—Robert Browning, *Essay on Shelley*.

Then there is Longfellow's familiar, " I know a Reaper whose name is Death."

Forest.—Emerson's greatest charm is that he suggests more than he says. There is no finality. . . . It is as though the reader is being guided through an endless forest. Long glades open on every side and tempt him to wander. Here the path is wide and there it is almost impracticable, but through the foliage at intervals come glimpses of sky and of blue distance inviting him on."—A Preface to Emerson's Works.

ILLUSTRATION

Various.—A core of scornful and melancholy protest, set about with a pulp of satire, and outside all a rind of thick burlesque—that is *Don Quixote*.—Francis Thompson, *Essay on Don Quixote*.

He [Coleridge] has incited in them the very sprouting of the laurel-bough, has been a fostering sun of song.—Francis Thompson, *Coleridge*.

If our dominions abroad are the roots which feed all this rank luxuriance of sedition, it is not intended to cut them off in order to famish the fruit.—Burke, *Thoughts on the Present Discontents*.

The popular vernaculars are vast speech jungles in which old forms are decaying and new ones continually springing into life, and this fermentation results in the creation of numberless new terms, which come to birth and live and die in tropical profusion.—L. Pearsall Smith, *Words and Idioms*.

Words of the kinds I have been describing . . . are continually finding their way from dialects and popular speech into the literary language, drifting like air borne seeds over the barriers and walls which guard its precincts.—Ibid.

The rhetoricians were teachers and being teachers knew the value of metaphor and simile which lend wings to the seeds of doctrine and which plant them in the field of the ear.—B. L. Gildersleeve in *A.J.P.*, xxiv, 1903.

> A crowd of hopes,
> That sought to sow themselves like winged seeds,
> Born out of everything I heard and saw,
> Flutter'd about my senses and my soul.
> Tennyson, *The Gardener's Daughter*.

The conditions have become too meticulous, hard, and acrid for that wayward crop, literature, to throw out those promiscuous spurts of growth which are the very routine of youth.—Daniel Corkery, *The Hidden Ireland*.

ANIMALS

VII. Animals

Oxen.—

And we shall feel like oxen at a stall
The better cherished, still the nearer death.

I *Henry IV*, v, 2.

Race-horse.—Mr. Vernède has a sprightly fancy and a gift of expressing himself with a laughing lightness that is not common. . . . So we feel slight dudgeon at finding his easy paces at times clogged by the mud of commonplace melodrama. That mud is exceptionally sticky. He is like a race-horse in a ploughed field—out of place. Happily it is not all ploughed land and he quickly kicks his heels free and is off at his own pace on the turf.—A Review in *The Academy*, October, 1913.

Of all the great men who have leaped upon the world as upon an unbroken horse, who have guided it with relentless hands, and ridden it breathless to the goal of glory, Caesar is the only one who turned the race into the tack of civilization and, dying, left mankind a future in the memory of his past.—Marion Crawford, *Ave Roma Immortalis*.

Horse.—The changeless amble of his (Southey's) blank verse, never breaking even into a trot, might almost make us regret that dissonant jolt which Byron substituted for the long easy canter of the Spenserian stanza under the guidance of its original master's serene and skilful hand.—Swinburne.

A miserable procession of knock-kneed, broken-winded metaphors.—J. Middleton Murry, *The Central Problem of Style*.

Eagle.—As fierce a beak and talon as ever struck—as strong a wing as ever beat, belonged to Swift. I am glad, for one, that fate wrested the prey out of his claws, and cut his wings and chained him. One can gaze, and not without awe and pity, at

ILLUSTRATION

the lonely eagle chained behind the bars.—Thackeray,
English Humourists.

> The eagle-wingéd pride
> Of sky-aspiring and ambitious thoughts.
> > *Richard II*, i, 3.

In some of these essays he (Emerson) is like a great
eagle, sailing in noble and ample gyres with deliberate
beat of the strong wing, round the eyrie where his
thought is nested.—Francis Thompson, *Emerson*.

> Though he inherit
> Nor the pride nor ample pinion
> That the Theban eagle bare
> Sailing with supreme dominion.
> Through the azure deep of air.
> > Gray, *The Progress of Poesy*.

SWALLOW.—

> . . . . Loosens from the lip
> Short swallow-flights of song that dip
> Their wings in tears and skim away.
> > Tennyson, *In Memoriam*.

LARK.—

> I was not therefore sad ;
> My soul was singing at a work apart
> Behind the wall of sense, as safe from harm
> As sings the lark when sucked up out of sight
> In vortices of glory and blue air.
> > E. B. Browning, *Aurora Leigh*.

BIRD.—For if, now and then, some straggling,
broken-winged thinker has cast an owl's glance
into this obscure region, the most have soared over
it altogether heedless.—Carlyle, *Sartor Resartus*.

> The bird of time has but a little way
> To flutter—and the bird is on the wing.
> > Omar Khayyam.

CORMORANT.—

> Light vanity, insatiate cormorant
> Consuming means, soon preys upon itself.
> > *Richard II*, ii, 1.

ANIMALS

FLIES.—

> To contemplation's sober eye
> Such is the race of man
> And they that creep and they that fly,
> Shall end where they began.
> Alike the busy and the gay,
> But flutter through life's little day,
> In Fortune's varying colours drest :
> Brushed by the hand of rough mischance,
> Or chilled by age, their airy dance
> They leave, in dust to rest.
>> Gray, *Ode to Spring.*

DOG.—Yet for all that, I am ill at ease ; and as I walked to-day, far and fast in the sun-warmed lanes, my thoughts came yapping and growling around me like a pack of curs—undignified, troublesome, vexatious thoughts ; I chase them away for a moment and next moment they are snapping at my heels.— A. C. Benson, *The Silent Isle.*

> For your own reasons turn into your bosoms
> Like dogs upon their masters worrying you.
>> *Henry V*, ii, 2.

HOUNDS.—

> O when mine eyes did see Olivia first
> Methought she purged the air of pestilence.
> That instant was I turned into a hart ;
> And my desires, like fell and cruel hounds,
> E'er since pursue me.
>> *Twelfth Night.*

> When the hounds of Spring are on Winter's traces,
>   The mother of months in meadow or plain
> Fills the shadows and windy places
>   With lisp of leaves and ripple of rain.
>> Swinburne, *Atlanta in Calydon.*

Erudition, like a bloodhound, is a charming thing when held firmly in leash, but it is not so attractive when turned loose upon a defenceless and unerudite public.—Agnes Repplier, *Points of View.*

325

Save that chained rage that ever yelped within.—
Tennyson.

He [Shelley] teases into growling the kennelled
thunder, and laughs at the shaking of its fiery chain.—
Francis Thompson, *Essay on Shelley*.

BEES AND WASPS.—When the Faith first emerged
into the world, the very first thing that happened to
it was that it was caught in a sort of swarm of mystical
and metaphysical sects, mostly out of the East ; like
one lonely golden bee caught in a swarm of wasps.
To the ordinary onlooker, there did not seem to be
much difference, or anything beyond a general buzz ;
indeed in a sense there was not much difference, so
far as stinging and being stung were concerned.
The difference was that only one golden dot in all
that whirring gold-dust had the power of going forth
to make hives for all humanity ; to give the world
honey and wax or (as was so finely said in a context
too easily forgotten) " the two noblest things, which
are sweetness and light". The wasps all died that
winter.—G. K. Chesterton, *The Everlasting Man*.

WILD BEASTS.—Such words were chamacicon
cloaks—" groundlion " cloaks, of the colour of the
ground of any man's fancy ; on that ground they lie
in wait, and rend him with a spring from it. There
were never creatures of prey so mischievous. . . .—
Ruskin, *Sesame and Lilies*.

The critic must not in too tiger-like a style tear a
defenceless metaphor to pieces.—Macbeth, *Might and
Mirth of Literature*.

HIND.—

> La biche illusion me mangeait dans le creux
> De la main ; tu l'as fait enfuir . . .
>
> V. Hugo, *Insommie*.

WILD GEESE.—I do not mean that in either case
I have space to deal with the multitude of fallacies
that rise flapping about me like a flock of wild geese

ANIMALS

wherever I move in the matter ; but in one or two cases I may warn Mr. L. away from a wild-goose chase.—G. K. Chesterton in *Dublin Review*, January, 1925.

FISH.—The whale is followed by waves. I would glide down the rivulet of quiet life, a trout.—Coleridge, *Anima Poetae*.

VARIOUS.—

> Michael comes
> And the savage truth appears and rips my life to thrums.
> John Masefield, *The Daffodil Fields*.

This is a day which shirks the labour of producing unified wholes, which dribbles away in snatches, mumbles and slathers the literary bone in its lazy jaws.—Francis Thompson, *Macaulay*.

Such writers have merely *verbal* imaginations that retain nothing but words. Or their puny thoughts have dragon-wings, all green and gold.—Hazlitt, *Table Talk*.

Wily thoughts that slip off into the darkness as we try to turn upon them the light of conscience.—B. W. Maturin, *Self-knowledge and Self-discipline*.

GULL.—His historical papers are unsystematic, skimming the subject like a sea-mew, and dipping every now and again to bring to the surface some fresh view on this or that point.—Francis Thompson, *Thomas de Quincey*.

DOVES.—

> Home from the horizon far and clear
>   Hither the soft wings sweep ;
> Flocks of the memories of the day draw near
>   The dovecote doors of sleep.
>
> Oh, which are they that come through sweetest light
>   Of all these homing birds ?
> Which with the straitest and the swiftest flight ?
>   Your words to me, your words.
>   Alice Meynell.

ILLUSTRATION

VIII. Arts and Crafts

Music.—How that dreary dull undertone of sadness rolls through all modern literature. Never a note of triumph, never a psalm of hope, never a glorious prophetic paean about the future that is to be. . . . But a low deep wail, musical enough if you like, echoing along the minor chords of human misery, and sobbing itself away into silence, unless the wind moaning among the tangled grasses and nettles amid the deserted and forgotten graves can be taken as the echo in Nature of the threnodies that wailed from such desolate and despairing lives.—Canon Sheehan, *Under the Cedars and the Stars*.

And thus the old house that I loved in my pleasant youth, the good days that I spent there year by year, are an earnest of the tender care that surrounds me. I will not regard them as past and gone ; I will rather regard them as the low sweet prelude of the great symphony ; if I am now tossed upon the melancholy and broken waves of some vehement scherzo of life, the subject is but working itself out, and I will strive to apprehend it even here. There are other great movements that await me, as wonderful, as sweet.— A. C. Benson, *The Silent Isle*.

> How light the touches are that kiss
> The music from the chords of life.
> C. Patmore, *The Angel in the House*.

Quite familiar now is the metaphorical usage of such musical terms as *gamut, diapason, key, harmony, melody*.

Mosaic.—It [literature] means a critical understanding of the value of the stones that make up the great mosaic of literature, and these stones are words.— Maurice Francis Egan, *A Gentleman*.

Weaving.—The black threads of this lament run hither and thither through the growing texture of poetry ; but there are other strands as well.—Professor Gummere, *Poetry and Democracy*.

Mr. Békássy's poetry is full of loose ends, of vivid threads which later experience would have woven into a pattern.—*Times Literary Supplement*, 14th May, 1925.

ARCHITECTURE AND BUILDING.—After all, why should we object to them, these odd crowding fancies of Crashaw ? They lend a sort of Gothic effect to his poetry. They are the flying buttresses, the gargoyles, the tooth-marks, and rose windows of Crashaw's Temple of the Lord. Looked at from a distance as a whole the edifice is a most sublime one. R. A. Eric Shepherd, Introduction to *Religious Poems of Richard Crashaw*.

High Air-castles are cunningly built of Words, the Words well bedded also in good Logic-mortar, wherein, however, no knowledge will come to lodge.— Carlyle, *Sartor Resartus*.

Only blood can bring together and cement the broken edges of the human and divine.—Lauchlan McLean Watt in *Expositor*, 1921.

Vallancey twisted language, towers, and traditions into his wickerwork theory of pagan Ireland ; and Walker built great facts and great blunders, granite blocks and rotten wood, into his antiquarian edifices.—Davis, *Essay on Irish Antiquities*.

It would have helped him [Carlyle] had he remembered that there were on all sides other workers engaged on the temple not made with hands, although he could not hear the sound of their hammers for the din he made himself.—H. Jones, *Browning as a Philosophical and Religious Teacher*.

THE JEWELLER.—The best work of Tennyson and Swinburne is not so wrought, but such work is more beautiful than the unpolished crystals of all but the greatest. Shakespeare or Blake or Shelley may cast from the crucible a flashing jewel that a single further touch could only spoil, but their temperature is their own secret ; other men must cut and polish more or less, though the stone lose a little in glow while it gains in lustre. Better at least the polished gem than the shapeless stone which now glows luridly and now is dull as glass, now glows like a carbuncle and now fades into a grey pebble.—E. G. Lamborn, *The Rudiments of Criticism*.

To become original passive reception of truths is not enough. . . . We must strike out our views, we must cut innumerable facets on the rough diamond of truth, transmitted to us from others.—F. P. Donnelly, *The Art of Interesting*.

EMBROIDERY.—"Very often in Tennyson and Swinburne, we can watch the hand of the conscious artist at work, charging every rift with gold, adding beauties till the simple texture of the original thought grows into a stiff brocade."—E. G. Lamborn, *The Rudiments of Poetry*.

PRINTING.—The sacred orator must melt down the stereotyped and run his language into new moulds for his audience.—Francis P. Donnelly, *The Art of Interesting*, 1921.

MINTING.—Let the worn-out thought be reminted in a glowing imagination and it will have all the brightness and ring of a first coinage.—F. P. Donnelly, *The Art of Interesting*.

METALLURGY.—

> Life is not as idle ore,
> But iron dug from central gloom,
>   And heated hot with burning fears,
>   And dipt in baths of hissing tears,
> And battered with the shocks of doom
> To shape and use . . .

Tennyson, *In Memoriam*.

330

OCCUPATIONS AND ACTIVITIES

IX. Occupations and Common Activities

WASHING.—The fact is in reporting one's conversation, one cannot help Blair-ing it up more or less, ironing out crumpled paragraphs, starching limp ones, and crimping and plaiting a little sometimes.—O. W. Holmes, *Autocrat of the Breakfast Table.*

There may be beliefs so sacred or so delicate, that, if I may use the metaphor, they will not wash without shrinking and losing colour.—Newman.

NURSE.—

> Time that aged nurse
> Rocked me to patience.
> Keats, Endymion.

AGRICULTURE AND HORTICULTURE.—He [Addison] was six and thirty. He had not worked crop after crop from his brain, manuring hastily, subsoiling indifferently, cutting and sowing and cutting again, like other luckless cultivators of letters.—Thackeray, *English Humourists.*

> Full seldom does a man repent, or use
> Both grace and will to pick the vicious quitch
> Of blood and custom wholly out of him,
> And make all clean and plant himself afresh.
> Tennyson, Geraint and Enid.

> Covering discretion with a coat of folly;
> As gardeners do with ordure hide those roots
> That shall first spring and be most delicate.
> Henry V, ii, 4.

His [Meredith's] style would be quite sufficient of itself to keep life at a distance. By its means he has planted round his garden a hedge full of thorns and red with wonderful roses.—Oscar Wilde, *The Decay of Lying.*

They [the profits] belonged to the party of progress in the best sense of the term, and their work was especially to break up the fallow ground of habit that had become hard and set and unfit to receive the seed of fresh teaching.—Hastings, *Dictionary of the Bible*, Art., Prophets.

GAMES.—Life consists not so much in holding a good hand as in playing a bad one well.—Father Bernard Vaughan, *What of To-day?*

POTTER'S WHEEL.—

> Ay, note that Potter's wheel
> That metaphor and feel
> Why time spins fast, why passive lies our clay.
> Browning, *Rabbi Ben Ezra*.

The whole poem is a working out of this metaphor.

SWIMMING.—I have swum in clear, sweet waters all my days ; and if sometimes they were a little cold, and the stream ran adverse and something rough, it was never too strong to be breasted and swum through.—Theodore Parker.

PILE-DRIVING.—I felt myself singularly without energy to carry out my hopes and schemes, and at the same time it seemed that time was ebbing away purposelessly and that I was not driving, so to speak, any piles in the fluid and easy substratum of ideas on which my life seemed built.—A. C. Benson, *The House of Quiet*.

SAILING.—A man who has always found it plain sailing, and has never failed to have sun and stars visible when he wanted them for observations may be sure he is sailing over a pacific ocean of his own, very different from the wild, uncertain, clouded seas, where saints so often find themselves at the mercy of wind and weather.—Father Faber, *Spiritual Conferences*.

DRINKING.—Even our puritan fore-fathers, with their hatred of art, were in love with ideas. They sipped theology with the air of connoisseurs : they drank down Hebrew virtues with a vigorous relish.—A. C. Benson, *The Silent Isle*.

OCCUPATIONS AND ACTIVITIES

JUDGE.—While Swift went about, hanging and ruthless—a literary Jeffreys—in Addison's kind court only minor cases were tried ; only peccadilloes and small sins against society.—Thackerary, *English Humourists.*

SINKING A WELL.—It was as if the Muse had said, I am weary of philosophy and satire, weary of faded sentiment, of refined and classic verse, and of stern pictures of misery, and I will have a something fresh at last ; and had driven a shaft down through layer after layer of dry clay, till she touched, far below, a source of new and hidden waters, that, loosened from their prison, rushed upwards to the surface, and ran away in a mountain torrent of clear bright verse, living, and life-giving.—Stopford Brooke, *Theology in the English Poets.*

DANCING.—The language has gained immensely, by the infusion, in richness of synonym and in the power of expressing nice shades of thought and feeling, but more than all in light-footed poly-syllables that trip singing to the music of verse.—Lowel, *English Poets.*

WEIGHING.—We weigh with minutest scales each ounce and drachm and scruple of the miserable alloy with which we are paying Him under the sweet-sounding name of love.—F. W. Faber, *The Creator and the Creature.*

RACING.—Good carries weight in the race with evil. It has not a fair start nor a fair field.—A. K. H. B., *Recreations of a Country Parson*, Second Series.

MINING.—When you come to a good book you must ask yourself, " Am I inclined to work as a Australian miner would ? Are my pickaxes and shovels in good order, and am I in good trim myself, my sleeves well up to the elbow, and my breath good, and my temper ? " And, keeping the figure a little longer, even at cost of tiresomeness, for it is a thoroughly useful one, the metal you are in search of being the author's mind or meaning, his words are as the rock which you have to crush and smelt in order to get it. And your pickaxes are your own care, wit, and learning ; your smelting furnace is your own thoughtful soul. Do not hope to get at any good author's meaning without those tools and that fire; often you will need sharpest, finest chiselling and patientest fusing, before you can gather one grain of the metal.—Ruskin, *Sesame and Lilies.*

USHER—Not every one can write a short history which makes good reading on its own account, and which yet possesses the higher and rarer merit of remaining after all the humble usher to a greater presence.—Robert Dewar, *The Year's Work in English Studies,* 1923.

WAR AND WEAPONS.—There were moments when the Roman cut his way with a sword-stroke of song out of the tangle of the mythologies.—G. K. Chesterton, *The Everlasting Man.*

An author's preliminary skirmish with his subject.—Lobban, Introduction to *English Essays.*

Irony in his [Addison's] hands was like a fine rapier which can wound without at once being felt, and no English writer has excelled him in the deft handling of the weapon.—The Same.

If a man is too fond of a paradox, if he is flighty and empty . . . stick a fact into him like a stiletto.—O. W. Holmes, *The Autocrat of the Breakfast Table.*

> Faintly venomed points
> Of slander, glancing here and grazing there.
> Tennyson, *Merlin and Vivien.*

They [the Reformers] exercised, at first clumsily, and in a limited field of the interpretation of Scripture, the weapon of independent criticism, which was later on to be melted down and forged afresh, and then skilfully wielded by free-thinkers against the inspiration of Scripture, and against Christianity itself.—Wilfrid Ward, *Problems and Persons*.

The logic-arrows how they glanced futile from obdurate thick-skinned Facts.—Carlyle, *Past and Present*.

It *was*, after all, mixing metaphors to say the jam was a slice of pie ; but then the way of escape was to withdraw either the jam or the pie, instead of forcing them together down our throats with a ramrod of apology.—Tract No. XI of the Society for Pure English, p. 10.

Anger is the sword which God puts into man's hand to fight the great moral battles of life. . . . Finding in his hand the sword of Anger he seizes it and fights with it his own battles, not the great moral battles for which alone it was intended. He draws it and strikes at everything that hinders him. . . . A wild mob with flashing swords of Anger, etc. [The metaphor is developed through several pages.]—B. W. Maturin, *Self-knowledge and Self-discipline*.

BATHING.—I am not a controversialist or a proselytizer, but I feel for those who stand on the edge and do not take the plunge. They seem to me to be always mentally and spiritually shivering in the cold as I did.—Father B. W. Maturin in a letter.

X.   THE SCIENCES

MEDICINE, PATHOLOGY.—For the last three centuries, above all for the last three-quarters of a century, that same Pericardial Nervous Tissue (as we named it) of Religion, where lies the Life Essence of Society, has been smote at and perforated, needfully and needlessly ; till now it is quite rent into shreds ; and Society, long pining, diabetic, consumptive, can be regarded as defunct ; for these spasmodic, galvanic sprawlings are not life ; neither will they endure, galvanize as you may, beyond two days.—Carlyle, *Sartor Resartus*.

Sir, this alarming discontent is not the growth of a day or of a year. If there be any symptoms by which it is possible to distinguish the chronic diseases of the body politic from its passing inflammations, all the symptoms exist in the present case. The taint has been gradually becoming more extensive and more malignant through the whole life time of two generations. We have tried cruel operations. What are we to try now ?—Macaulay, *On Parliamentary Reform*.

Religion was to Napoleon a useful vaccine against social distempers.—H. A. L. Fisher, *Napoleon*.

MATHEMATICS.—The Fraction of Life can be increased in value not so much by increasing your Numerator as by lessening your Denominator. Nay, unless my Algebra deceive me, Unity itself divided by Zero, will give *Infinity*. Make thy claim of wages a zero, then ; thou hast the world under thy feet.— Carlyle, *Sartor Resartus*.

ELECTRICITY.—His [Burns's] genius was the transmitter of the voice of Nature to the wireless receiver of every human heart.—D. McNaught, *The Truth about Burns*, 1921.

Semi-monastic quietness and solitude is not an end in itself ; it is merely the stillness of the power-house where unseen but energy-laden currents are generated.—Professor Alfred O'Rahilly, *Life of Father William Doyle*.

CHEMISTRY.—As a drop of prosaic feeling is said to precipitate a whole poem, so a drop of sentimental rhythm will bring a limpid tale or essay to cloudy effervescence.—E. C. Stedman, *Nature and Elements of Poetry*.

This incident, then, of historical, actual, or imaginary

336

life, will be as it were saturated with the quality of life which the writer discerns ; its various parts and characters will be of such a nature that the writer's accumulation of emotional experience will be able to form itself about them, like crystals about a string dipped into a saturated solution.—J. Middleton Murry, *The Problem of Style*.

A nature which had now not a little carbonized tinder, of Irritability ; with so much nitre of latent Passion, and sulphurous Humour enough ; the whole lying in such hot neighbourhood, close by a reverberating furnace of Fantasy : have we not here the components of driest gunpowder ?—Carlyle, *Sartor Resartus*.

Metre, therefore, having been connected with poetry most often and by a peculiar fitness, whatever else is combined with metre must, though it be not itself essentially poetic, have nevertheless some property in common with poetry, as an intermedium of affinity, a sort (if I may dare borrow a well known phrase from technical chemistry) of mordant between it and the superadded metre.—Coleridge, *Biographia Literaria*.

That chemistry of fate which brews effect out of cause and distils the imperishable essence of glory from the rougher liquors of vulgar success.—Marion Crawford, *Ave Roma Immortalis*.

Our costliest poetic phrase is put beyond reach of decay in the gleaming precipitate in which it united itself with his [Shakespeare's] thought.—Lowell, *The English Poets*.

The world is mind precipitated and the volatile essence is forever escaping again into the state of free thought.—Emerson.

The Gospel of John is a distillation of the life and teaching of Jesus from the Alembic of the Apostle's own mind.—G. B. Stevens, *N.T. Theology*.

Such thoughts, like chemical fluids, lay in solution

in Loyola's mind, awaiting the sudden troubling of the soul that should crystallize them into a definite form of devotion, self-consecration, and service.— Henry Dwight Sedgwick, *Ignatius Loyola*.

The most nobly conceived character in assuming *vraisemblance* takes up a certain quantity of imperfection ; it is its water of crystallization ; expel this and far from securing, as the artist fondly deems, a more perfect crystal, the character falls to powder.— Francis Thompson, *The Way of Imperfection*.

ASTRONOMY (Sunspots).—

> And was the day of my delight
> As pure and perfect as I say ?
> The very source and fount of day
> Is dashed with wandering isles of night.
> Tennyson, In Memoriam.

GEOLOGY.—This has been taken for a piece of the primeval rock of communism cropping up from underneath subsequent human formations.—Fr. Joseph Rickaby, *Moral Philosophy*.

Those magnificent crystallizations of feeling and phrase, basaltic masses molten and interfused by the primal fires of passion, are not to be reproduced by the slow experiments of the laboratory striving to parody creation with artifice.—Lowell, *English Poets*.

The Poetic Spirit becomes concrete through utterance, in that poetry which enters literature ; that is in the concrete utterance of age after age. Nothing of this is durably preserved, but that which possesses the crystalline gift of receiving and giving out light indefinitely, yet losing naught from its reservoir. Poetry is the diamond of these concretions. It gives out light of its own, but anticipates the light of after times, and refracts it with sympathetic splendours.—E. C. Stedman, *Nature and Elements of Poetry*.

THE SCIENCES

Max Müller's essay *On the Stratification of Language* [1] is one prolonged metaphor. The various stages through which a language passes are likened to strata, and geological phenomena such as the tilting of strata are used to illustrate linguistic phenomena. The following sentence is typical : " The primitive blocks of Chinese and the most perplexing agglomerates of Greek can be explained as the result of one continuous formative process."

And how happens it I can sit for hours turning over (with many a pooh ! and psha !) leaf after leaf of this same stratified debris.—John Mitchell, *Jail Journal*.

PHYSICS AND ELECTRICITY.—Mr. Carlyle desires to saturate language with meaning under the pressure of some half dozen atmospheres till it has gained something of the electrical effect of a moral discharge. —R. H. Hulton, *Brief Literary Criticisms*.

Wherever there was a shred of gold, a spark of the Divine, in the lost and sinful, Christ saw it by the instinct of His purity. He discovered it and drew it forth, as a magnet would draw from a heap of chaff one needle-point of steel.—Stopford Brooke, *Christ in Modern Life*.

> Something it is which thou hast lost,
>   Some pleasure of thine early years
>   Break, thou deep vase of chilling tears
> Which grief has shaken into frost.
> > Tennyson, *In Memoriam*.

They are fearful of exaggeration and extravagance. They harbour the suspicion that, if the pendulum is allowed to swing too far in the direction of fervour, it may on its returning arc register doubt and disbelief. —James J. Daly, S.J., *The Queen's Work*.

---

[1] In *Selected Essays on Language, Mythology, and Religion*, Longmans, 1882, vol. i, p. 27.

ILLUSTRATION

In morals, as in physics, the stream cannot rise higher than its source.—Newman, *The Tamworth Reading Room*.

This reference to something on one side or other of the actual thing meant by the word is another of the electrons clustering round the word-atom.— A. Williams-Ellis, *The Anatomy of Poetry*.

A void was made by the vanishing of the whole mythology of mankind, which would have asphyxiated like a vacuum if it had not been filled with theology. —G. K. Chesterton, *The Everlasting Man*.

Now this pure white light of style is as impossible as undesirable ; it *must* be splintered into colour by the refracting media of the individual mind, and humanity will always prefer the colour.—Francis Thompson, *The Way of Imperfection*.

PHYSICS (Light).—I may consider my soul as a ray of light flashed from the Sun of Justice, bearing wherever it shines an image of that Sun—like the ray, undivided in its action, yet having a triple force in the heat, light, and activism of the Memory, the Understanding, and the Will—like the ray again, when considered as refracted through the denser medium of sense-commencing knowledge, broken up into a spectrum of various qualities and powers, amid which the Will attains its maximum here, and the Understanding there, and each may be made to act apart—in all this like the Light of light who is undivided in Nature, triple in Personality, and refracted into variety of attribute in the feeble minds of His creatures.—F. C. Kolbe, *The Art of Life*.

Considering the short-circuit manner in which things happen in Mexico.—*Times Literary Supplement*, 5th June, 1920.

Love, beauty, passion, nature, art, life, the natural and theological virtues—there is nothing beyond his power to disenchant : nothing out of which the tremendous hydraulic press of his allegory . . . will not squeeze all feeling and freshness and leave it a juiceless jelly.—J. Russell Lowell.

His biographer, Dr. Furness, says of Emerson, that he grew up under " the pressure of I know not how many literary atmospheres ".

BOTANY.—There is a widespread wish to investigate personally these mysteries of root and stem, calyx and corolla, which in their union make up the flower of language. . . .—S. G. Ford, *Lessons in Verse Craft.*

L'histoire de la philosophie, veritable herbier des idées mortes et desséchées.—A. Sabatier, *L'Apôtre Paul.*

If we counted the wealth of English dialects and if we added the treasures of the ancient language from Alfred to Wycliffe, we should easily double the herbarium of the linguistic flora of England.—Max Müller, *Rede Lecture on the Stratification of Language.*

GEOMETRY.—This is partially true of all great minds, open and sensitive to truth and beauty through any large arc of their circumference.—Lowell, *English Poets.*

METALLURGY.—We do not mean what is technically called a living language—the contrivance, hollow as a speaking-trumpet, by which breathing and moving bipeds, even now, sailing over life's solemn main, are enabled to hail each other and make known their mutual shortness of mental stores—but one that is still hot from the hearts and brains of a people, not hardened yet, but moltenly ductile to new shapes of sharp and clear relief in the moulds of new thought. —Lowell, *English Poets.*

He [Shelley] is frequently diffuse and obscure. . . . The glowing metal rushes into the mould so vehemently that it overleaps the bounds and fails to find its way into all the little crevices.—A. C. Bradley, *Oxford Lectures on Poetry.*

ILLUSTRATION

BIOLOGY.—The ballad-dance remains a literary protoplasm : the primitive form up to which all other forms of literature ultimately may be traced.—Moulton, *The Modern Study of Literature*.

XI. MISCELLANEOUS

It [the principle of duty as opposed to that of love] never lets conscience alone. It wastes in a fruitless post-mortem examination of its actions the time that might have been spent in acts of heroic contrition. . . . Nay, it will even disinter again and again these actions, which had already passed the ordeal of so many examinations, and it will dissect and meddle, until it has acquired an inveterate habit of stooping and contracted a disease of the eyes.—F. W. Faber, *The Creator and the Creature*.

There is more meat on Mr. Bagehot's bones for the critics than on almost anybody else's ; hence his extreme utility to the nimble-witted and light-hearted gentry aforementioned. Bagehot crops up all over the country. His mind is lent out ; his thoughts toss on all waters ; his brew, mingled with a humbler element, may be tapped everywhere ; he has made a hundred small reputations.—A. Birrell, *Essays*.

> The lady failing to prevail her way,
> Upgathered my torn wishes from the ground
> And pieced them with her strong benevolence ;
> And, as I thought I could breathe freer air
> Away from England, going without pause,
> Without farewell, just breaking with a jerk
> The blossomed offshoot from my thorny life.
>   E. B. Browning, *Aurora Leigh*.

He [Shelley] plays truant from earth, slips through the wicket of fancy into Heaven's meadow, and goes gathering stars.—Francis Thompson, *Shelley*.

But he [Moore] never broods over his feeling until he has found his way down to its roots ; the song strikes off from the surface like the spurt of a match : there is no deep fire or steady flame.—A writer in *Everyman*.

We need not break conversational exaggeration on the wheel of exact inquiry.—*Times Literary Supplement*.

Archæology to them [the people of the Renaissance] was not a mere science for the antiquarian ; it was a means by which they could touch the dry dust of antiquity into the very breath and beauty of life, and fill with the new wine of romanticism forms that had else been old and outworn.—Oscar Wilde, *The Truth of Masks*.

Besides there is another thing about this talking which you forget. It shapes our thoughts for us ; the waves of conversation roll them as the surf rolls the pebbles on the shore. Let me modify the image a little. I rough out my thoughts in talk as an artist models in clay. Spoken language is so plastic—you can pat and coax, and spread and shave, and rub out and fill up and stick on so easily, when you work that soft material, that there is nothing like it for modelling. Out of it come the shapes which you turn into marble or bronze in your immortal books ; if you happen to write such. Or, to use another illustration, writing or printing is like shooting with a rifle ; you may hit your reader's mind, or miss it ; but talking is like playing at a mark with the pipe of an engine ; if it is within reach and you have time enough you can't help hitting it.—O. W. Holmes, *The Autocrat of the Breakfast Table*.

Let mystery always have its place in you ; do not be always turning up your whole soil with the plough-share of self-examination, but leave a fallow corner in your heart ready for any seeds the winds may bring, and reserve a nook of shadow for the passing bird ; keep a place in your heart for the unexpected guest, an altar for the unknown God. Then if a bird sing among your branches do not be too eager to tame it.—Amiel's *Journal*.

Burlesque, that smiler with knife under cloak, is always waiting round the corner for tragedy.—Professor Gummere, *Poetry and Democracy*.

In writing you are as a commander filing out his battalion through a narrow gate that allows only one man at a time to pass, and your reader as he receives the troops has to re-form and reconstruct them.—Sir A. Quiller-Couch, *The Art of Writing*.

Works of perfect art are the tombs in which artists lay to rest the passions they would fain make immortal. The more perfect their execution, the longer does the sepulchre endure, the sooner does the passion perish.—Geo. Wyndham, *Studies in Romantic Literature*.

The *Roman de la Rose* is a Coliseum out of whose ruins many cities have been quarried.—Ibid.

It [Webster's *Duchess of Malfi*] is just a box of tricks, of raw heads and bloody bones, left with the lid open.—Sir A. T. Quiller-Couch, *Poetry*.

Understanding is indeed thy window, too clear thou canst not make it ; but Fantasy is thy eye, with its colour-giving retina, healthy or diseased.—Carlyle, *Sartor Resartus*.

His study is relations. When he cannot discover them, he invents them—strings his fact-beads on the thread of hypothesis.

He is learned in the *peerage of words* ; knows the words of true descent and ancient blood, at a glance, from words of modern canaille ; remembers all their ancestry—their intermarriages, distantest relationships, and the extent to which they were admitted, and offices they held, among the national noblesse of words at any time, and in any country.—Ruskin, *Sesame and Lilies*.

MISCELLANEOUS

The solemn lady [George Eliot], who might seem such a terror to ill-doers, had yet a packet of the most delicious fondants in the pocket of her bombazine gown. The names of these sweetmeats, which were of a flavour and a texture delicious to the tongue, might be Mrs. Poyser or Lizzie Jerome or the sisters Dodson, but they all came from the Warwickshire factory at Griff, and they were all manufactured with the sugar and spice of memory. So long as George Eliot lived in the past, and extracted her honey from those wonderful cottage gardens which fill her early pages with their colours and their odours, the solidity and weight of her intellectual methods in other fields did not interfere with the power and intensity of the entertainment she offered. But from the first, if we now examine coldly and inquisitively, there was a moth sleeping in George Eliot's rich attire. This moth was pedantry.—Edmund Gosse, *Aspects and Impressions*, 1922.

Moreover, it is the few whom we may call half-cultured, or the hyper-cultured, who try positively to stand on the rickety pinnacle, as of atheism, so of complete extinction ; and, on the whole, if you watch carefully, you will find they do not keep their foothold there, but continually plunge off into the waves of superstitions that lap around them, fears of ghosts, of retribution, spiritualisms, fortune tellings, and the like ; and climb back dripping.—C. C. Martindale, S.J., *God and the Supernatural*.

The monograph-maker, with his habit of peering into crannies and raking the rubbish-heaps of the past to parade his particle of discovered truth, has much to answer for.—Robert Dewar in *The Year's Work in English Studies*, 1923.

A story that walks the highway of plain fact to the blistering of patience.—Ibid.

Mr. L. finds Father X. a particularly elusive nut

to crack. . . . He endeavours to peel off snippets of his works and pin them to the wall with a little jest or epigram of his own.—Shane Leslie, *Dublin Review*, January, 1925.

All these writers are of a revolutionary cast . . . crazy with the laughing gas of recovered liberty ; drunk with the wine-cup of their mighty Revolution, snorting, whinnying, throwing up their heels, like wild horses in the boundless pampas.—De Quincey, *Joan of Arc*.

Alas, what mountains of dead ashes, wreck, and dry bones, does assiduous Pedantry dig up from the Past Time, and name it History, and Philosophy of History ; till, as we say, the human soul sinks wearied and bewildered ; till the Past Time seems all one infinite incredibly grey void, without sun, stars, hearth-fires or candle light ; dim offensive dust whirlwinds filling universal Nature ; and over your Historical Library, it is as if all the Titans had written for themselves : Dry rubbish shot here.—Carlyle, *Past and Present*.

. . . Covered deeper than Pompeii with the lava-ashes and inarticulate wreck of seven hundred years.—Ibid.

The quest for this—the beautiful old life which rose like some undreamed-of human incense from the thurible of a sainted civilization, but kept the tang of earth and primitive emotion—was finally the only thing which drove him to write well.—G. N. Shuster in the *Month*.

The line of watershed between Poetry and Prose is a narrow edge, ticklish for the foot of travellers who like travelling along the crests.—John Earle, *English Prose*, 1890.

For the path of holiness is not the calm ascent of a marble stairway : it is for all of us . . . a life-long journey over a rugged and uncertain road, a stumbling over many stones, a wandering into many a bypath, a fall into many a snare : and when heaven's gates open to us at last, they open to a tattered traveller with a worn and weary soul.—Dr. Edwin Hatch, *The Heavenly and the Earthly Conflict* (quoted in John Earle's *English Prose*).

The wild regions of English that lie around the streets and suburbs of our polite vernacular.— L. P. Smith, *Words and Idioms*.

We ourselves, speaking the language which we speak, move about, as it were, in the innermost chambers, in the darkest recesses of that primeval palace, but we cannot tell by what steps and through what passages we arrived there, and we look in vain for the thread of Ariadne which in leading us out of the enchanted castle of our language would disclose to us the way by which we ourselves or our fathers and forefathers before us, have entered into it.—Max Müller.

The equilibrium of the style is so delicate, the weight of every word so justly felt and realized, that language under the poet's hand, instead of the jig-saw puzzle it is for most men, with a place for every piece, grows malleable and all but liquid ; the stream can be diverted at any moment in any direction ; old words come back to us shining like fresh coins from the mint. . . . —*Times Literary Supplement*, July, 1925.

In Shakespeare's *poems* the creative power and the intellectual energy wrestle as in a war embrace. Each in its excess of strength seems to threaten the existence of the other. At length in the drama they were reconciled and fought each with its shield before the breast of the other. Or like two rapid streams, that, at their first meeting within narrow and rocky banks, mutually strive to repel each other and intermix reluctantly and in tumult ; but soon finding a wider channel and more yielding shores,

347

blend and dilate, and flow in one current and with one voice.—Coleridge, *Biographia Literaria*, chap. xv.

> And now, thou elder nurseling of the nest ;
> Ere all the intertangled west
>   Be one magnificence
> Of multitudinous blossoms that o'errun
> The flaming brazen bowl o' the burnished sun
>   Which they do flower from.
>
> Francis Thompson.

The pure idea that dwells in a poem is suffused in the poetic utterance, as sunshine breaks into beauty in the mist, as life beats and flushes in the flesh, or as an impassioned thought breathes in a thinker's face.—H. Jones, *Browning as a Philosophical and Religious Thinker*.

A little deepening of the lines of character, the threads of habit woven a little firmer, the voice of conscience somewhat clearer or less distinct, the will sunk a trifle deeper into its ruts or lifted a little out of them. . . .—B. W. Maturin, *Self-knowledge and Self-discipline*.

We are surprised and shocked when we find some strong motive or passion or ambition standing like a draped form whose expression we cannot catch, in the very council chamber of the soul, etc.—*Ibid*.

> The lost days of my life until to-day,
>   What were they, could I see them on the street
>   Lie as they fell ? Would they be ears of wheat
> Sown once for food but trodden into clay ?
> Or golden coins squandered and still to pay ?
>   Or drops of blood dabbling the guilty feet ?
>   Or such spilt water as in dreams must cheat
> The throats of men in Hell, who thirst alway ?
>
> Dante Gabriel Rossetti.

Round the family do indeed gather the sanctities that separate men from ants and bees. Decency is the curtain of that tent ; liberty is the wall of that city ; property is but the family farm ; honour is but the family flag.—G. K. Chesterton, *The Everlasting Man*.

Have crystallized bits of their experience in shining phrases, enshrined them as it were in the amber of words. . . .—L. P. Smith, *Words and Idioms*.

His talk seems to open doors into gardens and corridors of the house of thought.—A. C. Benson, *From a College Window*.

His [Gerard Hopkins] poems are handed down by the initiated not like candles of flame or glowing coals, but like enamels that have run into each other with intensity of heat upon a reliquary.—Shane Leslie, Preface to *An Anthology of Catholic Poetry*.

INDEX

INDEX

INDEX

ADDENDUM—INDEX